Abraham's
Divided
Children

The New Testament in Context

Friendship and Finances in Philippi
THE LETTER OF PAUL TO THE PHILIPPIANS
Ben Witherington III

Walking in the Truth: Perseverers and Deserters
THE FIRST, SECOND, AND THIRD LETTERS OF JOHN
Gerard S. Sloyan

Church and Community in Crisis
THE GOSPEL ACCORDING TO MATTHEW
J. Andrew Overman

Letters to Paul's Delegates
1 TIMOTHY, 2 TIMOTHY, TITUS
Luke Timothy Johnson

Embassy of Onesimus
THE LETTER OF PAUL TO PHILEMON
Allen Dwight Callahan

Community of the Wise
THE LETTER OF JAMES
Robert W. Wall

To Every Nation under Heaven
THE ACTS OF THE APOSTLES
Howard Clark Kee

Fallen Is Babylon
THE REVELATION TO JOHN
Frederick J. Murphy

Abraham's Divided Children

GALATIANS AND THE POLITICS OF FAITH

Pheme Perkins

THE NEW TESTAMENT IN CONTEXT

Howard Clark Kee and J. Andrew Overman, editors

TRINITY PRESS INTERNATIONAL

Trinity Press International, P.O. Box 1321, Harrisburg, PA 17105
Trinity Press International is a division of The Morehouse Group.

Library of Congress Cataloging-in-Publication Data
Perkins, Pheme.
   Abraham's divided children : Galatians and the politics of faith / Pheme Perkins.
     p. cm.—(The New Testament in context)
   Includes bibliographical references and index.
   ISBN 1-56338-359-4 (alk. paper)
    1. Bible. N.T. Galatians—Commentaries. I. Title. II. Series.

BS2685.53 P47 2001
227'.4077—dc21   2001027486

Printed in the United States of America

01 02 03 04 05 06   10 9 8 7 6 5 4 3 2 1

Contents

Introduction

Where in the World?

Paul indicates that the recipients of his letter are "the churches of Galatia" (1:2). Right off the bat, we have a delivery problem. He is not addressing persons in a single city, "the church of God which is in Corinth" (1 Cor 1:2), for example. Paul writes to the inhabitants of a region whom he addresses as "Galatians" (3:1). As in the other NT references to this territory (2 Tim 4:10; 1 Pet 1:1), this designation tells us nothing about where these churches were or the ethnic makeup of their members. Does Paul consider "Galatians" an appropriate designation for all inhabitants of the territory that makes up the Roman province established in 25 B.C.? Or is it equivalent to "Celt," an ethnic term for tribes that had migrated to central Turkey and settled in the region around Ancyra ca. 278 B.C.E.? They had not adopted the civic institutions of Hellenistic city-states.

To further complicate the question, Paul suggests that he had not intended to evangelize this region (4:13) but took advantage of an illness that left him stranded in the area. Galatia lay on a major overland route between the Roman provinces of Asia and Syria. In the process of pacifying Pisidia to the south, the Romans had settled colonies of military veterans along a new road to the south, the *Via Sebaste*. Was Paul traveling the older route to the north or the new southern road between the Roman colonies? The latter fits Paul's ordinary sphere of activity. Philippi, Thessalonika, and Corinth were all founded or re-founded in the Roman period. Scholars who insist on fitting Paul's letters into the mission journey itineraries of Acts also favor this route. Acts 13:14–14:25 speaks of a circuit through Pisidian Antioch, Lystra, Derbe, and Iconium on the first journey.

1

Paul's second journey (Acts 16:1–18:23) included a second visit to those cities, and presumably to the mysterious Galatian churches as well (see Hansen 1994).

However, these visits are not accidental examples of church founding. Further, the churches established on the first missionary journey would appear to come under the authority of Syrian Antioch, the sponsoring church. Paul's argument requires that he was the sole apostle-founder (4:10–20). In addition, citizens of such hellenized towns as Pisidian Antioch and Lycaonia would hardly have accepted the ethnic designation "Galatians." Nor could the term be applied to persons in churches 172 miles apart (see Murphy-O'Connor 1996, 161). Therefore, other scholars locate the Galatian churches in the northern part of the province. Jerome Murphy-O'Connor takes Acts 16:8 as correct information concerning the final destination, Troas, which Paul reached by coming down through the region of Mysia; he proposes that upon reaching Antioch in Phrygia, Paul found that he could not journey through Roman Asia. Instead, he headed north along the Phrygian border to Pessinus, then headed west to Troas where he could cross to northern Greece (idem, 162–64). In this reconstruction, Pessinus would be the urban center for the churches of Galatia.

If the geographical location of Paul's addressees cannot be settled with any certainty, neither can the founding missionary activity. First Corinthians 16:1 refers to directions about the Jerusalem collection that Paul had given to the "churches of Galatia." That would seem to put Paul in Galatia after the Jerusalem agreement (Gal 2:9–10), before he wrote 1 Corinthians from Ephesus. In the interim, others had been preaching a different gospel in those churches (1:6–9). Paul's response to the threat that their teaching posed appears to be immediate, but he makes no reference to any further visits to the region. His activities have shifted to western Asia Minor and Greece. In order to accommodate the two visits assumed by Acts 18:23, Murphy-O'Connor places the foundation of these churches prior to the Jerusalem Council in the winters of 47 to 48 C.E. (1996, 26–29). Even if one rejects this hypothesis (see Betz 1979, 10–11), the best guess for the composition of the letter is the spring of 53 C.E. (Murphy-O'Connor 1996, 181–82).

The Roman historian Livy referred to inhabitants of Galatia as "Gallogrecians," Greek-speaking Gauls. They are depicted as fierce warriors, much like the highland Scots (Livy, *Hist.* 38.17, 3–9 [Foster, LCL]). A famous temple to the Phrygian mother goddess associated with the mountains, Agdistis or Cybele, was located at Pessinus (Strabo, *Geogr.* 12.5, 1–4). Her self-castrated devotees were known as *galli* and appear in Roman literature associated with the Syrian goddess Atargatis (see Apuleius, *Metam.* 8.25–30; Lucian, *Syr. d.* 27 and 50; Catullus 64). The north Galatia hypothesis puts Paul's audience in this cult center. However, the goddess was familiar in regional variations in the cities of south Galatia as well (see the evidence cited in Elliott 1999, 672–75). Elliott argues that Paul's identification of Hagar as Mount Sinai with her enslaved children (Gal 4:24–26) forges a direct link between Scripture and the pre-Christian cult of his addressees in Pessinus (Elliott 1999, 676–80).

However, the Roman conquest and veterans' colonies in the newly founded cities also brought new religious developments. Annius Afrinus, governor of the province from 49 to 54 C.E., was portrayed on the coins. The emperor's name was attached to some cities so that Derbe became Claudioderbe. Cultic devotion to the emperor drew citizens from the local aristocracy into its orbit by appointing persons for one-year terms as priests of the cult. A large temple to Augustus dominated Pisidian Antioch in Paul's day (Mitchell 1993, 1:103–107). Those who approached the city along the *Via Sebaste* would have no doubt that imperial Rome was the new source of wealth and prestige in the city. Beyond the upper classes, most of the populace was untouched by Hellenism. Roman ideas and the cult were innovations (Murphy-O'Connor 1996, 188–89).

Despite the suggestion that the Roman festival calendar would have posed a powerful counterweight to Christian evangelization (Mitchell 1993, 2:10), it may have had an unsettling effect on the populace. If they did not belong to the religious and cultural world of the newly Romanized cities, they could easily respond to Paul's apocalyptic preaching. According to Paul, believers have been separated from the old world (Gal 1:4) and already share the life of the new creation (6:14–15; Adams 2000, 226–27).

Jewish Presence in the Region

Paul's converts in Galatia were Gentiles (3:1–5; 4:8–11). His argument assumes an audience familiar with the Torah and the prophets. Unless there were Jewish communities with which they could identify, Judaizing could hardly pose the threat that Paul anticipates. As Rodney Stark's studies of conversion demonstrate, persons adhere to new movements when they have close personal ties with others in the group. The theological warrants that they give for their conversion represent learned behavior after association with the sect. Converts are instructed in core doctrines and how to testify to their beliefs (Stark 1996, 18–19). Archaeological remains from the third century and after indicate that Christians and Jews lived and were buried in close proximity to one another. Stark concludes that the impression Christians have gained from Galatians, Romans, and Acts of a failing mission to Israel supplanted by a non-Jewish church is wrong. Free of the ethnic particularities that separated Jews from their non-Jewish neighbors, the gospel preached by Paul after the Jerusalem Council appealed to assimilating tendencies in Diaspora communities (idem, 49–64).

Based on this model, Luke's picture of early Christian missionaries preaching first among those attached to Jewish synagogues and moving to non-Jewish patrons only when pushed out by local authorities reflects social reality. Unfortunately, we lack significant evidence about the Jewish presence in Anatolia and Asia Minor. Acts 14:1 refers to a synagogue in Iconium. A few inscriptions from the third century and after give evidence of Jewish names (Jacob, Estheras) and devotion to *theos hypsistos*, "God, most high" (see Schürer 1986, 1:34–36).

With virtually no evidence about Jewish communities in Galatia beyond these meager inscriptions and Philo's list of regions throughout the empire who call Jerusalem the site of worship of the "most high God" (*hypsistos theos*) their native home (*patris*; Philo, *Legat.* 281 [Colson, LCL]), scholars must rely on evidence from elsewhere to fill out the picture. All evidence for Jews in this region comes from the Roman province of Asia in western Turkey (Barclay 1996, 260). Trebilco opens his study of Jewish communities in the region with the caution that one should not assume that Jews had a universal Roman charter to live according to ancestral custom in the city-states of the region. Josephus reports scattered episodes in which Jews called upon the Romans to intervene in matters concerning their status (Josephus, *Ant.* 14.228–30; 19.290). Nor does hostility in one city imply that it existed in the rest of Asia Minor. Roman officials who issued decrees in favor of Jews were often reciprocating benefits received from Jewish rulers or members of the Herodian family (Trebilco 1991, 9–15).

Scholars recognize that a complex web of personal relationships based on the ability of individuals, families, and communities to secure powerful patrons was the glue that held ancient society together. It dictated relationships in the imperial court and relationships between Rome and its provincial subjects. By paying homage to their imperial benefactor, client kings like Herod enhanced their own power and influence (see Goodman 1997, 87–89; 107–12). Wealthy women from aristocratic families exercised considerable political and civic power as patrons and civic benefactors. They were priestesses in local and Roman cults, held honorific public offices, and in some instances were accorded the title "mother of the city"—or as in one Egyptian example, "father of the city" (Frantham 1994, 360–66). The prominence of women benefactors, patrons, civic leaders, and honorees in the cities of Asia Minor is reflected in Jewish sources as well. Jewish inscriptions refer to individual women as "leader of the synagogue," "ruler," "elder," and "priestess." Often inscriptions honoring women as donors to the synagogue link them with their husbands, but in other cases, they are named alone. The active involvement of women in the synagogues of this region reflects assimilation among Jews. They adopted sociocultural patterns of patronage in their own communities (see Trebilco 1991, 104–26).

Gentiles and Jews

How do Paul's Jewish credentials (Gal 1:13–14) play out in a non-Jewish world? Not well, if the negative characterizations found in Roman historians or satirists were to be believed (e.g., Tacitus, *Hist.*

4.5, 4; Juvenal, *Sat.* 6.544–45; Schäfer 1997, 32–86). Those who emphasize episodes of social conflict between Jews and non-Jewish civic authorities assume that Jewish refusal to participate in civil religion created permanent tensions with their neighbors. However, evidence suggests that Jews had lived in these cities for generations without such conflict (see Stanley 1996, 101–105). The contempt of elite Roman males should not obscure counter-indications that Jews had non-Jewish benefactors and sympathizers. Josephus crafted his account of Jewish history not only for those hellenized Jews who sought to understand their place in the world, but also for interested, educated non-Jewish readers (*Ant.* 1.10–17; Spilsbury 1998, 18–22). A dedicatory inscription for those who refurbished a synagogue in Acmonia indicates that the original building had been a gift of one Julia Severa. Coins indicate that she was active in the '50s and '60s C.E. Since she served as a civic magistrate and was honored as priestess of the imperial cult under Nero, she was a highly placed, non-Jewish patron. Her son L. Servenius Cornutus became a Roman senator and was pro-consul of Asia ca. 73 C.E. (Trebilco 1991, 58–60).

The earliest synagogues in Rome, founded near the end of the first century B.C.E., honored highly placed Roman benefactors (Richardson 1996, 20–23). Although there is no evidence of Jews actively seeking proselytes (Goodman 1994, 8–9; 60–72), the Jewish community was able to exert considerable social pressure in first-century Rome (Barclay 1996, 296). Patronage, politics, and civic unrest played out in the imperial actions against the Jewish community of Rome in the first half of the century. Under Tiberius (ca. 19 C.E.), Fulvia, wife of a Roman senator, provoked conscription of some four thousand Jews for the army in Sardinia and banishment of others (Josephus, *Ant.* 18.65–84; Tacitus, *Ann.* 2.85, 4; Suetonius, *Tib.* 36). She was said to have adopted Jewish practices and been defrauded of money and purple cloth donated for the temple in Jerusalem. A single episode could hardly have provoked such a punishment, but there is no reason to assume that the Jews were disciplined for converting Roman citizens as Cassius Dio alleges (*Hist.* 57.18, 5; Barclay 1996, 298–99). Actions taken by Claudius against Jews in Rome (Acts 18:2) are even more unclear. A harsh edict (41 C.E.) ended the strife between Jews in Alexandria and the ruling elite ("Greeks") over the desire of prominent

Jews to obtain citizen rights. Claudius may have prohibited Jewish
assemblies in the same year (Dio, *Hist.* 60.6, 6). Suetonius's reference
to expulsion of Jews for rioting at the name of "chrestus" (*Claud.* 25.4)
is usually taken as discord caused by Christian preaching and dated to
49 C.E. Some scholars have attributed all these references to a single
event under Claudius. Others believe that two separate incidents are
involved (see Barclay 1996, 305–307).

Throughout this period, Jews continued to have highly placed
patrons. Agrippa II grew up with Claudius, sided with Rome during
the Jewish revolt in Judea, and had the rank of praetor at Rome
(Josephus, *Ant.* 19.360–62; 20.10–12, 134–36; Dio, *Hist.* 66.15,
3–4). One sister, Drusilla, married the procurator of Judea, Felix (*Ant.*
20.141–44). Another, Bernice, rumored to be unnaturally close to
her brother, had an affair with Titus. He brought her to Rome but
sent her away for good before becoming emperor in 79 C.E. (Tacitus,
Hist. 2.2, 1; Dio, *Hist.* 66.15, 3–4; Barclay 1996, 308–309). Poppaea
Sabina, the mistress and later the wife of Nero, was also a political
patron of Jews. Josephus calls her *theosebēs*, "God-fearing," but
whether one can infer that she had also adopted Jewish religious practices remains unclear (*Ant.* 20.195; Barclay 1996, 307–308).

These examples indicate that non-Jews, especially civic officials and
others who also had to deal with the Roman authorities, might easily
perceive Jews as highly placed "clients" of the Romans. Stanley has
pointed out that when Jews are said to be in conflict with "Greeks" in
Diaspora cities, the term "Greek" does not mean non-Jew. No educated person would have used the term "Greek" to speak of the populace of Asia Minor. It refers to high-status persons, members of the
aristocracy able to appeal to actual or "remembered" Greek ancestry.
In some cases, several generations of Greek education might turn a
wealthy provincial family into "Greeks." For most cities, only members of this elite had citizen rights. However, Roman imperial power
disordered their inherited authority to govern. Although it was too
dangerous to attack Rome directly, attacks on their "clients" were not
unknown (Stanley 1996, 106–21).

Hostility was not the only response to the Jewish presence in Asia
Minor. Just as Acts depicts wealthy women as benefactors (13:50;
17:4, 12), inscriptions from Asia Minor include women as benefactors

and even as proselytes (Williams 1999, 77). The title "God-fearing" that Josephus used of Poppaea Sabina has been the subject of extended debate (see Lieu 1995). Was there a sociologically distinct group of non-Jewish patrons and sympathizers who participated in Jewish synagogue life without becoming proselytes, as Luke suggests (Acts 10:2, 22; 13:16, 26, 50; 16:14; 17:4, 17; 18:7)? Or is this an ideological construction on Luke's part? For most interpreters, the issue was decided with the discovery of a memorial inscription from the third century C.E. at Aprodisias in southwest Asia Minor. Members of the association that erected a building, part of which was to serve as a soup kitchen for relief of the poor, were clearly divided between Jews and proselytes on one side and *theosebeis* on the other. The first nine "God-fearers" are also identified as city councilors. A second-century C.E. inscription from the Crimea lists God-fearers alongside Jews as witnesses to a manumission that took place in the local synagogue (see Levine 1999, 1009–10; Levinskaya 1996, 51–82). However, the epigraphic evidence only establishes use of the term for patrons and benefactors. Judith Lieu's study of its literary use by Jewish and early Christian authors suggests that believers used the expression of themselves to contrast their adherence to the true God with the alleged piety of outsiders. *Theosebeia* was a preferred substitute for the Greek virtue of *eusebeia*. In persecution stories, it serves to demonstrate that the accused are not guilty of "atheism," of dishonoring the gods (Lieu 1995, 485–90).

The expression does not establish an intermediate category of persons. Rather it might be seen as a communal slogan or a sign of "party loyalty," which Jews at Miletus had inscribed on their theater seats (idem, 496–97). The heroic Maccabean martyrs are father or mother of the people: "But the daughter of the God-fearing *(theosebous)* Abraham remembered his bravery: O mother of the nation; avenger of the law and champion of piety *(eusebeia)* and victor of the contest of the heart" (4 Macc 15:28–29; Lieu 1995, 493). Extending the epithet *theosebeis* to the non-Jewish benefactor reinforces the demarcation between worship of the one God and the "piety" directed toward local, civic, and imperial cults. It does not tell us whether the persons so designated shared this conviction. Local magistrates probably did not, because their position would require some participation in civic cults.

Being Jewish in the Diaspora

Philo identifies as "Ioudaios" all those residents of the Diaspora whose true homeland is Jerusalem (*Legat.* 281). This usage retains the link between a geography, polity, and the religious and cultural practices characteristic of Jews. The definition becomes more problematic when one asks whether the Herodians were Jews. Geographically the family came from Idumea. Culturally, Herod sponsored and participated in non-Jewish cultic sacrifices (e.g., Josephus, *War* 1.248–49; *Ant.* 14.383). Dynastic alliances, not Jewishness, determined his selection of a husband for his sister. Thus, Morton Smith concludes that Herod may have been circumcised but he did not observe Torah (Smith 1999, 232–34; also see Cohen 1999, 13–19). No discernable differences in physical appearance, dress, or speech distinguished a Diaspora Jew from the non-Jew (idem, 28–35). Inscriptions show that Diaspora Jews might have pagan theophoric names; adopt local funerary customs; attend the theater, the hippodrome, and even local shrines or temples (Williams 1999: 82–83). In the western part of the empire circumcision might be a distinctive trait of Jews, but the evidence for the east is less clear. Both Egyptian priests and Arabs were said to have practiced circumcision. Some Jews underwent surgery to conceal the marks of circumcision (Cohen 1999, 44–45).

Josephus acknowledges the link between circumcision and endogamy. Abraham's offspring were not to mix with others (*Ant.* 1.192; Barclay 1996, 411–12). Non-Jews had to be circumcised in order to marry women in the Herodian family (*Ant.* 20.139, 145–46). This requirement did not involve other elements of Jewish practice such as participation in the synagogue, kosher food restrictions, and Sabbath observance. Aversion to pork had become the symbolic form of *kashrut*. Satirized in comedy (Juvenal, *Sat.* 6.157 60), it did not prevent the Herodians or Josephus from dining with Rome's elite (Josephus, *C. Ap.* 2.173–74, 234, 282; Barclay 1996, 436). Other products like wine and "impure oil" were more problematic. Our sources suggest that a variety of strategies were employed: bringing one's own food, eating only certain foods such as fruit and vegetables (Josephus, *Life* 14; Rom 14:1–2), or avoiding libations to pagan deities (*Aristeas* 184–85; Barclay 1996, 435).

Study of the progressive renovations of domestic insula-type houses adapted for synagogue use in Ostia shows a Jewish community able to balance the pressures of maintaining a distinctive identity and assimilation to the larger culture. The major second-century C.E. renovations that changed the architecture of the building involved local non-Jewish patrons. An inscription honors one C. Julius Justus as "gerousiarch." The "C. Julius" suggests that this individual may have been an imperial freedman (White 1996, 33–62). Such examples provide a different picture of Jewish life in the Diaspora than the one that emerges from the episodes of ethnic conflict or the depictions of Roman satirists. Jews associated with non-Jews and were even attached to the imperial household or administrative bureaucracy without abandoning social and religious ties to their fellow Jews. In part, the geographic associations of the word "Ioudaios," which could mean simply "a Judean," made it possible to understand why Jews had customs that distinguished them from others. Their ancestral home and their God were in Judea. Even after the destruction of the Temple, Diaspora Jews sought to be buried in Jerusalem (Williams 1999, 84).

However, the destruction of Jerusalem played an important political role in legitimating the new Flavian dynasty. Vespasian, Titus, and Domitian celebrated the victory with architectural monuments and inscriptions in the city of Rome. Hence, as Goodman suggests, the growth in anti-Jewish propaganda after 70 C.E. elicited the apologetic efforts in Josephus's *Jewish Antiquities* and *Against Apion* (Goodman 1999, 54–58). The encomium of Judaism in *C. Ap.* 2.182–272, which celebrates the excellence of the Jewish constitution in contrast to that of Greek cities like Carthage, never puts Rome in the negative column. Josephus draws a considerable list of parallels between Jewish values and those held dear by Romans (Goodman 1999, 57). Since *Against Apion* is Josephus's last work, written after the death of Domitian, its plea for rebuilding the Jerusalem Temple (2.193–98), the only place where Jews can worship, reflects a change in the political climate at Rome (Goodman 1999, 58). Josephus celebrates the piety of Moses as lawgiver whose code calls for harmony, justice, and fellowship between members of the community and in their relationship with outsiders (*C. Ap.* 2.170; 281; Spilsbury 1998, 65–66).

Josephus had a concrete political reason for praising the ancient constitution that governed those who belonged to the *polis* Jerusalem. Pride in the Law as the key to Jewish identity was hardly an apologetic fabrication. Epigraphic evidence from Roman Jews shows that such sentiments were shared at a more popular level. In addition to depictions of Torah shrines, epithets designated individuals as "student of the sages," "teacher," or "scholar of the Law." Or persons were said to be "law-loving" *(philonomos)* or "commandment-loving" *(philoentolos)*. The names "Philonomios" and "Entolios" also turn up in Diaspora inscriptions (Williams 1999, 83). Because the Law continued to be identified with the constitution of an actual city and with persons tied to it by descent, non-Jews who revered God, participated in some Jewish festivals, associated with Jews, or even kept some Jewish customs and rituals, might not be considered "Ioudaios." Cohen emphasizes the ambiguous identity that might lead such an individual to be considered a Jew in some contexts but Gentile in others. He suggests that while proselytes might be considered part of the Jewish *politeia*, they were not necessarily considered Jews within the Jewish community (Cohen 1999, 140–61). Exogamy further complicates the question of who is or is not a Jew, especially in the case of the wives of non-Jews who were reported to practice Jewish customs. Were they of Jewish origin? Or were they proselytes?

Paul exploited the uncertainty over Jewish identity in the Diaspora. From his standpoint as a Jew sent to Gentiles, he could only carry out his mission by identifying with the other. He was obligated (and Peter should also have been obliged) to live in a Gentile manner *(ethnikōs; Gal 2:14)*. He could live as "Ioudaios" and "under the Law" for the sake of winning over Jews and live outside the Law as well (1 Cor 9:20–21). J. D. G. Dunn has suggested that Paul would no longer have thought of himself as "Ioudaios" (Dunn 1999, 182; also Mason 1990, 183). But from the standpoint of the "other," Paul was insistent that no Gentile—not even those who share the faith of Abraham—could ever become "Ioudaios" (Gal 5:3). He even went out of his way to denigrate the "earthly Jerusalem," the *politeia* that was central to Jewish identity (Gal 4:21–30). Thus Paul's insistence upon the unity of God's people in Christ (Gal 3:26–28) has a disturbing corollary, a

deep division among the children of Abraham, a division that—with
the addition of Hagar's Islamic descendants—continues to threaten
political harmony around the globe almost two millennia later.
Troubled by Paul's politics of division, scholars often turn to Rom
9–11 as Paul's affirmation that God's plan has not been fully worked
out. Paul even presumed that his own apostolic mission was playing
a role in the working out of God's final plan (Rom 11:13–15; see the
discussion in Dunn, 1998, 526–31; for an argument that Romans
should be considered anomalous, see Mason 1990).

Judaizing in Galatia

The divisive rhetoric that dominates Galatians was provoked by
Gentile converts seeking to come under the Law (Gal 3:1–5; 4:21);
that is, they wanted in some context to be considered part of the
politeia that had its center in Jerusalem. For males, this transition
would involve being circumcised (Gal 5:2–3). Paul attributed this
development to unnamed outsiders who created doubts about Paul's
message in the minds of his converts (5:10–12; 6:12–13). That much
is clear. To fill in the picture, scholars reconstruct an ideological and
theological teaching of these opponents based on Paul's counterargu-
ments (see the sermons of the "teachers" in Martyn 1997, 117–26,
132–35; 302–306; 324–25; 434–41). Since Paul's letter insists that
his gospel reflects a direct calling from God that was only subse-
quently accepted by the apostles in Jerusalem (1:11–2.10), most
reconstructions assume that Paul was charged with distorting or dilut-
ing the preaching of Jerusalem authorities. The subsequent break with
Peter, caused by persons claiming ties to James in Jerusalem (Gal
2:11–14), is taken to imply that a move against Paul's preaching originated in Jerusalem. Noting the sharp warning against Jewish practices
in Phil 3:2–4:1 and the polemic against the fading glory of the Mosaic
law in 2 Cor 3:7–18, some scholars conclude that Paul faced unified
opposition from Judaizing apostles in all of his churches (Murphy-
O'Connor 1996, 229–30). Murphy-O'Connor, who opts for the
founding of the Galatian churches while Paul was an agent of the
Antioch church, thinks that the opposition in Galatia came from

Antioch (idem, 194–99). Much of the argument in the letter is addressed directly to them, not to the Gentile converts (idem, 200).

Such hypotheses are necessary if someone is writing a history of earliest Christianity or a biography of the apostle, but they require more than an analysis of Galatians. Scholars use the shorthand term "Judaizers" for the ideological position of Paul's opponents. Paul used the cognate verb *ioudaizein* in a rhetorical question that culminates his charge against Peter in 2:14: "If you being a Jew live like a gentile *(ethnikōs)* and not like a Jew *(ioudaikōs)*, how can you compel the gentiles to adopt a Jewish way of life *(ioudaizein)?*" The verb *ioudaizein* belongs to a group of verbs that have three possible meanings: to give political support to, to adopt the customs and manners of, or to speak the language of. When Cicero used the verb to mock an opponent, he could mean that the individual appeared to have adopted such Jewish customs as abstaining from pork, but he could also mean that the individual had allied himself with the political interests of Roman Jews (Cohen 1999, 179–81). In Gal 2:14, Paul used the term to mean "adopting Jewish customs."

Paul used the verb "compel" in connection with the Antioch episode. That links it to his earlier assertion that even in Jerusalem, Titus was not "compelled" to be circumcised. Yet this language is very puzzling given the overwhelming scholarly agreement that Jews did not proselytize Gentiles. Those Gentiles who did become proselytes were acting on their own, probably because they had close personal ties to the local Jewish community (Goodman 1994, 84–85). It was in the interest of the Jewish community to have Gentile sympathizers. Goodman concludes that Gentile sympathizers may have been encouraged to develop stronger links to the Jewish community so that they would act on its behalf with powerful friends (idem, 87–88).

Non-Jews would have recognized "Judaizer" as a term applied to those persons whose sympathies or political alliances lay with the Jewish community. Josephus reports on the ambiguities facing such persons during the turmoil of the Jewish revolt against Rome:

> Every city was divided into two military camps. . . . for when Syrians thought that they had destroyed the Jews, they held the Judaizers *(hoi ioudaizontes)* in suspicion also . . . and as each

side did not care to slay those whom they only suspected to be on the other (to amphibolon), so did they greatly fear them when they were mingled with the other (to memigmenon; "those of mixed ancestry"), as if they were certainly foreigners. . . . (War 2:462–63 [Thackeray, LCL])

Morton Smith points to the existence of three distinct groups of persons in this passage: persons clearly identified as Jews; persons from families in which Jews had married Gentiles; and "Judaizers"(Smith 1999, 246). The ambiguity attached to those of mixed ancestry suggests that they were not unambiguously Jewish. Technically the Judaizers remained Gentiles. Goodman insists that while Jews did accept proselytes who were circumcised and intended to observe the Law (e.g., Josephus, C. Ap. 2.210), they never assumed that male converts could avoid the obligation of circumcision or the obligation to follow a Jewish way of life (Goodman 1994, 81–85). Consequently, some scholars have presumed that the pressure to bring Paul's Gentile Christians into Jewish observance resulted from a growing Jewish nationalism in Judea. Jewish Christians in Jerusalem had to prove their loyalty. Association with Gentiles would compromise their position with fellow Jews (Jewett 1971). Lacking persuasive evidence for this political dynamic, scholars who are inclined to accept it point to the need to explain the extremely negative reaction of Paul in Galatians (Davies 1999, 698–99).

These various theories adopt without comment Paul's rhetoric of compulsion (2:14) and enslavement (5:1). Troy Martin rightly recognizes that the Galatians are not compelled. He concludes that they were not in danger of adopting Jewish customs but of defecting to paganism (4.8–10; Martin 1995): "There is absolutely no evidence in the letter to prove the Galatians desired to live according to the Jewish Law" (idem, 455). This conclusion depends upon a formal analysis of the rhetorical construction of the letter, which relocates the points being proven away from the issue of Judaizing. It also manifests a rarely challenged assumption that Gentiles would not have chosen to assimilate to Jewish customs as part of their Christian faith. The evidence for proselytes, Judaizers, and persons of "mixed parentage" in the Diaspora suggests that Gentiles did identify with Jews in the

Diaspora. Goodman asks what would cause non-Jews in a city like Antioch to identify themselves with the minority Jewish community. They must have associated some advantage—either in this world or in the next—with this connection. He proposes that Jewish associates encouraged such "Judaizers" because they required sympathizers in order to maintain their political independence (*isopoliteia;* Goodman 1994, 87–88).

Stark's sociological reconstruction of the expansion of early Christianity highlights another flaw in historical reconstructions based on the Pauline epistles and Acts: the assumption that Jews ceased to join the new sect by the end of the first century, that Paul's mission to the Gentiles was a growing concern, while Peter's to Israel ("the circumcision"; Gal 2:9) was failing. He points to evidence of Judaizing among Christians into the fifth century C.E. Christians could well have been the product of families in which Jews had married non-Jews. Cities with identifiable Christian churches in the third and fourth centuries also had important synagogues (Stark 1996, 65–69). Jews who assimilated into a non-Jewish environment might refer to their ethnic origins as "Ioudaios" even when they no longer followed Jewish practices. Presumably, Christian Jews who regularly associated with non-Jewish Christians belonged to the "high assimilation" end of the spectrum (Barclay 1996, 326). Scholars who insist that the Judaizing trend in Galatia originated in political and religious tensions originating in Jerusalem or Antioch emphasize the paucity of evidence for local Jewish communities. One might reject the lack of evidence as the basis to conclude that such synagogue communities did not exist. If the dynamics of Judaizing require Jewish communities with which such persons may be socially or politically allied—a reality in the case of Syrian Antioch—then the possibility of local, Diaspora support for Judaizing Christians emerges. Smiles argues that Jewish Christians living among Gentiles in the Diaspora were more likely to demand separatist behavior of fellow believers than were emissaries from Jerusalem, which did not regulate conduct in the Diaspora (Smiles 1998, 14–15).

Because he assumes that persons from a sociologically distinct group, "God-fearers," formed the basis for Paul's Gentile churches, O'Neill concludes that the threat posed by Judaizing in Galatia was that such Christians would become proselytes. They would return as "Jews" to the synagogues they had once attended (O'Neill 1998, 82–83). O'Neill's assumptions about the presence of God-fearers as a sociological group and the extent to which Jewish synagogues would have encouraged such conversions are dubious. If the non-proselytizing stance of Diaspora Judaism bought civic harmony, Christian proselytizing could have caused considerable difficulty for fellow Jews in cities like Rome or Antioch (see Walters 1996, 182). Walters concludes that Jews probably reacted to these new pressures by distancing themselves from the Christians. Measures were taken to clarify the boundaries, such as the synagogue discipline enacted against Paul (2 Cor 11:24); Jewish-Christian denial of table fellowship with non-Jewish Christians (Gal 2:11–14); and expulsion of Christians from local synagogues (John 9:22; 12:42; 16:2; Walters 1996, 182–83) However, O'Neill rightly identifies the social implications of the term "Judaizing." It implies that non-Jews are engaging in some form of alliance with Jews—perhaps as political benefactors or clients, perhaps because of marriage, or perhaps through adoption of Jewish religious practices. Though Paul's argument in Gal 5:2–6 presumes that such individuals would become proselytes, they need not have done so. A non-Jewish Christian with a Jewish or Jewish-Christian wife might have been circumcised for the sake of his wife or her family without considering himself obligated to adopt other Jewish customs, for example. These observations make it more plausible to assume that the Galatians' interest in things Jewish involved interaction with local Jewish communities than that they were befuddled Gentiles being pushed into a new way of life by authorities in Jerusalem or Antioch. Outsiders may have sparked the interest, just as persons from Jerusalem had done in Antioch (2:11–14), but there had to be a preexisting community of Jews in order to make "Judaizer" a plausible social or religious identity.

Paul and the Gentiles

Given the general consensus that Diaspora Jews were not engaged in proselytizing among non-Jews, Paul's view of his call to preach Christ among the Gentiles (Gal 1:16) cannot be a simple transformation of a prior engagement with a Pharisaic mission to the Gentiles (so Fung 1988, 71–72). What does cohere with Paul's self-confessed zeal for ancestral tradition (Gal 1:14; Phil 3:6) is his strong opposition to blurring the lines between Jew and non-Jew. Though he agrees that the distinctions are no longer relevant "in Christ" (3:26–28), the only way they impinge upon the social life of actual communities is for the Jew to "live in a gentile manner" when associating with non-Jewish fellow Christians (2:14b). Paul's assertion that he once "preached circumcision" (Gal 5:11) must not refer to proselytizing among Gentiles (against Donaldson 1997, 282–83), but to Paul's efforts to persuade fellow Jews to adopt a particular standard of Torah observance. Perhaps it involved the activities by which he himself was persecuting and trying to wipe out the emerging Christian movement (1:13). Paul is equally determined to promote the truth of the gospel, as Barton observes:

> For in Galatians, Paul is hardly a model of what we might call tolerance. On the contrary, he repeatedly pronounces anathema on anyone who perverts the gospel of Christ (see 1:8, 9), recalls for his readers the occasion at Antioch when he "opposed Cephas to his face" for his damaging act of hypocrisy in withdrawing from Gentile table-fellowship (2:11–14), and is quite vituperative towards his opponents (5:12)! (Barton 1998, 126)

Paul stakes his entire apostolic authority on an understanding of the gospel that his converts must accept. To do otherwise is nothing less than apostasy (4:19; Barton 1998, 127).

This dualism fits Barclay's observation that Paul retains a negative view of the non-Jewish world as marred by sin and ignorance of God (Gal 2:15; 1 Thess 4:5; Rom 1:28–35; Phil 2:15). His converts are no longer "Gentiles" in that sense (1 Cor 12:2). Thus Paul's view of the Gentiles must be distinguished from the attitudes of Jews who have assimilated the positive values of Hellenistic culture (Barclay 1996, 388–91). Donaldson has sketched a grid of possible Jewish views concerning the inclusion of non-Jews in the age to come (Donaldson 1997, 52–74). As aliens to God's covenant, the non-Jew is permanently excluded. *Jubilees* makes this point, combining the requirement of circumcision and descent from Abraham:

> And anyone who is born whose own flesh is not circumcised on the eighth day is not from the sons of the covenant which the Lord made for Abraham since he is from the children of destruction. And there is therefore no sign upon him so that he might belong to the Lord because he is destined to be destroyed and annihilated from the earth and to be uprooted from the earth because he has destroyed the covenant of the Lord, Our God. (15.26 [Wintermute, OTP])

This passage is a polemic against Jews who might dispense with circumcision in assimilating to their environment as well as against non-Jews. Such sentiments also make the case for those who advocated circumcision for non-Jewish Christians. We have seen that the proselyte has entered the covenant community but remains somewhat anomalous because he or she cannot claim to be "from Judea" in the ethnic sense. More assimilated Jews such as Philo of Alexandria recognize a category of persons that Donaldson refers to as "natural Law proselytes" (idem, 60). While remaining uncircumcised Gentiles, such persons are devoted to the one God, reject idolatry, and live moral lives that correspond to the rational virtues found in God's law, virtues that were spontaneously followed by those who lived before the Mosaic law was promulgated (Philo, *Abr.* 3–6). Donaldson also argues that the rabbinic distinction between righteous Gentiles and the wicked who forget God (b. *Sanh.* 13.2) already existed in the first century (idem, 65–69). In the *Sibylline Oracles*, prophetic traditions concerning the restoration of Israel as a time in which Gentiles would also be drawn to worship Israel's God (3.657–808) provide for an end-time expansion of God's people. This restoration eschatology presumes that the nations will be subordinate to the "sons of the Great God," the restored Israel.

Where does Paul appear in this spectrum? Allegiance to the crucified and risen Christ has replaced the Law as the criterion for participation in God's eschatological restoration of the covenant people (Hengel 1997, 13). Paul insists that Gentiles are included within this

new Israel without becoming "Jews" (Gal 6:16; Dunn 1998, 507).
But, as Martyn maintains, the break in Paul's view of salvation does
not permit a developmental view of salvation history—as though the
Gentile Christians were incorporated into "Israel," God's existing people (Martyn 1997, 348–52). Paul denies that the promise to Abraham
that is fulfilled in Christ has any ethnic or geographic parameters. Thus
Barclay rightly observes that Rom 14:1–15:6 can be read as a concession on Paul's part to law-observant, Jewish Christians. While they can
keep dietary rules and associate with fellow Jews in synagogues, the
socioreligious language that Paul uses for Christian life undermines the
point of doing so (Barclay 1996, 385–86). Christians have an alternate
cult, the true worship of God (Phil 3:3; 2 Cor 3:15). Enthusiasm for
maintaining cultic worship of God in the Jerusalem Temple would be
undermined by Paul's repeated insistence that the Christian community see itself as the temple of God (1 Cor 3:16–17; 6:19–20; 2 Cor
6:16; Barclay 1996, 386).

The most stunning rhetorical identification with non-Jews comes
in Paul's repeated use of expressions associated with circumcision as
the ethnic designation for Jews (e.g., Gal 2:9). Although Jews recognized circumcision as the special mark of their covenant with God
(*Jubilees* 15.26), it was ordinarily an ethnic designation only in
polemical contexts. Within Judea in the Maccabean period, circumcision was the marker of Jewish identity. By the first century B.C.E.,
Roman satirists had begun to recognize it as a way to ridicule the Jew
(e.g., Horace, *Sat.* 2.9, 69–70; Petronius, *Satyr.* 102.14; Cohen 1999,
39–44; Barclay 1996, 438–39). Given the repugnance shown for the
practice in such writers, Paul can be read as hoping to awaken disgust
in his non-Jewish audience (so Mason 1990, 183–205). Non-Jewish
authors sometimes equate the practice of circumcision with the
Phrygian practice of castration (Mason 1990, 189); however, such an
identification would not necessarily turn the stomachs of the Galatians,
since they were familiar with the castrated devotees of the Anatolian
mother goddess (Elliott 1999, 679). Paul's vicious slap at those who
have suggested circumcision—they deserve accidental castration
(5:12)—shows that he is familiar with the satirical use of this equation.

Paul may have misjudged his Galatian audience by assuming that
they would share the same sentiments of revulsion evident among the

Roman intellectual elite. We cannot be sure. We can conclude that
Paul exhibits such an identification with the non-Jewish perspective
that it would not have been unreasonable for other Jews or Jewish
Christians to doubt his loyalty to ancestral tradition. Barclay argues
that even in Romans, where Paul attempts to make more accommodating statements about the Mosaic law (Rom 7:12, 14), the overall
impact of his remarks is negative. He does not defend the Torah, as
did other Hellenistic Jews. Christ is the "end" (Gk. *telos*) of the Law
(Rom 10:4) in the sense that belief in Christ is its goal. Christians are
dispensed from obligation to follow it (Rom 7:1–6), since its vulnerability to the power of sin made it unable to render persons righteous
(Rom 7:7–8:4; Barclay 1996, 387). Paul's "zeal" for the Law in his
past way of life "in Judaism" (Gal 1:12–13) aligns his religious sentiments more with the position reflected in Maccabees (1 Macc 1:60–63;
Dunn 1999, 183–85) than with the assimilation to Greco-Roman culture of other Diaspora Jews. Dunn suggests that it is that sense of
"Judaism" that the apostle abandoned. When Paul's ethical sentiments
about idolatry or sexual morality are invoked, he remains firmly in the
Jewish camp (idem, 191–92). Thus, even if Paul did recognize the
attraction circumcision could hold for Galatian Christians, he would
be equally horrified. For him, it could only represent a lapse back
toward the veneration his converts had shown to the cult of the mother
goddess. He made this point by treating the Galatians' desire to come
under the Law as though it were a lapse back into paganism (4:8–11).

Galatians and Rhetoric

The question of the impact of Paul's line of argument opens up a
larger debate over the rhetorical strategies being employed in the letter. Hans Dieter Betz's commentary demonstrates that one could ana-
lyze the structure of the letter using the formal categories of classical
legal rhetoric (Betz 1979, 14–25). He agrees that the epistolary form
deprives Paul of the advantages and techniques of an actual speech
delivered in court, but insists that the best way to understand the
dynamic of this letter is to read it as Paul's defense of himself: "The
apologetic letter such as Galatians, presupposes the real or fictitious

situation of the court of law. . . . In the case of Galatians, the addressees are identical with the jury, with Paul being the defendant and his opponents the accusers" (Betz 1979, 24). Scholars have since objected that elements such as the ethical advice on Christian life (Gal 5:13–6:10) are out of place in the defense speech and that other criteria should be used to determine the structure of the letter (e.g., Longenecker 1990, cix–cxix; Boers 1994, 43–47; Kern 1998).

Even if the entire letter is not framed as a piece of forensic rhetoric, Betz's analysis has demonstrated the necessity of reading the letter as a piece of persuasion that is addressed to an emotionally charged situation. Bachmann suggests that the polemical letter in which a teacher of the Essene sect addressed other Jews over differences in halachah (4 QMMT) is a closer rhetorical analogy to Galatians than Greco-Roman rhetorical theory (Bachmann 1998, 95). However, 4 QMMT only provides an analogy for the three-cornered rhetorical pattern in which the sender seeks to enlist the addressees on his side against the halachah of another group. It does not provide a model for the forms of rhetorical argument found in Galatians. Bachmann points out that the issue of inclusion and exclusion forms the key to Gal 3:1–4:7. If the Galatians adopt the Judaizing policy of the opposition, they will be excluded from their relationship with the apostle (Bachmann 1998, 97). The latter is Paul's positioning of the issue. Being circumcised implies deserting Christ to come under the Law. The Galatians did not necessarily hold this view. They may have seen the rite as little more than a sign of the covenant (so Boers 1994, 63–64) or, as our discussion of Judaizing has suggested, a declaration of political, social, and religious loyalty to the God of Israel.

Did Paul succeed in winning back the loyalty of the Galatians whom he describes with extraordinary pathos as wayward children who have left him at his wits' end (4:18–20; Betz 1979, 236–37)? Did they agree to take action against those who were preaching a false gospel, as the allegory of Hagar and Sarah suggests they should, by throwing them out (4:21–5:1)? It is difficult to imagine that such a rhetorically powerful presentation of the gospel failed to achieve Paul's practical objectives. Yet many prominent scholars have argued that Galatians was a failure. The crucial evidence for their view comes from Romans. W. D. Davies suggests that the conciliatory language about the Law, Israel, and Christians who continue ancestral Jewish practices resulted from the failure of Galatians. He also concludes that Paul's anticipation of Jewish and Jewish-Christian opposition when he gets to Jerusalem (Rom 15:22–33) flows from the success of the opposition in Galatia (Davies 1999, 725).

To answer the question of whether or not Galatians succeeded by referring to hypothetical reasons for the composition of Romans merely substitutes one set of unknowns for another. Much depends upon our assessment of the dual audience. Paul may have crafted a successful appeal to his Galatian converts that left the more ideological advocates of Judaizing unmoved. Murphy-O'Connor presumes that the former would not have understood much of the exegetical, Jewish argumentation in Galatians. That argument was directed at the "intruders" who were still present (1:7; 5:10). Even if they were not persuaded, Paul's letter could have created disarray in the ranks (Murphy-O'Connor 1996, 200–203).

If the Galatians had only relatively weak links to the social, political, or religious interests of Jews—combined with an affinity toward Jewish festivals and even circumcision drawn from their prior religious practice—then Paul's sharply worded condemnation would seem to be adequate to its task. The famous fourth-century C.E. rhetorician-turned-Christian, Victorinus, defined Paul's task as deliberative. Paul demonstrated that: "To believe in Christ and follow the works of the law is inconsistent and self-contradictory. For since the law failed to justify human kind on the basis of its works, Christ came for that reason" (Cooper 2000, 119). Victorinus differs from modern commentators like Betz in his understanding of Galatians' opening claims about authority. Paul is not responding to a personal attack, but asserting the authority of the gospel that his audience already knew to be divine revelation (Cooper 2000, 122–25). Based on his reading of Victorinus, Cooper concludes that the episode with Peter (Gal 2:11–14) has also been misread in contemporary analysis. The audience was intended to consider Paul's intervention a success: "Prior to embarking on the series of arguments in ch. 3–4, the *narratio* thus serves to prepare the Galatians to be corrected by offering a precedent, inasmuch as Peter himself is depicted as having been rebuked for failing to make his own behavior conform to what he had already admitted to being the nature of the gospel" (idem, 125). The autobiographical elements in Paul's account serve to establish his character as a reliable and truthful witness to the gospel (idem, 126).

Whether one treats the rhetorical agenda of Gal 1–4 as Paul's defense against accusations directed against his ministry (apologetic) or as a strong intervention calling the Galatians back to the apostle's teaching about salvation (deliberative), the shift to ethical exhortation in chs. 5–6 is not directly related to the rhetorical genre. Victorinus comments: "at this point, as if the previous question and issue had been left behind, Paul now seems to give a precept for exhortation so that they would not love discord but mutually cherish one another," (CSEL [Corpus scriptorum ecclesiasticorum latinorum] 83.2, 164.12–14; Cooper 2000, 127). The conclusion in Paul's own hand (6:11–17) returns to the issue of Judaizing as disloyalty to Paul's gospel; therefore, commentators often fill in the unexpressed link between paraenesis and argument. For example, Betz suggests that the Galatians turned toward the Law as a resolution to the problem of transgressions, of life governed by the passions of the flesh. Life "in the Spirit" did not transform the moral conduct of believers (Betz 1979, 8–9). Or, as in Martyn's case, they may appeal to the view that Galatians is a substitute for the sermon Paul would have preached had he been present (Martyn 1997, 23). Exhortation in Christian living is part of the sermonic agenda along with rhetorical devices from both forensic and deliberative speeches. However, Martyn concludes that the hortatory section must answer a charge of "ethical chaos" made by those advocating Jewish practices (idem, 27).

Given a powerful incentive in their personal experience for adopting the Law, Martyn also concludes that Galatians failed to win the day. He agrees with those who cite as evidence of Paul's failure the fact that Galatia is not mentioned as contributing to the Jerusalem collection in Rom 15:26 despite the fact that he had made an appeal there (1 Cor 16:1). However, Paul may have been referring only to those accompanying him to Jerusalem. If the Galatian churches were in the northern territory, rather than the south, a land route from Ephesus would not bring him anywhere near the Galatian churches (see Map 3 in Mitchell 1993, opposite p. 40). Acts (20:15–16; 21:1–4) has Paul sail from Macedonia to Miletus and then on to Tyre (see discussion in

Murphy-O'Connor 1996, 343–47), even further removed from
Galatia. A second difficulty with reconstructions that assume the
Galatians were motivated to adopt the Law by experiences of moral
weakness lies in the assumption that non-Jews would instinctively view
law as the solution. Jewish apologists depicted the Law in such terms
and underlined the moral depravity of non-Jews deprived of its knowledge of God (Wis 13:1–14:31; Philo, *Spec.* 1.15; *Opif.* 45). Romans
1:18–2:29 employs that tradition (see Dunn 1988, 61). However, Paul
introduces an unusual twist in the argument. The pagans once had
knowledge of God but rebelled. Their moral depravity is God's punishment for suppressing the truth about God (see Gaca 1999,
170–77). Such arguments encouraged insiders to remain loyal to their
Jewish or Christian tradition. They did not advocate introduction of
the Law as a cure for the social problems of immorality. Seeking to win
a sympathetic hearing from non-Jewish readers in Rome at the end of
the first century, Josephus accentuated the coherence between Jewish
ideals and traditional Roman values (see Goodman 1999, 57). Instead
of reading the hortatory section as Paul's reply to a hypothesized argument for the Law as an ethical guide, one should see it as a positive
appeal to patterns of group solidarity and mutual love established
when Paul founded the churches in Galatia. Paul's letter begins the
general exhortations with the love command as fulfillment of the Law
(5:13–14) and concludes with a general maxim, "do good to all, especially those of the household of faith" (6:10). The community is able
to remain self-sufficient. It does not require the political, social, or religious links with Judaism associated with Judaizing in the first century.

Neither Romans nor Acts provides evidence for the success or failure of this letter. We do know that in the third and fourth centuries
C.E., rural Anatolia converted to Christianity. Christians had forged a
religious language about God and the cosmos that resonated with
ancestral, pagan beliefs in "the most holy, highest God" and with reverence for prophetic oracles (see Mitchell 1993, 2:37–63). Some areas
and cities had adopted Christianity in the third century while neigh-
boring territory remained pagan until the imperial establishment of
Christianity in the fourth century. This expansive growth in the later
centuries would not have occurred without the consistent presence of
Christians in the region (see Stark 1996). The gospel was not lost

because of the crisis referred to in Galatians. Scraps of evidence suggest that some forms of Judaizing Christianity existed in the region during the later centuries. The cemetery of a village near Tavium contains both Jewish and Christian graves (Mitchell 1993, 2:36). With Christians and Jews continuing to live in close proximity, the social and religious issues posed in Galatians must have remained alive. Paul's refusal to compromise with the Judaizing views of the opposition in Galatia (see Gaventa 2000, 271) made it impossible for Christians to slide over into the margins of the Jewish community. However the recipients may have responded to Galatians, its success in drawing a sharp line between Christian identity and that of Abraham's Jewish offspring is striking.

The theological premise behind this division is fundamental to Paul's understanding of salvation. Martyn catalogues the apocalyptic expressions in Galatians. He argues that Paul adopts a cosmological vision of the human plight. Anti-God powers had taken over the world and led humanity into slavery. God freed humanity by conquering the powers of the "present evil age." This "apocalyptic invasion" occurred with the coming of the Son (4:4; Martyn 1997, 97–105). The "new creation" (6:15) that followed this divine act of liberation obliterated all the conventional marks of identity (3:28). Gaventa observes: "As the gospel's arrival obliterates the Law, it also obliterates those other "places" with which people identify themselves, even the most fundamental places of ethnicity, economic and social standing, and gender. The only location available for those grasped by the gospel is "in Christ" (Gaventa 2000, 272). While it is easy to state the principle that Christians have their identity in Christ, not in social or religious codes devised by human beings, determining the consequences of that insight for Christian life is more difficult. The pastoral dimensions of Paul's letters are most evident when they intervene to put various churches back on track.

Theological Assumptions in Galatians

Modern readers can be as fascinated with the social dynamics of early Christianity as ancient readers were with discovering elaborate allegorical

meanings in every passage of the Bible. The primary purpose of reading the Bible is not instruction in social history or in unraveling some
coded message. Most people read the Bible because they want to
know what the word of God has to say about their lives. Even if they
would never use the term "theology," that is what most people expect
from Scripture. However, the twenty-first-century Christian rarely
hears even the most basic theological words used outside the church
doors. Even coffee-hour fellowship in the church hall lapses into discussions about newspapers, sports, television, and so on. A fiction
writer proposed a scene in which God's loneliness and passionate
desire to communicate with humanity led him to start calling Oprah!
Paul's world was much different. Religion was not a marginal question. Each city had its calendar of religious festivals and sacrifices.
Public office required individuals to sponsor, participate in, and even
officiate at such events. Because Jews would not do so, outsiders often
said that they were "haters of humanity." Everyone agreed that divine
powers, whether pagan gods or the God of Israel, were the most
important forces behind whatever happened in the world.

   People today assume that the basic theological question is whether
there is a God at all. Then, if there is, does God really act to change
things in the universe? Or is God just an inspiring, comforting image
in our minds? The first-century question was much different. For
pagans, who lived in a world populated with many gods, goddesses,
and other spiritual powers, the problem was to figure out which ones
were likely to help you (Klauck 2000, 1–68). What sacrifices, prayers,
and other rites were you required to perform so that your divine benefactor would come through when you needed help? The religious system also included sacrifices offered for the dead on fixed dates. Meals
could be offered at the grave or liquids poured down specially
designed tubes. Klauck comments: "Two potential meanings for the
feeding of the dead have been indicated above: the appeasing of the
spirits of the dead and the conviction that the dead depend on the living for nourishment to sustain their existence in the afterlife. Another
driving force could have been the wish to deny the reality of death by
continuing table fellowship: by giving the dead a share of one's own
food, one maintains a link with them" (idem, 77).

When one adds to the routine, public expressions of religion, special cults that provided secret initiations into the divine realm, popular oracle and healing shrines, and the myriad items of magic, it is easy to see that the religious scene was bustling. No one could ignore it. The Jewish and Christian belief that there is only one God cut through the complexity of competing divinities. Paul presumes that his Galatian converts will look back on their old religious behavior as slavery to "elemental powers of the universe" (4:8–11).

Another key item in the Jewish understanding of God is that God created everything in the universe. Nothing stands outside of God's power. That too could have been attractive over against the pagan myths in which gods could operate against one another. Paul could assume that the Galatians had experienced God's effective power firsthand. Their conversion was accompanied by miraculous signs (Gal 3:5). Another example of God's power that would have been familiar from Paul's initial preaching is the power over death. Galatians 1:1 reminds readers that God has raised Christ from the dead. The realization that God raised Jesus from the dead was the central element in Paul's transformation from zealous Jew and persecutor of the church to preacher of the gospel to the Gentiles (Gal 1:15–16). Resurrection of the dead should not be seen as equivalent to philosophical beliefs concerning the immortality of the soul or whatever uncertain connections to the dead were embedded in meals and food offerings. Resurrection belongs to the constellation of hopes associated with the new creation. The resurrection of Christ indicates that the new age is underway even though the old order has not been brought to an end (Achtemeier 1996, 140–41). Thanks to the cross, Christians belong to the new creation, not to the old order with its distinction between Jew (circumcision) and Gentile (non-circumcision; Gal 6:14–15).

This understanding of creation is more developed in other letters (see 1 Cor 7:32–35; 8:4–6; 15:27–50; Rom 8:19–22, 39; and discussion in Adams 2000, 105–90). Adams sees an important qualification in Rom 8:11–23. Instead of speaking of the coming new age and the resurrection body that corresponds to it as though it were a substitution for the present creation, Paul speaks of freeing creation from its bondage. This emphasis on continuity corresponds to the universalist vision of salvation in Romans. All are under sin (Rom 1:18–3:20; 5:15–19); all are saved through Christ's death (3:21–26). Paul rejects the common apocalyptic dualism between a remnant of the righteous, saved at the Parousia, and the masses of wicked Jews and Gentiles who are condemned (Adams 2000, 188–93). Galatians does not take sides on the theological question of whether the new creation is a replacement of the old creation or if it is the old creation liberated from the powers of decay, sin, and death. Paul uses the terminology of old creation (*stoicheia tou kosmou*, 4:3; *kosmos*, 6:14) and new (*kainē ktisis*, 6:15) to argue for a point of discontinuity. Religious and social divisions characteristic of the old creation no longer obtain in Christ (see Gal 3:26–28; Adams 2000, 227–28). "The antithesis of *kosmos* and *kainē ktisis* in this passage thus has a very clear social function. It serves to underline the social and religious distinction between the Jewish community and the Galatian churches. Judaism (cf. 1:13–14), as a social, cultural and religious entity, belongs along with paganism to the dying *kosmos*" (Adams 2000, 228).

However, there is another important point of continuity in Paul's thought. The new creation that comes to be realized in Christ belongs to a plan of salvation that has been God's intention from the beginning. Those who are "in Christ" become heirs to God's initial promise to Abraham (Gal 3:29). Because God knew that Abraham's descendants would be Gentiles as well as Jews, God inscribed that promise in Scripture (Gal 3:8). Paul argues that the "nations" mentioned in the blessing of Gen 12:3 are the Gentile converts to faith in Christ, not merely the nations of the world (see Martyn 1997, 301). Jewish authors in the first century C.E. saw Abraham himself as the exemplary convert. While still an idolater in Mesopotamia, Abram recognized the truth that there is only one God, the Creator; rejected idolatry; and was persecuted for trying to get others to do the same. Just as Galatians treats "subjection to the elemental powers" (4:3) as a key feature of paganism, Josephus argues that Abraham rejected the Chaldean view that stars and planets were divine beings (Josephus *Ant.* 1.154–57; see Nickelsburg 1998, 160–61). Such traditions about Abraham would have been a natural way of showing Gentile converts the wisdom of leaving their old customs of idol worship and astrology (Gal 4:8–10) behind (Nickelsburg 1998, 168–71). The faith that Abraham demonstrated in leaving behind home and religion was amply rewarded by the Lord (Gen 15:6; Gal 3:6). However, Gen 17:1–14 imposes the obligation to circumcise male descendants and even slaves purchased by Abraham as a sign of the covenant with God; therefore, Paul's opponents could appeal to the same tradition as evidence that these new Gentile converts should be circumcised (see Martyn's hypothetical sermon in Martyn 1997, 302–306). Paul makes a different move. He develops the baptismal tradition of incorporation into Christ (3:26–27) as the basis for a new relationship between believers and God; they are descended from God, "adopted as sons" (Gal 4:4–7; Martyn 1997, 306). Thus White argues that a radical change has occurred in Paul's idea of God. God is no longer identified as the lawgiver and judge in the Mosaic covenant. God is the Creator who establishes a "family" through adoption (White 1999, xx–xxii).

Since God's plan has been revealed in Scripture, Paul presumes that the truths of salvation in Christ are to be found there. However, Jews are not likely to agree with Christian reinterpretations of Scripture, as 2 Cor 3:14–16 acknowledges. Paul's reading of Scripture follows a narrative structure that lays out the story of God's promises and faithfulness. The prophets, especially Deutero-Isaiah, point forward to the death of Christ as the way in which God has reconciled a fallen humanity to God's self, thereby demonstrating God's righteousness (see Hays 1989, 156–64). Although Paul insists that Christ has ended the obligation to follow regulations of the Torah (Gal 5:1; Byrne 2000, 295–99), he assumes that Scripture provides a vision of life according to God's will that is the basis for ethical life (Rom 13:8–10; Gal 5:14). He can speak of the "just requirement" of the Law being fulfilled in life according to the Spirit (Rom 8:3–4; Hays 1996, 35–39). Scripture is not the only source of moral insight in Paul, as studies of philosophical traditions in his epistles have shown (for example, Engberg-Pedersen 2000). However, Scripture interpreted in light of the gospel message is the only all-embracing framework for discerning how God intends the faithful to live (Hays 1996, 46–47). Having allegorized the story of Sarah and Hagar to identify those who insist on circumcision and Torah obedience as slave descendants of Abraham, Paul personifies Scripture. She gives the Galatians a direct command: "drive out the slavewoman [= those advocating circumcision] and her son" (Gal 4:30 quoting Gen 21:10; Hays 1996, 43). The allegory that leads up to this application of Scripture to the immediate situation will play a key role in patristic theories concerning the multiple senses of Scripture. Paul's reference to things spoken as allegory (Gal 4:21) provided the validation for attributing allegorical or spiritual meaning to Biblical texts generally (de Lubac 1959, 371–83). Paul himself does not treat this example as a paradigm case for Christian reading of Scripture. He has generated the allegory to meet the rhetorical needs of the moment. It does not return when he picks up the Abraham story again in Rom 4:1–25. There Paul uses the fact that Abraham's faith is credited as righteousness prior to the demand for circumcision as evidence that God does not require circumcision of those made righteous through faith (Rom 4:9–12). In the Romans example, Paul's midrash on the Abraham story shifts toward an explicitly Christian affirmation at the end. The same creative power by which God gave the barren, aged couple a son (4:8–19) has raised Jesus from the dead "for our justification" (4:24b–25; Bryan 2000, 117–18).

Paul's methods of interpreting Scripture are tailored to the particular needs of his discourse. In some instances he may intend the audience to recall much more of the story than his citations suggest. In others, such as the reference to Lev 19:18 in 5:14, he clearly means only the text cited. In still other cases, one cannot tell. He presumes an audience familiar with large portions of the Abraham story, but does he really intend that they remember the command to circumcise, let alone Abraham's submission to the rite in Gen 17:24–27? It would certainly undermine the rhetorical effectiveness of his argument were they to do so. Therefore, it seems more likely that Paul treats Scripture as a text whose authority lies in the specific words cited and their interpretation as offered by the apostle. He does not envisage readers who have independent access to these texts beyond what they hear read and preached.

No one can read Paul's letters without recognizing that the cross is central to God's saving action in Christ (Gal 1:4; 2:19–21) and to Paul's self-understanding as an apostle (Gal 6:17). He uses a rhetorical topos, the requirement that an orator set his subject visibly before the audience, to assert that his preaching had so presented Christ crucified (Gal 3:1; cf. 1 Cor 2:2). Christian life is marked by the cross (Gal

2:19; 6:14). Thus anyone who deviates from Paul's understanding of the gospel can be accused of evading persecution by nullifying the offense of the cross (5:11). Paul can presume that his readers know instinctively what modern readers do not, that crucifixion is the most degrading, humiliating, and tortured death devised for human beings; that no person of stature would be so executed (see Brown 1993, 855; 1209–10). Paul adds to the offense the testimony of Scripture itself, that persons hanged on a tree fall under God's curse (Gal 3:13 citing Deut 21:22–23).

This shift from crucified messiah as a challenge to the cultural and religious assumptions about religious power and authority among the audience (as in 1 Cor 1:18–25; 2:1–9) to the Christ condemned by the Law typifies the rhetorical style of Galatians. Paul sharpens the antithesis between faith in Christ and the Law at every turn. Martyn has emphasized this feature of Paul's argument in Galatians (see Martyn 1985). He describes this move in Galatians as a battle between Christ, born under its enslaving power (Gal 4:4; Phil 2:7), and the Law that speaks in curses. Its curses affect both humanity in general (Gal 3:10; 4:3) and the one who died on the cross for our sins (Gal 3:13). As such, the Law is in collusion with the elemental powers of the cosmos (Martyn 1996, 53). Since Christ triumphed in the contest, he has liberated humanity from its bondage (Gal 5:1). Circumcision becomes like the branding of a slave, the sign of subjection to the Law in its old power (Gal 5:2–3).

The theological problem of accounting for the soteriological effectiveness of the cross is not solved by the appeal to the curse of the Law. Do we perhaps hear the voice of Paul, the zealous persecutor, arguing against the emerging Jesus movement? Paul must be convinced that his Galatian audience remains sufficiently loyal to Christ to turn against the Law for its curse. When Paul employed the language of slavery and freedom, he invoked an established set of cultural relationships. Aageson has pointed out that power relationships are key to the use of slave metaphors, not ownership. Persons were transferred from one domain to another, from one master to another. With each change, individuals had to reconfigure their behavior to the requirements of a new set of power relationships (Aageson 1996). In some way that remains unspecified, the death of Christ for us effects such a transfer.

A second account of the cross focuses on the necessity for sinners to become righteous. For Paul the Pharisee, careful observance of the prescriptions of the Law would have been the condition for attaining righteousness (Pss 7:9–12; 119:1–8; Josephus, *C. Ap.* 2.41). For the Essenes a meticulous devotion to the Law as interpreted within the sect was combined with the confession of the sinfulness of humanity before God. God enables members of the sect to walk in the path of holiness (1 QS 11.9–12; 1 QH 9.32–34; 14.15–16). For Paul the apostle, no form of law observance establishes the sinful human as righteous before God. If it could, Christ's death would have been without purpose (Gal 2:20–21). The tradition that the death of Christ was "for our sins" antedates Paul. He refers to it in formulae that he expects his audience to recognize as traditional (e.g., Rom 3:24–26; 1 Cor 15:3; Gal 1:4).

Romans 3:25 treats the blood shed on the cross as a sacrifice to expiate sin, *hilastērion*. Four Maccabees 17:22 uses the phrase "their expiating death" for the Maccabean martyrs. God's wrath was turned away from a sinful nation thanks to the death of these faithful martyrs (Dunn 1998, 215). Or one might take the phrase as nominal, referring to the cross as the place of such sin-offerings, the "mercy seat" in the Holy of Holies (cf. Heb 9:5; so Fitzmyer 1993, 351–52). While the formula in Rom 3:25 has assimilated the death of Christ to a cultic act that reestablishes the people as righteous before God, that in 1 Cor 15:3 points in another direction. Christ's death for our sins is "according to Scriptures." First Corinthians does not indicate what Scripture texts were used to support the affirmation. One has to look elsewhere in the NT for clues. The OT background to the Passion Narratives provides such familiar examples as the Suffering Servant (Is 53:6–12) and Pss 22:7–9 and 69:4, 22. Though this language emerges in sectarian hymns from Qumran (e.g., 1 QH 5.5–19), there is no evidence for an expectation that God's agent of final salvation would be such a suffering righteous one. The collection of OT texts as testimony to the place of Jesus' death in God's plan reflects the exegetical effort of early Christians (Brown 1994, 1449–63).

These two lines of tradition establish fundamental Christian convictions about the death of Jesus. It was foreseen in God's plan of salvation and prophesied in texts concerning the suffering of the righteous. It represents the definitive offer of God's forgiveness to a sinful humanity. In a culture familiar with sacrificial rituals, the cultic atonement sacrifice and the sacrifice of the Passover lamb (see 1 Cor 5:7), a symbol of freedom, provided the most natural comparison. Paul does not have to elaborate on this tradition in his letters. He alludes to it only in formulaic phrases because Christians were familiar with its outlines in their ritual celebration of the Lord's Supper (e.g., 1 Cor 11:23–26; Mark 14:23–24). The ritual requirement that a sacrificial animal be without blemish is reflected in the sinlessness of Christ, who offered his life on the cross (2 Cor 5:21; Dunn 1998, 221).

Because Paul's letters incorporate such a range of metaphorical traditions to express the importance of Christ's death on the cross, some scholars argue against treating them all as a single, coherent theology (see Achtemeier 1996, 136–37). Dunn pieces together the various ritual images to argue that Paul understood the sacrificial victim as embodying "the offerer *qua sinner*, so that the offerer's sin was somehow identified with the animal and its life stood for his. The only difference in Christ's case is that the initiative came from God rather than from the sinner (Rom 8:3; 2 Cor 5:21)" (Dunn 1998, 220). Thanks to this identification, Paul goes on to conclude that the animal's death is the death of the sinner as a sinner (Rom 6:6; idem, 221). The same transfer of sin to the sinless victim is presumed in texts like Gal 4:4–5 and 3:13 (idem, 222). This shift of sin from sinner to victim in order that sin be put to death fits the agenda of Romans by highlighting that it is illogical for those who share the death of Christ in baptism to think of sin ruling their lives. But that is not Paul's difficulty in Galatians. There he must show that the demands of the Law themselves are to be set aside. The images of Christ as victor and as the one who redeems slaves that Paul uses to establish that point are not derived from the complex of ideas derived from sacrificial cult, as Dunn admits (idem, 227–31). Therefore, it is more appropriate to speak of fundamental convictions about the death of Christ that Paul expresses in a number of striking metaphors than of a systematic theological perspective on how the death of Christ works to bring about righteousness before God.

All of Paul's letters devote space to ethical exhortation. The life of holiness is a consequence of entering into this new relationship with

God through Christ. Galatians 5:13–14 makes the shift from the disruption caused by the debate over circumcision to paraenesis very deftly. The freedom bestowed in Christ is not license for desires but the transfer to a new mode of obedience, an obedience expressed in the command to love one another. Some interpreters assume that the difficulty of living the Christian life without a more explicit ethical code impelled some Galatians to seek out obedience to the Law (so Betz 1979, 273). However, the content of Paul's comments in Gal 5:13–6:10 is quite general. It does not suggest any instances of serious moral difficulty in the Galatian churches. When Paul returns to specifics in 6:11–16, he again sets loyalty to the cross of Christ over against those who advocate circumcision. So the ethical traditions invoked in 5:13–6:10 are more likely a source of agreement, designed to emphasize what Paul and his audience hold in common rather than what divides them. As we have noted above, Paul does not consider adopting the Law a philosophically enlightened solution to the problems of passion in the moral life. It served to guard God's people until the fulfillment of God's promise in Christ (Gal 3:6–24). Now the heirs of that promise exist because of their common baptism into the Spirit (3:25–29). Communal and ethical solidarity between members of this new community can be adequately fostered by the single command that sums up the Law: "You shall love your neighbor as yourself" (Gal 5:14).

Paul's depiction of the "crucifixion of the passions" and the high moral calling of Christians fits the socioreligious argument advanced earlier in the letter. The apparent universalism of its conclusion, "whenever we have an opportunity, let us work for the good of all, and especially for those of the family of faith" (Gal 6:10), codes an item of difference. "The family of faith" is distinct from all others. This division fits the apocalyptic categories that divide the time of salvation from "the evil age" or the age of bondage that preceded it, as we have seen. That division makes it impossible to assimilate across the boundaries back toward a group formed during the past age. Whatever benefits the "Judaizers" sought from forging political or religious ties to Jews, whether locally or as adherents of a cult center in Jerusalem, cannot be retained. However, benefits may be conferred on those others, as in the collection for poor coreligionists in Jerusalem (Gal 2:9–10), insofar as it is encompassed by the phrase "do good to all."

Galatians 1

───────────────────────────────────────

1 Paul, an apostle—not thanks to human choice or through a human appointment but through Jesus Christ and God the Father, who raised him from the dead—and all those[1] who are with me to the churches in Galatia: Grace and peace be with you from God our Father and the Lord Jesus Christ,[2] who gave himself for[3] our sins in order that he might rescue us from the present evil age according to the will of our God and Father, to whom be glory throughout all ages,[4] Amen. (1:1–5)

A typical letter opening includes designations of sender (Paul), recipients ("churches in Galatia"), and greeting ("grace and peace"). Paul typically includes God and the Lord Jesus Christ as the source of the blessing implied by the greeting (see Rom 1:7). Since Paul directs this letter to Christians in a region of Galatia, rather than to the church or churches of a particular city, one might expect what follows to take the form of a public address. Two unusual features of Gal 1:1–5 foster this expectation: (1) its extensive authorization for the author (v. 1); and (2) the final benediction (v. 5). Galatians is the only Pauline epistle that ends with such a liturgical formula (Martyn 1997, 106). A third expansion (v. 4) introduces a formulaic saying that summarizes the message of salvation. This formula first (v. 4a) celebrates the death of Jesus as atonement for sin, an application of Isa 53:6, 12 to the death of Jesus that is pre-Pauline (see 1 Cor 15:3; Bruce 1988, 75). However, the second phrase (v. 4b), which characterizes salvation in apocalyptic terms as "rescue . . . from the present evil age," appears to be Paul's expansion. The argument to follow warns against returning to the slavery from which the death of Christ has liberated us (2:20–21; 4:3–4, 8–9; 5:1; Smiles 1998, 74). Another element in traditional formulae, God having raised Christ from the dead (cf. 1 Cor 15:4; Rom 4:25), is attached to the reference to God the Father in v. 1. Martyn points to traditional Jewish prayers that describe God as "the one who raises the dead." For Christians, this stock epithet now refers to a specific resurrection, that of Jesus (Martyn 1997, 85).

Use of these set formulae assures the audience that what follows concerns the core of the gospel that they received when Paul first preached to them. Resurrection does not reappear as part of the argument in Galatians. Its presence here indicates that Paul is appealing to foundational beliefs that he shares with the audience (Dunn 1993, 29). It is gratuitous to assume that Paul emphasizes the death of Christ for sin because his opponents alleged Jewish sin to be less than that of Gentiles (despite Smiles 1998, 71). Intra-Jewish polemics evident in the Pseudepigrapha and the Dead Sea Scrolls demonstrate that Jews were most concerned with a sinfulness that infected their own people. In some instances reference to Gentile sinfulness is evidence for concern over assimilation to the dominant culture (see Elliott 2000, 57–113). For example, *Psalms of Solomon* 17:14–15 blames Pompey for luring Jerusalemites into pagan practices (idem, 112).

Though the traditional formulae have not been dictated by the preaching of opposing missionaries, Paul's self-designation appears to be another matter. The double negative that follows "apostle" excludes any form of human appointment. The autobiographical argument later in this chapter makes Paul's independence of human authorities evident (1:11–19; 2:1–9; Smiles 1998, 31). There the authorities in question are apostles in Jerusalem. However, if there is any factual background to the stories of Paul's early missionary efforts in Acts, Paul was authorized by the church in Antioch and evangelized cities in southern Galatia as their apostle (Acts 13–14; Dunn, 1993, 25–26). In secular Greek, the word "apostle" designates an envoy or ambassador. In 2 Cor 8:23, representatives of the Corinthian church taking the collection to Jerusalem are referred to as "apostles of the churches." How such an ambassador is received reflects the relative status of the sender and recipients as well as the friendship or hostility that exists between them. To be "sent by God" implies that the apostle's word carries the authority of God (Martyn 1997, 82). Paul will describe his conversion as a direct commission from God to preach among the Gentiles (1:15–16). By insisting upon the divine source of his mission, Paul contributes a religious connotation to the term "apostle." God's choice must be discerned in the mission at hand. It also serves to distinguish some Christian missionaries from others. When Paul speaks of those in Jerusalem "who were apostles before me" (1:17), he also employs this restricted sense. The criterion for designating a person "apostle" appears to be a divine commission through a vision of the risen Jesus. In 1 Cor 15:3–10, Paul attaches his own calling to a list of such resurrection witnesses that is largely focused on apostles. The link between resurrection visions and the commission to preach occurs in later gospel narratives of resurrection appearances (Luke 24:47–48; Acts 1:8; Matt 28:16–20; John 20:21).

Paul evidently had to struggle to maintain his claim to be "apostle" among those who could claim to have been original followers of Jesus (1 Cor 9:1–2; 2 Cor 11:5; 12:12; Rom 1:1). Luke only speaks of his hero as "apostle" once, in Acts 14:4, 14, while he was still an emissary from Antioch. Paul appears to employ another criterion in his use of the word "apostle" beyond that of "resurrection vision." Apostles have been sent by God to found churches (1 Cor 9:1–2). Churches can only have one "apostle-founder" to whom they owe special loyalty (2 Cor 10:13–16; so Dunn 1998, 540–41). Paul summons his audience to attend once again to the God who called them into existence through the agency of their apostle-founder.[5] Others unfamiliar with the peculiarities of Paul's use of the term "apostle" might nevertheless find a powerful claim to authoritative truth in v. 1. No less a cultural icon than the philosopher Socrates claimed to have Apollo's authorization for his wisdom (Plato, *Apol.* 20E; so Betz 1979, 39).

Scholars have also pointed out the important role that the metaphor of God as "Father" (v. 1) plays in Galatians. Initially the expression serves to establish the relationship between God and Jesus, who is "son" to God in a unique way and shares God's name and power as risen Lord (Rom 1:4; Phil 2:9–11).[6] Galatians emphasizes the consequence of that relationship for believers. They are adopted as children of God thanks to the gracious action of God as Father (vv. 3–4; 4:2–6; Betz, 1979, 39 n. 27; Martyn 1997, 84). Since this new relationship is conferred and affirmed in liturgy and prayer where the Spirit permits believers to address God as "Abba, Father" (4:6), the prayer formula in v. 5 brings Paul and his audience together in the language of worship.

> I am shocked[7] at how quickly you have deserted the one who called you by the grace of Christ[8] for another gospel—not that there is another one; just that there are some people upsetting you and intending to pervert the gospel of Christ. But even if we or an angel from heaven should preach a gospel to you different from the one we have preached to you, let him be cursed! I am saying yet again what I have said, "If someone preaches to you something different from what you have received, let him be cursed!"
>
> For am I still currying favor with people or with God? Or am I seeking to please people? If I was still pleasing people, I would not be a slave of Christ. (1:6–10)

The rhetorical unity generated by Paul's use of liturgical motifs in the prescript is immediately shattered by the accusation in v. 6. The Galatians are not loyal to the apostle or to the gracious God who adopted them as children. They are deserters. The verb *metatithēmi* in v. 6 is used of those who fall away, desert a military post, or are apostates (Herodotus, *Hist.* 7.18, 3; Plato, *Resp.* 1.345b; Sir 6:9; 2 Macc 7:24; Josephus, *Ant.* 20, 38). The charge becomes most severe, apostasy from God, if the expression "so quickly" is taken as an allusion to the story of Israel and the golden calf. The Greek translation speaks of the Israelites having "turned quickly from the way you commanded them" (Exod 32:8 LXX; Longenecker 1990, 14–15). Paul's astonishment at this development is heightened by the fact that he omits the thanksgiving prayer formula that ordinarily follows the prescript of his letters (see 1 Cor 1:4–9 for example). He will later treat the Galatians' interest in aligning themselves with Jewish customs as if it were apostasy, a turning back to the idols they had once worshiped (Gal 4.8–11). The charge must have hit Paul's audience like a lightning bolt out of the blue sky. Those who were encouraging the adoption of Jewish customs must have presented circumcision and closer ties with Judaism as a way of demonstrating loyalty to the God of Israel. As Martyn observes, they might even have presented the "Law as the good news" (Martyn 1997, 121–22).

Paul sets out what is to be demonstrated in the letter: there cannot be a gospel concerning Christ that differs from that which he had preached in founding the church. He uses a dramatic curse formula to exclude that possibility. Not even he, himself, or an angelic mediator could say something different (vv. 7–9). Modern readers have nothing in their experience that corresponds to the power of the ancient curse or oath formula. Scholars have pointed out that in the ancient Mediterranean world a person or persons whom others thought had been cursed by the gods would be driven out of the community. Failure to do so could result in divine retribution against the whole community.[9] Paul demanded that the Corinthians exclude a fellow Christian who had married his stepmother for this reason (1 Cor 5:1–6). He will propose that the Galatians do the same with those who are advocating this "other gospel" (Gal 4:28–31). Of course, the two cases are not evidently similar. The latter involves a public display of immorality that even pagans found repulsive (1 Cor 5:1). From the ordinary Jewish perspective, the Law is quite different. It was given to protect and preserve the holiness of God's people. What is so offensive about non-Jews adopting some of its precepts that those who advocate this policy should be treated as cursed objects?

By opening with such a dramatic antithesis, Paul has set the bar very high for a successful argument. But before he turns to the matter at hand with the introductory, "I want you to realize"[10] in v. 11, he interjects a comment on the motivation of the contending parties. Commentators and translators remain puzzled over where to place v. 10 in the argument. It does not clearly follow the curse formulae in v. 9. Nor can it introduce the next topic, since v. 11 begins with a standard verb for initiating a topic of discussion.[11] Boers (1994, 57–58) divides the phrase, treating the first part as a sarcastic question that embodies a charge made against Paul, that he had not required Jewish practices of Gentiles in order to make the gospel easier to take. Verse 10b provides an answering response: if he were acting on such motives, he would not be a slave of Christ. Our translation follows this general suggestion. However, considerations of ancient rhetoric make it unnecessary to see Paul responding to a particular charge made against him. The question of whether or not the speaker seeks to flatter his audience is part of a stock theme concerning character.

Flatterers are not to be believed, since they will adapt the truth to the tastes of their listeners (Betz 1979, 55 nn. 111–13; Dodd 1996, 93–94).

Verse 10 provides two bits of evidence[12] that would distinguish Paul from the practitioners of false rhetoric. He himself continues to be persecuted, and he is a slave of Jesus Christ. Both themes will be picked up in what follows. He was once a zealous persecutor of the church (1:13, 23). Those who now seek closer ties with Judaism even at the cost of being circumcised are adopting a course that lessens the danger of persecution (5:11; 6:12; Dodd 1996, 94). Paul cannot be charged with seeking to avoid persecution, since his sufferings as an apostle show that he identifies with the crucified Christ (2:19–21; 3:13; 5:24–25; 6:14–17). Presumably, the phrase "slave of Christ" refers to this latter argument. Paul sets before his audience the choice of either being flatterers or "God-pleasers." If they opt for the latter, they will take the same view of persons who are stirring up turmoil in the churches as Paul does (Dodd 1996, 96). Paul's account of his conversion and relation to other apostles, which follows in Gal 1:11–2:14, also demonstrates his integrity. Once he became an apostle of Christ, no form of human pressure could get him to abandon the true gospel (Dodd 1996, 100–102).

> For[13] I want you to realize, brothers,[14] that the gospel I preach is not of human origin. For I did not receive it from a human being nor was I taught by anyone, but [I learned it][15] through a revelation of Jesus Christ.
>
> For you have heard about how I used to live as a member of the Jewish community,[16] that I was persecuting the church of God vigorously and trying to destroy it, and I was advancing in the Jewish community[17] beyond many of my own age among my own people because I was such a zealot for my ancestral traditions. Now when the one who set me apart from my mother's womb and called me through his grace[18] determined to reveal his Son to me[19] so that I might preach him among the Gentiles, I did not go up to Jerusalem to those who were apostles before me, but I went down to Arabia and again returned to Damascus. (1:11–17)

Verses 11 and 12 emphasize the divine origin of Paul's preaching. The double negative, not received from or taught by someone else, points forward to Gal 2:7. Paul's apostolate is no less divinely authorized than the teaching of the Jerusalem apostles (Smiles 1998, 35–36). Paul equates his vision of the risen Lord to that of the earlier apostles while intimating in 1 Cor 15:8–10 that his was the last such resurrection commissioning (Murphy-O'Connor 1996, 72). However, this phrase poses a problem. Does Paul affirm only that God called him to preach Christ among the Gentiles, leaving to the apostle's own discernment the content of that message? Or does Paul imply, as Donaldson holds, that Paul's message of salvation through faith without obligations to the Law was part of that initial revelation? For Donaldson, that conclusion requires the assumption that Paul had been actively engaged in encouraging Gentiles to join the Jewish community as proselytes (Donaldson 1997, 273–77). However, many scholars challenge the presumption that first-century Jews actively sought to increase their numbers by encouraging Gentile conversion.[20] Rather than set up a scenario according to which Paul's conversion experience reversed his evaluation of a project of bringing Gentiles under the Law, we presume that Paul remained consistently a separatist. He had never favored the conversion of Gentiles to Torah observance.

Martyn has pointed out an extraordinary claim for himself that Paul embeds in his affirmation that he did not receive the gospel through any form of human mediation. Paul must be equating himself with Moses receiving the Torah from God, though Paul never makes such a link explicit. He is more inclined to compare his call to that of the prophet Jeremiah; Martyn therefore concludes that "no human mediator" reflects the apocalyptic side of Paul's thought. This perspective determines the tone of the narrative of events that follows: "[I]n his historical narrative Paul shows that the gospel marches through the world under the banner of apocalypse and not under the constraints of tradition" (1:12, 1:16–17, 2:2; 2:5–6; 2:14; Martyn 1997, 150). The gospel that calls non-Jews to participate in God's salvation belongs to the new age, not to the old.

Paul introduces the narrative that is intended to demonstrate the truth of his claims with information that the audience must have heard from the apostle himself.[21] When he was living according to the Jewish law, Paul persecuted the church with the intent to destroy it. Scholars remain sharply divided over the question of what provoked Paul to engage in such persecution. Donaldson presumes that Paul saw the Christian sect focused on Jesus as a rival to his own attempts to win over Gentiles (Donaldson 1997, 275–78). Others insist that we have no evidence for Paul's pre-Christian activities or motives and should make our reading of his words independent of any such hypotheses (Udoh 2000, 216–20). Both his general zeal for ancestral tradition and his persecution of the church provide the evidence for asserting that Paul's conversion cannot be a change of heart motivated by human concerns or persuasion. As Paul had said, he is not engaged in rhetorical tricks to gain fame and fortune by telling people what they want to hear (Gal 1:10). Paul's assertion that his persecuting activities were near to wiping out the church must be rhetorical intensification.[22]

The account that he goes on to give of his conversion from persecutor to apostle underlines the divine initiative. The God whom he had unwittingly opposed in his zeal has been guiding Paul to the moment in which God will call him to preach Jesus among the Gentiles (vv. 15–16). The language of zeal for ancestral traditions (v. 14) originated in the priestly class but was adopted by the Maccabees. In that context, "zeal for the Law" was a call to arms against those who would eradicate the practice of Judaism (1 Macc 2:26; see Collins 1995, 85). This model suggests a strong emphasis on Jewish identity and a willingness to use the sword against those who threaten it (Dunn 1999, 184). Whatever form Paul's activities took, persecuting the church appeared to be an option for God's holiness at the time. Dunn cites a funerary inscription from Italy that praises a woman "who lived a gracious life inside Judaism" (Dunn 1999, 183). Paul need not have been a political zealot to engage in harassment of Christians for violating the boundaries that protected such a gracious life. Murphy-O'Connor perceives this zeal as a competitive spirit typical of members of elite groups. He suggests that Paul did not begin life in such circles but entered Pharisaic circles when he came to Jerusalem to study. Comparing himself to contemporaries reflects the determination of a newcomer from the Diaspora who got a late start.[23]

Paul tells us little about this shift in his position, preferring to emphasize the divine agency involved.[24] He compresses the entire account into a single sentence (vv. 15–17). The conversion report (vv. 15–16) forms a temporal clause dependent upon the assertion that Paul did not go up to Jerusalem to confer with "those who were apostles before me" (v. 17; Martyn 1997, 156–57). Yet the account provides some clues about how Paul understands himself. The phrase "set me apart from my mother's womb" combines Isa 49:1, 6 and Jer 1:5 LXX, inviting us to see Paul in the mold of the Hebrew prophets. Whatever Paul may have done in persecuting the church out of a misplaced zeal is irrelevant. He responded immediately to God's call when it came to him. There is no reason to assume that he engaged in a period of instruction or study. Nor is there any reason to think that his conviction that Christ is to be preached to the Gentiles developed because of earlier efforts among Jews. Paul went to preach among the Gentiles from the beginning (so Murphy-O'Connor 1996, 80–82). At the same time, Paul makes himself a paradigm case for the thesis that God's call depends entirely upon God's grace, an experience with which his audience should be familiar (Gal 3:2–5; Smiles 1998, 52–53).

He proceeds to the Nabatean kingdom, later the Roman province of Asia, which included the Transjordan from parts of Syria to the Gulf of Aqaba and the Sinai from the Negev to Egypt. This area controlled important trade routes from the Mediterranean across the Jordan valley. The Romans confirmed Aretas as its king (Bowersock 1983, 2–11; 52–57). If he also controlled Damascus as Paul suggests when he later refers to his ignominious flight from the city (2 Cor 11:32–33), that would put Paul's initial missionary activities there sometime in 38–39 C.E., prior to Aretas's death.[25] We have no indication of the reason for Paul's initial choice. Some scholars assume that he knew of Christian missionaries already at work in that region (so Hengel and Schwemer 1997, 109). However, since Paul insists that his calling was to preach Christ among non-Jews, he may have turned to a region with which he was already familiar. Soldiers and merchants passing along its trade routes would have provided the apostle with ample opportunities to ply his trade of tent making.[26] Though we often imagine the earliest missionaries preaching in synagogues, the homes of wealthy patrons, or hired lecture halls, the workshop itself may have been an important locus for evangelization (so Hock 1980).

Paul provides no details of his activities in Arabia or Damascus. The geographical references only serve to demonstrate that he had not gone to Jerusalem. He may be answering a charge that he was dependent upon Jerusalem for his call to preach. However, he will admit that the other apostles could have caused his efforts to be in vain if they had refused to acknowledge Gentile believers (2:1–10; Dunn 1993, 68–69). Paul reports fleeing Damascus in 2 Cor 11:32–33. His activities must have sparked discord in the city, probably among Jews (Dunn 1993, 72). Though the method of escape, being let down along the wall in a basket, is sometimes referred to as humiliating, Paul has considerable ancient precedent for the detail: Joshua's spies escaping Jericho (Josh 2:15; Josephus, *Ant.* 5.1, 2); David from Saul (1 Sam 19:12); Athenians from the tyrant Athenion (Athenaeus, *Deipn.* 5.214a). Thus Paul may have been creating a heroic pedigree for himself in 2 Corinthians. Galatians is only concerned with proving that Paul was well established as a missionary to the Gentiles before he had formal contacts with Jerusalem.

Then three years later I went up to Jerusalem to get acquainted with[27] Cephas[28] and I stayed with him for two weeks, but I did not see any other apostle except James, the brother of the Lord.

What I am writing to you, I swear before God that I am not lying.

Then I went to the districts of Syria and Cilicia. But I remained unknown in person to the Christian[29] churches of Judea. They had only heard that the man who once persecuted us is now preaching the faith which he was once trying to destroy, and they were glorifying God because of me.(1:18–24)

The rest of Paul's autobiographical account (1:18–2:14) consists of a series of episodes introduced by "afterwards, next" plus an indication of the number of years which had passed (1:18; 2:1), "afterwards" with no indication of time (1:21), or "when" (2:11). This sequence conveys the impression that Paul has summarized his entire career, though he says nothing of how he came to be associated with the church in Antioch (see Acts 11:22–26). The purpose of the account is to demonstrate his independence of the Jerusalem apostles. If Acts is correct in attributing the move from Cilicia to Barnabas, a member of the Jerusalem church sent to supervise Antioch, then Paul would weaken his case by including that detail. The details of Paul's first visit, a two-week stay with Peter, have also been subject to considerable speculation. Relying upon the fact that the verb *historēsai* ("visit, get to know") appears in contexts that allude to gaining information, some scholars favor that translation here. Paul did not visit Jerusalem to get to know its leading apostle(s). He visited to gain information about Jesus.[30] By highlighting the hospitality received from Peter, Paul may also wish to imply that he knows Peter better than those who suspect him of breaking away from Jerusalem tradition. Though Paul always uses the Latinized "Paul" for himself,[31] he employs the Aramaic form of Simon's nickname, Cephas ("rock").

The visit is described as a private affair, which may have been necessary if Paul's presence in the city would have stirred up conflict (so Hengel and Schwemer 1997, 144–46). Paul minimizes his contacts with other apostles, although he does acknowledge meeting James during the visit. An oath formula (v. 20) highlights the significance of that part of the account. Paul was never subordinate to or commissioned by the apostles in Jerusalem. Though Paul speaks as if he turned to his home district of Cilicia and then went to Syria, he may have gone to Cilicia as a missionary from Antioch as Acts suggests. Cilicia, lying to the south of Galatia, would have been familiar to the audience (Martyn 1997, 175). Other scholars suggest that Paul's geography has been laid out to fit ancient traditions concerning Abraham's journey around the land promised to him (Hengel and Schwemer 1997, 174–75). However, the most immediate rhetorical function of these geographical notices is demarcation, not focus on the promised land. They create the illusion of two distinct regions, one centered in Jerusalem and Judea, the other a group of surrounding territories. The former is evangelized by Peter, James, and other apostles in Jerusalem; the latter, by God's newly elected apostle, Paul. The linguistic distinction maintained when the new apostle refers to Peter by the Aramaic "Cephas" and to himself with the Romanized "Paul"[32] also contributes to this differentiation.

The fact that Acts presents a more complex picture of the evangelization of the Nabatean region and Syria, with well-established churches in Damascus and Antioch prior to Paul's arrival, should not obscure Paul's presentation here. He has not given a complete, historically accurate account of his life in this period. That his audience may have been familiar with some of the missing details could be implied. Paul says that he "returned *again* to Damascus" (v. 17), suggesting that the audience knows that his vision of the Lord occurred in the vicinity of Damascus. Paul takes Barnabas, otherwise unidentified, to Jerusalem (2:1). Peter's presence in Antioch, Barnabas's authority there, and the links between that church and the Jerusalem church that created the conditions for the episode in Gal 2:11–14, assume that Paul is a subordinate player in Syria's most important church. Therefore, Paul's rhetoric should not be construed as an attempt to deceive the Galatians by hiding information about his past. Rather the territorial designations permit him to argue independence from Jerusalem and its territory, Judea. From the civic point of view, Judea is a distinct region. The cultural, personal, and religious ties, which in fact link Christians in Jerusalem with those in Antioch, Syria, and the Nabatean territories around Damascus, are passed over in silence.

Paul, himself, is not completely unknown in Judea. The fact that he spent two weeks as a guest of Peter indicates that he had some form of introduction to the apostle.[33] Paul insists that it was his reputation, not his person, that was known to Christians in the Roman province of Judea (vv. 22–24). However, this assertion creates a dilemma, since they are said to praise God because "the person who was once persecuting *us*" has reversed his position. Was the persecution to which Paul refers within Judea, as his words suggest, or outside the province in Damascus as Acts 9:2 implies (Hengel and Schwemer 1997, 37; Hultgren 1976)? We have no clear evidence to resolve the historical issue.[34] What, then, is the rhetorical significance of Paul's statement? The oath formula in v. 20 may be taken to cover all the details that follow in vv. 21–24, although Paul's narrative does not specify the precise point at issue. Betz suggests that the opposition to Paul's gospel had originated in Judea. Paul's countermove exploits a standard topos in martyrdom traditions, God's miraculous conversion of the persecutor (Betz 1979, 79–81). Hence the oath addresses the question of how Paul was viewed by Christians in these churches, not the associated geographical movements. If the churches in Judea are giving thanks to God for the divine miracle of Paul's conversion and preaching, then no one who denigrates the apostle or his message can claim to represent the teaching of those churches. To follow the example of their fellow believers in Judea,[35] Paul's Galatian converts must join in praising God for the apostle's conversion from persecutor to evangelist.[36]

Chapter Two

Galatians 2

Then fourteen years later, I again went up to Jerusalem with Barnabas, also taking Titus along; now I went up as a consequence of a revelation and I put before them the gospel which I preach among the Gentiles, but in private, before the important people,[1] lest somehow I am putting out the effort[2] or had done so in vain. But Titus, who was with me, although he was Greek, was not compelled to be circumcised in any way;[3] now because of false brothers brought in surreptitiously, who slipped in to spy on the freedom which we have in Christ Jesus, in order to enslave us[4]—to whom we did not yield submissively even for a moment[5] so that the truth of the gospel might continue unchanged for you. Now from those regarded as important— what sort of persons they were makes no difference to me. God is no respecter of persons—for the important people added nothing to me, but quite the opposite, seeing that I had been entrusted with the gospel for the uncircumcised just as Peter had for the circumcised,[6] for the one who activated Peter for apostleship to the circumcised also [activated] me for the Gentiles, and recognizing the grace that had been given to me, James, Cephas, and John, those who were considered pillars, extended the right hand of partnership to me and Barnabas, so that we [would preach][7] to the Gentiles, and they to the circumcised. [They] only [asked][8] that we remember their poor, the very thing which I was eager to do. (2:1–10)

Having established a geographical distinction between his activities and those of the Jerusalem apostles, Paul turns to incidents in which he is face-to-face with Christian authorities from Jerusalem. The reference point for the "fourteen years" is unclear. Does Paul mean fourteen years after his call to be apostle to the Gentiles? Or fourteen years after the initial visit with Peter? Either is possible, although the reference to his conversion in Gal 1:23 makes it plausible that the "then" resumes the sequence of events to be narrated and the years are counted from that conversion rather than from the prior visit.[9] Difficulties in reconciling Paul's account of his second visit to Jerusalem in Gal 2:1–10 with the Jerusalem Council in Acts 15:1–29 have led some scholars to argue against identifying the two meetings (see Achtemeier 1987). However, elements in both versions make it more probable that the same event is at issue:[10] (a) agitation by some who seek the circumcision of Gentile converts; (b) Paul and Barnabas as representatives of Gentile converts; (c) Jerusalem leaders, Peter and James, central to the decision; (d) Gentile converts are not required to adopt circumcision (Barrett 1998, 710–12; Fitzmyer 1998, 543–44; Perkins 1994, 118–20).

Galatians 2:1–10 does not present a historical account of the events connected with the visit to Jerusalem (Betz 1979, 84). Without the version in Acts 15, one might infer that Paul took his missionary associates on a semiprivate visit to Jerusalem to confer with church leaders about his preaching to the Gentiles. Yet Paul can hardly have doubted the gospel that he had been preaching for fourteen years. Only a more dangerous threat that would undermine the existence of the Gentile churches could have elicited such a visit (Murphy-O'Connor 1996, 137; Smiles 1998, 39).[11] Paul is careful to mention that he was directed to undertake this visit by God (v. 2a). This remark recalls the divine origin of Paul's gospel for the Gentiles and sets the tone for the rest of the account. Paul acts as God's agent on an equal basis with the other apostles (Smiles 1998, 36–38). The expressions that Paul uses in referring to other participants create uncertainty about his view of the other apostles. The Greek *hoi dokountes* ("important persons"; vv. 2, 6, 9) can be taken in a more negative or ironic sense. Such persons only seem to be important or are held in esteem on false premises (Betz 1979, 87).[12] However, the force of Paul's concluding argument, that these prominent men had accepted his mission (v. 9), would be considerably lessened by sarcasm. Therefore we have opted for a more neutral rendering of the expression. James, Peter, and John really are the most prominent members of the Jerusalem church. Yet Paul is compelled to mitigate a view of their authority that would make these apostles superior to himself. Consequently, he imports two maxims into the presentation: (a) the wise man's indifference to the threats or pretensions of the powerful ("what they once were[13] is nothing to me"); and (b) God's impartiality in judging humans (v. 6).[14]

The situation becomes even more problematic if one sets aside the model suggested by Acts 15:1–5 of an irenic appeal to Jerusalem for help in settling questions about Gentile converts that had been introduced by persons from Judea. Philip Esler has suggested that Paul is responding to the challenge of persons from Judea with a provocation of his own. He insists on being on equal terms with the Jerusalem authorities. To make matters worse, he has brought along Titus, an uncircumcised Gentile, to force a confrontation. However, Paul attempts to restrict discussion to the leaders rather than to involve the larger community out of consideration for the honor of James, Peter, and John—should they concede that Paul's gospel is correct (Esler 1995, 292–94). The challenge proved a victory for Paul's position because the Jewish-Christian leaders received Titus without the demand that he be circumcised (Betz 1979, 88–89).[15] But Paul must still explain where the controversy over Gentile converts originated. He does so by shifting metaphors from hospitality and consultation among equals to conspiracy. Paul introduces a third party of "false brothers," smuggled in as spies with the purpose of destroying the freedom of the Gentile believers (v. 4; Bruce 1988, 112–13).[16] But he does not indicate whose spies these false brethren are. The metaphor may suggest a third group where none existed as analogous with what has happened to the churches in Galatia or to the episode at Antioch in the next section (Gal 2:11–14). In those instances, outsiders sparked controversy over the presence of Gentiles in the community.

Since Paul wishes the Galatians to expel the agitators from their community, the metaphor of false Christians as spies sneaking in to destroy a city facilitates that emotional transfer on the part of the audience. It also enables Paul to mask the possibility of disagreement between himself and other apostles. Luke assumes that the agitation over circumcising Gentile converts was caused by Christians who belonged to the Pharisee party (Acts 15:5).[17] This guess has sparked more elaborate reconstructions of political turmoil in mid-century Jerusalem. Conflict between native populations, Jews, and Roman authorities, which under Claudius led to the expulsion of Jews from Rome and a severe edict warning Jews in Alexandria to cease agitating for citizenship, must have had their repercussions in the city. Caligula's demand to install his statue in the Temple had already sparked dissent in Alexandria and Jerusalem but was resolved by the emperor's death (Murphy-O'Connor 1998, 138–41).[18] Some Christians might have sought to ameliorate tensions with fellow Jews in this troubled city by insisting that Gentile converts become Jewish proselytes (so Jewett 1970, 205). Murphy-O'Connor, who otherwise agrees with this depiction of political turmoil in Jerusalem, doubts that it would lead to proselytizing among Gentile Christians. On the contrary, these tensions could lead Christian Jews to dissociate themselves from the Gentiles altogether. He comments: "[E]ven though they had no attachment to Judaism; they were followers of Christ, not of Moses. What loyalty could the Jewish people expect of such individuals when hostile pressures began to take their toll?" (Murphy-O'Connor 1996, 141).

What loyalty indeed? As we have seen in the Introduction, "to Judaize" had a wide range of associations in the ancient world. It could refer to Gentiles who advocated for the Jewish community in a political context without any suggestion that these patrons were also proselytes (Cohen 1999, 181–85). Would the Christian Jews in Jerusalem expect some degree of political support or patronage from these new Gentile believers? Without a doubt, as the agreement reached at the conclusion to the meeting suggests. The collection for the poor in Jerusalem (vv. 9b–10) was not Paul's compromise proposal but a requirement imposed by James, Peter, and John. Esler sees it as a face-saving move by the apostles. They are "able to claim before the Jerusalem church that they had extracted a valuable concession in return" (Esler 1995, 297). Was the concession purely financial, as Esler's statement suggests? That would be no small gain for a group whose Galilean origins would have left it with little in the way of patronage or financial resources in Jerusalem. Or did it carry broader sociopolitical implications, creating a general network of benefactor-client relationships between Jerusalem Christians and the Gentiles of the Diaspora churches? If the polarizations that would become evident in the Judean-led revolt of 66 C.E. were already taking shape, the practical considerations that led James to agree that Gentile believers could belong to the church as such (so Murphy-O'Connor, 1996, 141) may have been fueled by political needs as much as by financial ones.[19]

Such an agreement is fraught with ambiguities. Paul repeatedly insists that his view of the gospel prevailed. He did not defer to the authority of the Jerusalem apostles, since his apostleship is equal to theirs (v. 6). He was eager to carry out the collection for the poor among the Gentiles (vv. 9b–10). As Esler puts it, "James and Peter really got nothing out of him at all in return for the agreement. . . . This means that he has got the better of them in the exchange and his honor is enhanced at their expense" (1995, 297). If the collection is perceived in ordinary social terms as the gift of a benefactor to a client, then the asymmetry tips the balance of power toward the Gentile churches.[20] Paul wishes his Galatian audience to form this impression from his account. If, on the other hand, the collection is perceived as an acknowledgment of Jerusalem as the religious center of the movement, then it might be understood as acknowledging the religious authority of its apostles. Such ambiguities cast doubt on the form of the agreement itself. Scholars have generally concluded that the "right hand of *koinēnia*" (v. 9) implied a full, mutual agreement[21] as to the principles of Paul's mission among the Gentiles (Dunn 1993, 105–15). Esler challenges this consensus. He points to instances in which "giving the right hand" does not mean equality or mutual agreement. In Maccabees, for example, it refers to establishing a peace after hostilities (e.g., 1 Macc 6:58; 11:50, 62, 66; 13:45, 50; 2 Macc 4:34; 11:26; 12:11; 13:22; 14:19). The commander or superior party "gives the right hand" while the inferior, sometimes portrayed as a suppliant, takes it (Esler 1995, 298–99). Paul's persistent assertions that he does not regard the Jerusalem apostles as superior to himself have successfully obscured this element in the exchange from the eyes of most scholars, as was his intent with regard to the original audience.

Esler's proposal carries the political metaphor of spying and conflict from v. 4 into the concluding agreement. If we are to envisage the conclusion under the rubric of a peace treaty, then we should treat its other stipulations in similar fashion. The division of mission responsibility has long baffled commentators. Does Peter's charge with preaching "to the circumcision" and Paul "to the uncircumcision/Gentiles" (vv. 7–9) imply an ethnic or a geographical division (Bruce 1988, 125–26)? Paul could hardly agree that the content of the gospel preached to Jews would involve a Torah obligation that was rejected in his own preaching to Gentiles (Bruce 1988, 124). He has insisted that there is only one gospel (1:6–9). Both the geographic and the ethnic interpretations pose difficulties for the picture of mixed early Christian communities that we find in most of the New Testament writings (Murphy-O'Connor 1996, 142). Murphy-O'Connor concludes that Paul has incorporated the geographical division agreed to with Peter on his prior visit to Jerusalem (1996, 93–94).[22] If, on the other hand, we view this agreement as the peace treaty that followed hostilities, then the stipulation of either geographic or ethnic separation on paper may not have anything to do with realities on the ground. The uneasiness that some scholars have noted concerning the collection for Jerusalem fits this pattern as well.[23] In the ancient world, the persons who "pay up" to settle a conflict are the losers, not the victors. Are we to imagine the Gentile churches as captive slaves purchasing their freedom (v. 4) from the victorious generals?[24] Paul shunts aside that implication by appealing to his continued enthusiasm for the collection (v. 10). Who is to pay? Some exegetes take the simple past tense, "I was eager," as evidence that the collection in question only bound Paul and Barnabas upon their return to Antioch. They conclude that the collection efforts that figure so prominently in Paul's letters (1 Cor 16:1–4; 2 Cor 8–9; Rom 15:25–27) refer to a second effort initiated later by the apostle himself (see Martyn 1997, 222–28). However, Paul's argument implies that the Galatians are familiar with this collection and with Paul's enthusiasm for it, and should draw on that personal knowledge to back up his claim in v. 10.[25] Once the ambiguity and fragility of the Jerusalem agreements are recognized, the collapse of this accord (2:11–14) becomes more easily intelligible.

Now when Cephas came to Antioch, I opposed him to his face, that he was condemned [by his actions].[26] For before certain people[27] came from James he used to eat with the Gentiles, but when they came,[28] he drew back and separated himself because he feared the circumcision advocates.[29] And the rest of the Jews[30] joined him in the pretense, so that even Barnabas was carried away by their hypocrisy. But when I saw that they were not on the right road towards the truth of the gospel, I said to Peter in front of everyone, "If you, who are a Jew, can live in a non-Jewish way and not in a Jewish one, how is it that you compel the Gentiles to adopt Jewish ways?"[31] (2:11–14)

Since this episode lacks the introductory "then," some scholars have assumed that the crisis over commensality between Christian Jews and their Gentile converts occurred prior to the Jerusalem meeting. However, there is no reason to assume that Paul has put the events out of order, especially if the minimal requirements for Gentile dietary practice mentioned in Acts 15:13–29 were dispatched independently of the Jerusalem agreement (Bruce 1988, 128; Fitzmyer 1998, 552). The incident in question probably occurred very shortly after the Jerusalem meeting. Murphy-O'Connor indicates that Paul and Barnabas would have returned to Antioch before the winter. Given Paul's urgent pursuit of his missionary activity, he is likely to have set off northward as soon as travel became possible the following spring (Murphy-O'Connor 1996, 29). No indication of Peter's reason for coming to Antioch is given, but he was there for some time before the arrival of persons associated with James. Antioch had a large, ancient, and well-established Jewish population.[32] According to Josephus (*War* 7.45), a large number of Greeks were Jewish sympathizers. Roman rule supported the privileges claimed by Jews to follow ancestral customs, and the city appears to have escaped the waves of anti-Jewish reprisals that followed the outbreak of the Judean rebellion of 66 C.E. in other cities (Smallwood 1999, 187).[33] Thus the Christian Jews of Antioch began accepting Gentile believers in an environment of friendly relationships between Jews and non-Jews.

Given the fragility of the Jerusalem situation, one should hardly be surprised that it had not created unanimity of spirit or settled the most important issues: under what conditions would Christian Jews share table fellowship with non-Jewish believers (Davies 1999, 696). Given the centrality of commensality to the identity of Jews as a group and to early Christian communities, a willingness to associate with Gentiles in the public square, the marketplace, the baths, or even in gatherings for preaching, teaching, and prayer, would not necessarily carry over to the intimate sphere of the table (Holmberg 1998, 398–402).[34] Evidently, Antioch Christians had been accustomed to gather for the communal meal at the homes of Gentile believers without incident. Whether the hosts in question had taken care to avoid meat from pagan sacrifices and the like so as not to offend Jewish food laws (*Aristeas* 181; Murphy-O'Connor 1996, 150), we do not know.[35] There is no reason to doubt Paul's statement that Peter was willing to "live in a Gentile manner," that is, to share the Lord's Supper with Gentile believers, prior to the arrival of persons associated with James (2:11, 14).

Those from James are unwilling to share table fellowship with non-Jewish Christians under any circumstances.[36] Peter led the Christian Jews in accommodating the demands of the visitors for separate gatherings of Jewish and non-Jewish believers. He may have seen this action as no different from the hospitality accorded Titus earlier (2:4).[37]

Paul alleges that Peter acted out of fear (v. 12), a charge that exegetes have generally taken at face value. They suggest that Peter fears losing his authority in Jerusalem (Betz 1979, 107–109) or reprisals against the Jerusalem church if it became known that one of its leaders was fraternizing with Gentiles (Longenecker 1990, 75). However, Paul may have attributed this motive to Peter as a bit of character assassination. He wishes to undercut the standing of the Jerusalem apostles with his Galatian audience. Peter's cowardice is being contrasted with the bold speech of Paul in delivering a public reprimand to this pillar of the Jerusalem church.[38] This face-to-face confrontation (v. 11) bears out Paul's earlier claim to a divine indifference to an individual's standing (v. 6). Since even Barnabas went along with the other Christian Jews in following Peter's lead (v. 13), Paul appears to have failed in stemming the trend toward separation. The defection of someone with whom he had long been engaged in missionary activity would have been particularly painful (Bauckham 1979).[39] From Paul's perspective, the agreement in Jerusalem concerning the Gentile mission has been broken. Esler concludes that this breech is result of disaffected Christian Jews in Jerusalem who were humiliated by the events surrounding the earlier agreement (Esler 1995, 304–307). They were able to pressure James and Peter to "break the peace."

How far did this change of heart go? Esler infers from the phrase "compel to Judaize" in v. 14 that everything was canceled. Peter now agreed that Gentile believers should become proselytes (Esler 1995, 307). However, this conclusion only holds if the identity of the community requires a common table fellowship of Christian Jews with their non-Jewish counterparts, as Paul certainly thinks that it does. For the Jew, whether Christian or not, to whom table fellowship with non-Jews is equivalent to apostasy, Paul seems to require just that (so Holmberg 1998, 414).[40] Why does the door only swing one way? The Christian Jew can assimilate to the culture of non-Jews who now believe in the same God. Paul does not criticize Peter for living in a Gentile manner while at Antioch after all. But the non-Jewish Christian cannot adopt Jewish customs or even become a Jew out of solidarity with his new Christian Jewish brothers and sisters.[41] Why? Paul construes the situation as one in which those who advocate circumcision are *compelling* non-Jewish believers to become proselytes (2:3, 14; 6:12; Martyn 1997, 235–36; Cosgrove 1988, 129–33).

However, outside of the incorporation of the Idumean populace into the Hasmonean kingdom (Josephus, *Ant.* 13.257–58), we have little evidence for forced circumcision (Cohen 1999, 110–25). Certainly the Hasmonean policy provided an impetus to the view that circumcision was a necessary identity marker by which aliens are incorporated into the people of Israel (Cohen 1999, 125), but actual practice in the first century C.E. was much less rigid. Gentiles might adopt a wide range of Jewish belief and practice without becoming proselytes. In some circumstances they might have been considered "Jews," while from within the Jewish community they would have remained non-Jews (Cohen 1999, 140–62).[42] The behavior of Peter and the others, which Paul describes as hypocrisy or "play acting," might be considered a normal reflection of first-century identity politics among first-century Diaspora Jews and their non-Jewish sympathizers. From their point of view, Paul is as intolerant of the Gentile who assimilates to Jewish habits and religious practices as the sharp-tongued Roman satirists who make fun of such Judaizing.[43] Perhaps Paul realizes the dilemma his narrative has created. He breaks off the account in v. 14

and introduces a summary argument intended to demonstrate that his position is the only one that upholds the truth of the gospel.

> We, Jews by birth and not Gentile sinners; knowing that a person is not righteous by fulfilling stipulations of the Law,[44] but through faith in Christ,[45] and we have believed in Christ Jesus so that we might be righteous through faith in Christ and not by fulfilling stipulations of the Law because no one[46] becomes righteous by fulfilling stipulations of the Law. Now if, while seeking to become righteous by means of Christ,[47] we ourselves were found to be sinners, would Christ then [be] an agent[48] of sin? No way! For if I am building up again, the same things I destroyed, I present myself as a transgressor. For I put the Law to death through the Law so that I might live for God. I have been crucified with Christ. Now I live no longer [as] "I" but Christ in me. What [life] I now live as a human being[49] I live by faith in the Son of God[50] who loved me and gave himself up for me. I am not going to nullify the grace of God. For if righteousness [is obtained][51] through the Law, then Christ died uselessly. (2:15–21)

Paul might be seen to continue paraphrasing a speech given against Peter in verses 15–21, since there is no indication of a shift in audience between vv. 14–15. The "we" who are born Jews includes Peter, Barnabas, and the other Christian Jews (vv. 15–17). The shift to "I" in v. 17 refers to Paul's own personal plea. However, the Antioch setting disappears from view.[52] The plural "you" that corresponds to the "we" appears in 3:1, Paul's Gentile converts in Galatia. They have been the focus of Paul's narrative, which had been designed to clarify the choice before them: Paul and the truth of the gospel or Peter and the vacillations of fear, hypocrisy, and broken promises. Peter has been described as making demands that are equivalent to those of the "false brothers" in the Jerusalem meeting and of the interlopers in Galatia (Bachmann 1992, 26–29; Betz 1979, 113; Smiles 1998, 11). This section formulates principles at stake in the decision.

Betz treats this section as the *propositio* of a formal speech (Betz 1979, 114; Longenecker 1990, 80–81). Arguments for the propositions advanced follow in the demonstrative section of the letter (3:1–4:31).[53]

He proposes a useful analysis of verses 15–21: (a) vv. 15–16 establish a principle that should be clear to all parties; (b) vv. 17–18 point to the issue under dispute employing phrases from the opposition; (c.) vv. 19–20 contain a set of theological propositions; and (d) v. 21 concludes with a sharp denial of the charge (Betz 1979, 114–15). This schema overrides the shift between "we" and "I" in vv. 17 and 18 (Bachmann 1992, 26). However, Rom 7:7–8 uses the diatribe form to make a similar transition between a first-person plural (vv. 6–7a) and the first-person singular elaboration (vv. 7b–12), so one should take the transition as part of Paul's rhetorical style.

The section opens with such a blatant example of Jewish ethnic stereotyping, "born Jews" against "Gentile sinners" (v. 15), that one wonders how a person who has spent at least fifteen years preaching to and living with Gentiles came out with it. The continued identification of proselytes as such on their tombstones leads Cohen to argue that many first-century C.E. Jews would have made this division. Anyone not born a Jew is a Gentile, even if he or she becomes part of the Jewish community through conversion (Cohen 1999, 161–62). All parties to the earlier conflict would have accepted this statement, which is generally taken to be the reason Paul speaks as he does (Betz 1979, 115).[54] What did this phrase sound like to Paul's audience in Galatia? By using the expression "born Jews," he makes it clear that there is a boundary that they can never cross, not even by being circumcised. He may also evoke memories of tense, boundary-enforcing encounters with Jews. In short, Paul is using this bit of ethnic stereotyping to send a message to those seeking to assimilate to Judaism:[55] "Don't think that you can pass for Jewish. They won't let you." Paul is not simply making common ground with Christian Jews who opposed him. For the purposes of his own argument, Paul has drawn the line of ethnic division where it cannot be bridged. Though he will argue that the categories do not apply "in Christ" (Gal 3:28) and has agreed that Christian Jews should "live like Gentiles" when among non-Jewish Christians, Paul resists any possibility that the differences would be erased by Gentiles assimilating to Jewish practices.

Verse 16 claims to present the principles on which Christian Jews base their faith in Jesus. From that point of view, being made upright or righteous through belief in God's Messiah does not exclude faithful observance of Torah. The either "Torah obedience" or "faith in Christ" but not both of Paul's theology should not be imported into the argument (Betz 1979, 118). Paul's views on the Law in his various letters are too complex to be surveyed here.[56] The sharp "us" (Jews) vs. "them" (Gentiles) division in the opening clause presumes Jewish pride in the Law as the ancient, divinely given constitution that governs the Jewish polity. Paul never overrides that function of the Law. What he contests is its ability to generate the righteousness with God characteristic of the age of salvation inaugurated by the death and resurrection of God's Messiah (Byrne 2000, 303).

The conflict over Paul's position with regard to the Gentiles suggests that the other apostles disagreed with him over the significance of the Law for a person's righteousness before God as well. The Greek phrase, *erga tou nomou* ("works of the Law"), which Paul employs three times in this verse and picks up in the next section of the argument (3:2, 5, 10), has been clarified by the use of the Hebrew phrase, *ma'ăśê hattôrāh* ("deeds of the Law") in the Dead Sea Scrolls (4Q Fl 1.7; 4QMMT 3.29; and "his deeds in the Law," 1 QS 5.21; 6.18). The expression reflects a pre-Pauline, Palestinian-Jewish way of referring to deeds done in obedience to Torah (Fitzmyer 1993, 338). It cannot be limited to a subset of Jewish practices, such as keeping the Sabbath, kosher dietary practices, and circumcision, which distinguish Jews from Gentiles. However, it may have been used among sectarian Jews like the Essenes for the forms of Torah obedience or interpretation that distinguished their group (Dunn 1993, 136–37; Bachmann 1998, 101–109). In that sense, "deeds of the Law" make one group of Jews the righteous remnant, the people of the new covenant, in contrast to the rest of humanity, Jew and non-Jew, who will be subject to God's wrath. Such a phrase would have come naturally to Paul during his earlier life as a Jew filled with zeal for ancestral tradition (1:13–14; Bachmann 1992, 100–101). Thus the question of how a person is to become righteous in v. 16a initially came down to a choice between competing ways of living in obedience to the Torah—as a member of a Jewish sect or as a follower of the Messiah Jesus. That the two were in conflict we know from Paul's testimony that he had persecuted the church (1:13, 23).

Verse 16b repeats what has just been said. Although some scholars maintain that the genitive in the expression "faith of Christ" should be read as subjective, that is, Christ's faith or faithfulness (see Hays 1991, 715–25), its use in parallel with the expression "we have believed in Christ Jesus" tips the balance in favor of treating the expression as a reference to the faith of Christians. Williams makes the link between the two aspects of faith by commenting that such faith in Paul's usage of the phrase has a distinctive relationship to Christ. Christ's death and resurrection inaugurated the eschatological age. Believers must have the same confidence in God's promises that Jesus had. Like him, they will experience crucifixion (2:19) and new life (6:15; Williams 1997, 67–70). Williams cautions against reading Paul to say that faith is somehow the cause of righteousness before God. Only God confers righteousness, thanks to the death of Jesus (Williams 1997, 71).

Finally, Paul wraps up this overloaded assertion of shared convictions about salvation in Christ with a citation of Ps 143:2 (v. 16c). Paul has modified the phrase "all flesh is not justified" from the psalm with the addition of "by works of the Law" (also in Rom 3:20, 28). What had been a confession of human unworthiness to receive God's salvation and loving-kindness now becomes an affirmation that the source of righteousness is not Torah observance (Bruce 1988, 137). The psalmist might agree insofar as it is God's faithfulness, righteousness, and loving-kindness that are exhibited when God rescues the suppliant from the enemy. God's spirit will instruct the psalmist in how to live as God wills (Ps 143:10). Faith in God is the necessary characteristic of persons who are God's servants (Ps 143:8). Betz sees the emergence of a second type of testimony in the use of Ps 143:2. Paul has been appealing to witness testimony, his own conversion, and the experiences of other Christians. He will add to those sources the testimony of Scripture (Betz 1979, 119).

Verse 17 breaks into the train of thought with a rhetorical question typical of Paul's diatribe style. The "let it not be" at the end of the verse indicates that what precedes it should be treated as a question that contains some elements of impossibility (Stowers 1981). The absurdity appears in the clause introduced by an interrogative particle *(ara)* that anticipates a negative response:[57] "Christ, servant of sin." The phrase may have been a slogan used against Christians in general or against Paul's Gentile mission in particular. Sectarian polemicists would see the halachah of a different Jewish group as sin. The Essene writings use an epithet, *moreh sedeq*, "Teacher of Righteousness," for their founder. The opposition between the Teacher and other Jews makes him a "snare for sinners" and "the foundation of truth and understanding for them whose way is straight" (1 QH 2.6–13). As Elliott observes: "The *moreh* had in effect become the instrument of division in Israel" (Elliott 2000, 460). By calling into existence the eschatological remnant of the righteous, the Teacher, at the same time, makes those who oppose his divinely inspired instruction sinners.

Assuming that we are still confronting bits of sectarian rhetoric makes it unnecessary to attach the slogans in v. 17 to Jewish-Christian protests against Gentile converts who are not obligated to obey Torah or an implicit reduction of Jews to a status no better than that of Gentiles.[58] Just as the Teacher is a "snare," so Christ may be a "servant" of sin insofar as those who reject God's eschatological call to join the elect remnant, the recipients of the new covenant, are sinners. From the point of view of those who have placed their trust in the Teacher or in Christ respectively as the way to be righteous before God, the absurdity would be if they were somehow found to be sinners. Read in this vein, without the diatribe form that Paul has imposed on this sectarian slogan, v. 17 makes good sense as a continuation of the common Christian-Jewish convictions introduced in the previous verses.

Paul has introduced the diatribe question to force the absurdity of the "Christ, servant of sin" phrase as a lead-in to the shift into the first person in v. 18. Williams suggests that one consider this usage a "hortative I": Paul is now encouraging the audience to learn from his example (1997, 73). Verse 18 states the general principle: Paul would be a transgressor if he were to turn around and begin to build up what he had destroyed. He does not specify the objects of these actions, but the audience can fill them in based on the preceding autobiography. Paul cannot return to zeal for the Law as the basis for righteousness or to the way of life that characterized his pre-Christian life. Paul has substituted the term "transgressor" for "sinner" not because he has violation of a particular statute in mind, but because he would be setting aside the Law's intent (Longenecker 1990, 90–91).

The series of statements in vv. 19 to 20 anticipate the more detailed arguments to follow (Betz 1979, 121–25). How it is that Christians participate in the death of Christ in such a way that they are led by the Law to die to it (v. 19a) requires the curse that the Law lays on the crucified (3:10–14). The apostle bears the marks of suffering for the gospel on his body (6:17) and may be the vehicle through which the crucified was presented to the Galatians in visible form (3:1). Therefore, the basis of his claim to be crucified with Christ (v. 19b) should be familiar to his audience. How the Galatians should go about living this life as not just a bodily existence but "in Christ" (v. 20ab) will be described in the exhortation section of the letter (5:2–6:10). Paul is not arguing freedom from obligations to the Law frivolously, as his opponents may have charged. All of these principles refer back to the cross. Verse 20c cites a formula that identifies Christ as the Son of God who gave his life out of love to rescue a sinful humanity (cf. Rom 5:6–11). Such expressions must have been familiar ones in Paul's evangelization. This time it sets the stage for Paul's final gambit. Were Paul to return to zeal for the Law or were his Gentile converts to adopt a Jewish way of life, they would be rejecting the grace of God that called them into Christ (1:6, 15). Even worse, it would imply that Paul had been preaching a false gospel about the death of Christ as the source of our righteousness before God. If being an observant Jew—albeit in a sectarian sense of following the halachah of the group that constitutes God's elect—were sufficient to attain God's eschatological gift of righteousness, then the death of Christ has no religious or theological significance (v. 21). As Williams observes: "To nullify God's grace would be to scrap the gospel he preached and admit that his life's work as a slave of Christ was a huge mistake" (1997, 75–76). Paul has raised the stakes well beyond what those advocating assimilation to Jewish patterns of life, even circumcision, are likely to have imagined. There is no middle ground in which loyalty to God and to the Son who gave his life for us can be combined with adopting a Jewish way of life. What's more, as we have seen, for Christian Jews the one-way door means that fellowship with non-Jewish believers requires partial, temporary, or perhaps even permanent surrender of critical identity markers. It could well mean being considered apostate by one's Jewish relatives, friends, and associates.[59]

Chapter Three

Galatians 3

You idiot Galatians! Who has cast a spell on you before whose very eyes[1] Jesus Christ was exhibited as crucified? I would just like to learn this one thing from you: did you receive the Spirit from fulfilling prescriptions of the Law or from hearing of faith? Are you such idiots that having begun with the Spirit you would now finish up with the flesh? Have you suffered so much in vain? If it really was in vain. Therefore did the one who supplied you with the Spirit and worked miracles among you [do so] by fulfilling precepts of the Law or by the hearing of faith? (3:1–5)

Paul now returns to his audience in Galatia with yet another piece of ethnic prejudice. He calls them *anoētoi* ("unintelligent," "foolish"), a reference to the ancient view that ethnic Galatians were uncivilized or stupid (Willliams 1997, 83). Hurling insults at an opponent was an established part of ancient rhetorical use of the diatribe, as was the charge that the opponents must have bewitched the audience with underhanded sophistry (Plato, *Apol.* 17a; *Resp.* 413b)[2] and the orator's claim to have presented the subject so clearly that the audience could see what was described as with their own eyes (Aristotle, *Rhet.* 3.1.6; 3.11.1–5; Betz 1979, 130–31). Since Paul's own body is marked by the cross (6.17), he may have pointed to it as he made appeal for faith in the crucified.[3] The verb *prographô* ("show publically") can refer to something posted as a placard or public announcement (Longenecker 1990, 100). One would presume that an orator who could make his audience see the facts of the case could overcome the sophistries of false preachers. The insulting comments about his audience, that they must be "thick-headed" or victims of magical attack,[4] may be intended to shame them into agreeing with Paul.[5]

Paul shifts the grounds of argument back to experience, that of the Galatians when they heard him preaching the gospel. Conversion was regularly accompanied by manifestations of the Spirit in early Christian churches, although it is not clear how baptism was connected to reception of the Spirit (Betz 1979, 132; Rabens 1999, 172).[6] The implicit response to the question of how they received that Spirit, believing the gospel preached by the apostle or adopting a Jewish way of life, is obvious. Faith in the gospel preached to them was the source of the Spirit (Bruce 1988, 149). In the dichotomizing that he employs throughout the epistle, Paul forces an exclusion of Jewish observance by the Spirit. He leads his audience to infer that Gentiles who assimilate to Judaism will lose the Spirit. Paul's Jewish contemporaries would not have accepted this theological inference. The Essene writings indicate that an elaborate doctrine of the presence of God's Spirit in the community supported the sect's halachah. Because they possess the Spirit, the righteous are assimilated to God's holy angels (Elliott 2000, 408–16).[7] One cannot tell from Galatians whether or not those advocating circumcision also argued that Jewish observance would confirm or enhance the blessings of God's Spirit, but they might have done so.[8]

In order to undercut the possibility of such an accommodation, Paul, with another dig at his audience as *anoētoi*, opposes the *Spirit* received from accepting the gospel to the *flesh*, which they now propose to mark with circumcision (v. 3). The ethical exhortation that follows the argumentative section provides the positive answer to the question of what should follow upon this beginning in the Spirit. A Christian life of continued obedience to the Spirit will bring with it all the virtues the Galatians may hope to gain by adopting Jewish practices (Betz 1979, 133).[9] The note of exasperation in v. 4 contains a subtle irony in its reference to suffering. Paul can assume that all converts pay a price of persecution when they reject ancestral and civic traditions about proper piety toward the gods to follow Christ (cf. 1 Thess 2:14; 2 Thess 1:4–5; Bruce 1988, 150). But as we have suggested in the Introduction, the suffering associated with the ritual of circumcision may have been perceived as a good thing among the Galatian populace. Devotees of the popular mother goddess Cybele (Mitchell 1993, 20–23) might be seen to draw blood in castrating or mutilating themselves. So Paul must indicate to his audience that they have already demonstrated their devotion to God in suffering. To adopt this new rite would render that earlier sacrifice useless (v. 4). The brief tag at the end of the verse, "If it really was in vain," holds open the door. The Galatians can accept Paul's argument and draw back from what they are proposing to do (Bruce 1988, 150). He shifts the rhetorical question that repeats the basic antithesis of this section: the Spirit with its gifts is received through faith, not through Torah observance (v. 5). The formulation throws weight on God who has given the Spirit and continues to do so.[10] This shift prepares the audience for a transition in the argument. Paul will turn from commenting on their religious experience to a theological argument about God's plan of salvation as revealed in Scripture.

As in the case of Abraham: "He believed God and it was credited to him as righteousness."[11] Therefore you recognize that people of faith, they are sons of Abraham. And Scripture, seeing in advance that God would make the Gentiles righteous on the basis of faith, preached the gospel in advance, saying: "All the Gentiles will be blessed on account of you."[12] So, people of faith are blessed with the faith of Abraham.

For those who are engaged in fulfilling precepts of the Law are under a curse; for it is written: "Cursed is anyone who does not keep all the things written in the book of the Law to put them into practice,"[13] and it is clear that no one is righteous before God by means of the Law, [it says]: "The just person will live by faith."[14] Now the Law is not by means of faith, but [it says]: "The one who does these things will live by them."[15] Christ ransomed us from the curse of the Law by becoming a curse on our behalf, as it is written: "Cursed [be] everyone who is hanged on the wood,"[16] so that the blessing of Abraham might come to the Gentiles by means of Christ Jesus, so that we might receive the promise[17] of the Spirit through faith. (3:6–14)

Not only is Abraham the ancestor of the Israelites, he is depicted in Jewish sources as the model of faith in God. While still a pagan, Abraham was said to have discerned the truth that God is one from observing the heavens, to have been persecuted for preaching monotheism, and to have left his homeland in response to God's call (*Jubilees* 11–12; Josephus, *Ant.* 1.154–57; Philo, *Migr.* 176–86; *Abr.* 66–88).[18] Paul probably introduced his converts to these stories in his initial preaching. But Abraham could just as well be the hero of those advocating circumcision, since as Sir 44:19–21 puts it: "Abraham was the great father of a multitude of nations . . . He kept the law of the Most High, and entered into a covenant with him; he certified the covenant in his flesh, and when he was tested he proved faithful. Therefore the Lord assured him with an oath that the nations would be blessed through his offspring *(sperma)*." Abraham's faith (Gen 15:6) is linked with his acceptance of circumcision (Gen 17:4–14) in Jewish sources (Longenecker 1990, 110–11).[19] Paul once again creates a disjunction between what Jews would ordinarily consider together by insisting on the priority of Gen 15:6. God's covenant with Abraham consists solely of the divine promise to Abraham as the man of faith who "believed God" (v. 6). It has no connection with Abraham's subsequent deeds of obedience (Reinbold 2000, 94).

Paul's initial interpretation of Gen 15:6 states a noncontroversial proposition: the "children of Abraham" are those who are "from faith," that is, descendants of Isaac, not the other offspring of Abraham mentioned in Scripture (cf. *Jubilees* 16:16–18).[20] However, sectarian Jews in the first century would concur with the use of an attribute such as "from faith" to make a distinction among the descendants of Isaac as well. Abraham prays that God will preserve him and his offspring from being led astray by the evil spirits that "rule over the thought of the heart of man" (*Jubilees* 12:20). God promises that Abraham will have righteous seed, even though much of Israel will go astray. However, the preferred maxim of such sectarian "seed theology" is "doing righteousness" (*Jubilees* 36:16), not having faith (Elliott 2000, 219–23). Paul connects faith, being righteous, and the Gentiles in his interpretation of Abraham's role as a source of blessing for the nations (vv. 8–9). Righteousness based on faith is the blessing for the nations (Reinbold 2000, 95).

Verses 6–9 are not controversial.[21] The challenge comes when Paul, true to form, separates those whose relationship to Abraham is based on faith from those who base that relationship on observing Torah

(v. 10). Instead of finding themselves recipients of covenant blessings, persons who are under the Law find themselves faced with a curse (v. 10b; Deut 27:26). Paul formulates an elaborate chiasmus in vv. 10–14. The two statements about curses pronounced by the Law (Deut 27:26 and Deut 21:23) serve to frame the two Scripture quotes that promise salvation to persons of faith (Hab 2:4; Lev 18:5; Garlington 1997, 85). Verse 10 cannot but jar the ear of a Jewish reader. The whole purpose of concern about the exact requirements of Torah is to avoid coming under the curse that the Law pronounces against the unrighteous.[22] Paul extracts his surprising conclusion from an exegesis of Scripture in two steps, an appeal to the testimony of the Law about itself (vv. 11–12) and an appeal to the Christ-event (vv. 13–14). Verses 11–12 demonstrate that Scripture itself speaks of faith as the source of righteousness and of precepts of the Law as something that must be carried out (Reinbold 2000, 97). Verses 13–14 connect the crucifixion by which Christ has come under the curse of the Law with the blessing of the Gentiles through Abraham. Thus Paul is able to set the promise and its fulfillment in Christ over against the Mosaic law (White 1999, 170). When the Messiah comes under the curse of the Law as a consequence of his death, it becomes evident that the Law has not produced the righteous descendants for Abraham that its advocates claim (Martyn 1997, 310–11). The extension of Deut 21:23 to victims of crucifixion is attested in the Dead Sea Scrolls (4 QpNah 1.7–8; 11 QT 64.2–3). Paul himself may have used this passage of Scripture in arguments against Jesus as Messiah before his conversion (Dunn 1998, 209).

Paul's formulation of the Christ-event, death on the cross to liberate humanity from the curse of the Law, is so concise that it creates several puzzles. Presumably humanity is under a "curse of the Law" not because the Law itself is the agent of alienation from God,[23] but because humanity is alienated from God by sin. Thus the curses of the covenant in the first sense fall on humanity.[24] As Paul insisted earlier, Torah observance was unable to reverse that condition. Only the death of God's Messiah has done so (2:15–21). However, the Law cannot be accused of false testimony about righteousness. It preached righteousness based on faith to Abraham and in the phrases that Paul cites in verses 11–12 (Reinbold 2000, 99). Paul is careful to distinguish the cursing voice of the Law from God's voice of promise (Smiles 1998, 197). He does not wish to leave the impression that on the cross Christ was separated in any way from God. Christ's sacrifice on the cross is the example of obedience to God (Bruce 1988, 165–66).

Scholars also remain divided over how to read the first-person plural, "us," in v. 13. Is Paul still referring to Christian Jews as "us" and reserving "you" for his Gentile audience? If so, does he mean to imply that until God had delivered those Jews who are the elect from the curse of the Law, the Abrahamic promise of righteousness through faith for the Gentiles could not be realized (so Donaldson 1997, 182; Boers 1994, 69)?[25] Or, more likely, has he used "us" as a universal term for the entire human race, once caught under sin and now called to faith in the gospel (Williams 1987, 91)?[26] Verse 14 further complicates the picture. Two purpose clauses spell out the soteriological consequences of Christ's death on the cross: the blessing of Abraham is extended to the Gentiles and "we," presumably all believers, receive the Spirit. By returning to the experiential dimension, receiving God's Spirit, Paul demonstrates to his audience that they already possess the promise to Abraham. Nothing has been left incomplete (Betz 1979, 152–53). Williams defends an inclusive reading of the entire verse on the grounds that the promise to Abraham, righteousness through faith, is not reserved only for Gentiles in Paul's view. Jewish believers must also share Abraham's faith in order to be righteous (Williams 1987, 92).

Brothers, I am using a human analogy, just as no one nullifies or adds a codicil to someone's legally ratified will. Now the promises were made to Abraham and to his seed. It[27] does not say, "to his seeds," as if speaking of many but as if speaking about one, "And to his seed"[28] which is Christ. Now I say this: with respect to a will ratified previously by God, the Law that came 430 years later does not annul [it] so as to cancel the promise. For if the inheritance [was conveyed] by the Law, [it would] no longer [be] based on the promise. But God granted Abraham a favor through the promise. What about the Law, then? It was added because of transgressions until the seed to whom the promise was made should come, [the Law] having been ordered through angels by the hand of a mediator. Now the mediator is not one, but God is one. (3:15–20)

Paul elaborates on the distinction introduced in the previous section between the promise to Abraham and the Law. The address, "brothers" (v. 15), signals an epistolary seam or division in the argument, as well as a reminder of the relationships of family-like affection that bind Christians together (Longenecker 1990, 126).[29] Paul has shifted his tone away from the posture of ethnic superiority in the earlier half of the chapter. Before returning to Abraham in v. 16, Paul introduces an example from civil law. The point is clear enough. Paul wishes to argue that God's promise has the force of a will that has been ratified. Nothing added later can change it. However, the analogy limps because we do not know what civil code he has in mind (Betz 1979, 155). Roman testaments could be changed by codicil at any time, and legal disputes often ensued that could be argued based on what the testator intended to do. At least in theory, the sealing of a Roman will was accompanied by an elaborate ceremony involving several witnesses, a "purchaser" of the estate, and someone to weigh out the price. Even the wills of those in humble circumstances exhibit the same linguistic formalities as those of the wealthy (Crook 1967, 118–32). Paul may have had the impressive formalism of sealing a will in mind when he concluded that once a will was enacted it could not be altered.

Verse 16 picks up the promise to Abraham from v. 14. As with any will, it becomes necessary to determine who are the heirs of the estate. Paul has indicated already that not all the physical descendants of Abraham belong to the elect. Here he plays on the fact that the term "seed" is a singular, not a plural noun.[30] It is to that descendant, namely Christ, to whom promises are made (Williams 1988, 717–18). Williams suggests that the content of those promises goes beyond the "many nations" of Gen 15:5–6, as implied in Gal 3:6, to include the gift of the Spirit by which the Gentiles become children of Abraham (3:14). Paul returns to the role of the Spirit in the adoption of those who believe in Christ as children and heirs in Gal 4:5–6 (Williams 1988, 714–15).

At this point in the argument, Paul is not concerned with the content of the promise but with its irrevocability. The Law that was not

enacted until 430 years later[31] cannot annul the covenant with Abraham
(v. 17). So far, Paul's remarks would not surprise a first-century Jewish
audience. Abraham's recognition of the one God, even when he was
still a pagan, would indicate an exemplary concern for the first and
most important command of Torah. He even receives Hebrew lessons
from the angel of the presence (*Jubilees* 12:1–24; Nickelsburg 1998,
152–55). Any possibility of Abraham's positive relationship to the
Law unravels in what follows. Paul first drives a wedge between the
Law and the promise to Abraham. If the inheritance is linked to the
Law, then the promise is negated—an impossibility, since God gave
the inheritance to Abraham through the promise (v. 18). Why the disjunction? All Jewish sectarian movements had to come to terms with
the Law. Paul diverges from the more common patterns of halachah
for the righteous elect because in the death and resurrection of Christ,
the messianic age has begun (Davies 1999, 707–708). The Messiah's
appearance has delivered believers from the present evil age (1:4–5).
Believers have died to the Law with its curse (2:18; 3:13). The promise to Abraham is fulfilled (3:16). This eschatological turning point
has demonstrated that grace, faith, and possession of God's Spirit are
the conditions for inclusion among God's righteous people. The prior
history of God's dealings with his people must be consistent with
God's purposes as revealed in God's Messiah (Dunn 1993, 185–86).[32]
For Paul, that implies a distinction between God's word of promise
and God's word of command in Torah.

The question that opens v. 19 indicates that Paul has made a shift
away from ordinary Jewish views that treat blessing and promise as
part of a covenant relationship with God that requires Torah observance. *Jubilees*, for example, recognizes a multiplicity of covenants
that begin with Noah. Elliott notes that the Mosaic covenant is not
described as such. Moses is told to "write the divisions of the days"
(1:1). Apparently the content of the Mosaic covenant—Sabbath laws,
for example—was understood to have already been revealed to the
patriarchs (*Jubilees* 50). Sectarian divisions over interpretations of
Torah, calendar, and festival observance probably underlie this shift
away from emphasis on the Mosaic covenant (Elliott 2000, 251–52).
Thus Paul's initial shift from Moses to Abraham can be understood to
fit an established pattern of internal, sectarian dispute among Jews.

He differs in restricting knowledge of Torah to the Mosaic covenant.[33] Without knowledge or obedience to Torah either explicitly or implicitly attached to the covenants with the patriarchs, the question "Why the Torah?" must be addressed.[34]

The reply in v. 19 takes the form of four propositions: (a) because of transgressions; (b) until the seed to whom the promise was made should come; (c) decreed by angels; and (d) through a mediator (Betz 1979, 163). Each proposition poses exegetical difficulties. Because Paul presumes that Torah had no association with God's prior self-revelation and promise, he can speak of God "adding" it to the covenant with Abraham (Longenecker 1990, 138). Paul has made it clear already that "added" cannot mean a change in or supplement to the promise. The word *charin* ("because of") can be taken to imply that the Law was put forward as a way of dealing with transgressions that had already occurred (Dunn 1998, 139). Or it can be understood to imply that transgressions would follow from the enactment of the Law, as Paul asserts in Romans (4:15; 5:13; Betz 1979, 165). Relying on this latter possibility, Martyn translates the phrase: "It was added in order to provoke transgressions" (Martyn 1997, 352). In what follows in vv. 21–25, Paul can be seen to play on both possibilities: the Law as source of transgressions as well as the Law as restraint of the tendencies that lead to them. His image of the Law as *paidagogos* ("guardian") inclines toward the latter.

Since Paul has already identified the "seed" used in the singular to be Christ, the second phrase states that the Law was given only until the arrival of the Messiah. Christ is the "end" of the Law in a temporal sense because he initiates the fulfillment of the promise to Abraham (Betz 1979, 166). The second two phrases indicate an inferiority of the Law to the promise based on its mode of delivery: from angels to Moses; from Moses, the mediator, to Israel. The unexpressed contrast to this mediated relationship is the direct covenanting between God and Abraham in Gen 15. The view that the Law was given to Moses through angels who accompanied the divine presence on Sinai already appears in the Septuagint (Deut 33:2).[35] It occurs regularly in Jewish authors from this period (*Jubilees* 1:29–2:1; Philo, *Somn.* 1.143). For these authors angelic mediation is not a discrediting factor. It can be used to assert the superiority of the Jewish law

over the codes and constitutions of other nations (so Josephus, *Ant.*
15.136). Nor did the fact of Moses' mediation carry negative overtones. The tag attached in v. 20 clearly intends to support that conclusion by contrasting the plurality of what comes through a mediator
with the confession that God is one (Betz 1979, 170–73). How the
audience is to draw this conclusion from the Shema is obscure.
Martyn suggests that this ambiguity introduces a radical conclusion,
not finally shared by Paul himself: "There, without fully accepting
it—and without Paul's intending them fully to accept it—they have
to look at the vision of a godless Law. For the syllogism yields the
conclusion that Moses, the mediator of the Sinaitic Law, does not
speak for God" (Martyn 1997, 358). The passive verb "was added" in
v. 19 refers to God as responsible for providing the Law so the Law
cannot be God-less, but its mediated reception may have distorted the
signals. Paul turns to this problem in the next section.

> Is the Law therefore against the promises of God? No way! For if
> a Law had been given which was able to give life, righteousness
> would certainly be based on the Law, but the Law confined all
> things under sin so that the promise might be given to believers
> on the basis of faith. Now before faith came, we were held under
> the Law, confined until the intended faith was revealed, so, the
> Law was our slave-guardian[36] until Christ so that we might
> become righteous on the basis of faith; now since faith came, we
> are no longer under a slave-guardian.
>
> For all are sons of God through faith by means of Christ Jesus;
> for those who have been baptized into Christ, have put on Christ.
> There is neither Jew nor Greek; not slave nor free man; not male
> and female; for you are all one in Christ Jesus. And if you are
> Christ's, then you are seed of Abraham, heirs according to the
> promise. (3:21–29)

The diatribe question voices the suspicion that the voices of promise and Law might be opposed to one another. Paul wards off this
radical conclusion, which an opponent might draw from his antithesis
(Martyn 1997, 358). The two do have contrasting roles in God's overall plan of salvation. The Law cannot "make alive," that is, produce

persons who are righteous before God (Bruce 1988, 180).[37] Nor had God ever intended it to do so.[38] In two parallel expressions, Paul describes the function of the Law as imprisoning an "us" until the realization of the promise (vv. 22–23). Sin is responsible for locking up the "us" (v. 22), while the Law serves as jailor (v. 23; Bruce 1988, 181–82). The first expression in which Scripture confines all things under sin presents as universal a case as possible. All humanity is consigned to life under sin, not merely the Israelites who received the Law from Moses (Longenecker 1990, 144). However, the "we" in custody under the Law in v. 23 can only refer to Israel. In both cases, the restraint has a limit, the coming of Christ (Dunn 1993, 196–97).

The metaphoric link between sin, Law, and imprisonment would support reading *charin* in v. 19 as a statement concerning the transgression-reckoning (Rom 5:13) function of the Law. Imprisonment ends because the due penalty has been paid thanks to the death of Christ on behalf of sinners (Rom 5:6–11).[39] But Paul cannot leave his account of the function of the Law on such a negative note without risking a complete divorce between God's promise and God's command, so he reformulates the contrast between the Law prior to Christ and salvation now made available through faith (vv. 24–25). In this comparison, the Law takes on the function of the *paidagogos*, a slave assigned by his parents to watch over a young boy. The slave was to accompany him to and from school, to see to discipline, and to keep his young charge from harm. The *paidagogos* was not a tutor. The "up to Christ" of v. 24a should not be construed as if the Law were a lower stage of schooling required as preparation for Christ (Lull 1986). In some instances, adults express great fondness for the slaves who had been their childhood companions and disciplinarians, since those slaves were more intimately linked to the family than others (Dixon 1992, 154). Therefore, some scholars have read this image as an allusion to the harsh punishments regularly meted out to children or to the boorish figure of Roman comedy (so Betz 1979, 177). Others point to the important role of the *paidagogos* in child-rearing and the affection evidenced toward these slaves in inscriptions as evidence that Paul has shifted to a more moderate image for the function of the Law (Dunn 1993, 199–200). In this reading, the Law does not serve to create or reckon transgression but to control the unavoidable tendencies to sin in those unable to govern their own behavior. After the Spirit is given to believers, they no longer need such a governor (v. 25), since the Spirit becomes the principle of Christian life (5:5; 6:8; Williams 1988, 711–13).

Verse 26 shifts from the first-person plural to the second person "you," including Paul's non-Jewish audience along with the "we," once restricted by the Law, now righteous through faith (v. 24). The heirs of Abraham's promise include all who belong to Christ, not a subset of Torah observers (v. 29; Dunn 1993, 201–202). In order to underline this appeal to his audience to see themselves as descendants of Abraham because they believe in Christ, Paul once again turns back to their experience of conversion with an appeal to the entry rite characteristic of the new Christian movement, baptism (vv. 27–28).[40] Although uncertainty about the shape of that ritual in this early period makes some scholars hesitant to assume that this passage correlates with actual practice (so Dunn 1993, 201–204), given the Galatian interest in ritual there is no reason to infer that Paul's references are only metaphorical. The NT speaks of "putting on" Christ in three senses: (a) in baptismal contexts, referring to the clothing of the baptized after they emerged from the water (Col 3:10; Eph 4:24); (b) in ethical contexts, referring to the new moral life led by Christians (Rom 13:12, 14; Col 2:12, 3:9–10; Eph 4:22–24, 6:11, 6:14; 1 Thess 5:8); (c) in eschatological contexts, referring to the transformation of the resurrected into the image of Christ (1 Cor 15:53–54; 2 Cor 5:3).[41]

The question of whether or not v. 28 corresponds to an actual formula used during the ritual of baptism is somewhat more controversial. Similar expressions occur in 1 Cor 12:13 to remind a divided community that in baptism all came to share one Spirit and in Col 3:10–11 as part of an ethical exhortation to be clothed with the new life of virtue. Neither of these examples contains the suggestion that gender division has been transcended in Christ. The expression "not male and female" alludes to Gen 1:27. It suggests an interpretation of Christian baptism as a restoration of the original nature of human beings before their division into male and female with the subsequent history of subjection to bodily passions and the like (Meeks 1973/74). Such an erasure underlines the radical difference between life derived from the power of the Spirit in the new creation (6:15) and the categories that govern the old creation (Martyn 1997, 380–81).

Ritual abolition of social categories was by no means unknown in the ancient world. The problematic question is whether such ritual declarations have any consequences for communal life or social interaction with others. The phrase "not male and female" may have dropped out of Paul's usage when he came to insist upon maintaining gender asymmetry in the dress and behavior of Christian prophets (1 Cor 11:11–12; Betz 1979, 200). Similarly, the declaration that as Christians persons are neither "slave nor free" coheres with Paul's comments in Philemon but contradicts his expressed preference for the Christian slave to remain content with his or her situation (1 Cor 7:20–24; Betz, 1979, 193–95).[42] Neither of these divisions appears to have been contested in Galatia. The ethnic, social, and religious division between Jew and non-Jew underlies the desire of some non-Jewish Christians to be circumcised. But the phrase "neither Jew nor Greek" is not equivalent to "neither Jew nor Gentile." For the cities of the Roman East, "Greek" meant those whose Greek ancestry gave them the privileges of being enrolled as citizens (Stanley 1996, 109). Jewish agitation for such citizen rights in Alexandria had been roundly quashed by Claudius in 41 C.E. (Barclay 1996, 55–71). Ethnic tensions between "Greek" and "Jew" after Claudius's intervention continued to spark episodes of civic unrest as well as literary mockery of Jews. Josephus and Philo depict the conflict as one between Jews and the ethnic Egyptians (Josephus, *C. Ap.* 2.28–32, 65–67, 121–24; Philo, *Flacc.* 17, 29, 33–34; *Legat.* 120, 132, 160, 171). Shifting the blame to the lower orders of society enables both writers to insist that Jews remained friendly toward the "Greeks" as well as loyal subjects of Rome (Barclay 1996, 72–75).

In light of these grim contemporary developments, Paul must have been aware that concrete attempts to unite Jew with Greek in the ranks of the governing aristocracies of local cities could be a recipe for disaster (Stanley 1996, 123). Given the ethnic makeup of central and northern Galatia, one cannot assume that his Gentile audience would have been considered or considered themselves "Greeks" in the ethnic and civic sense. The expression employed in Col 3:11 seems to have been expanded in a way that provides a closer match to the situation in these cities: "there is not Greek and Jew, circumcision and uncircumcision, barbarian, Scythian, slave, free." The list descends the social ladder to include "barbarians," persons without the veneer or claim to Greek culture, and "Sythians," whom Josephus describes as "delighting in murder of people and little different from wild beasts" (*C. Ap.* 2.26). Paul may not wish to remind his Galatian audience of such civic struggles, particularly if those seeking assimilation to Judaism were non-Greeks with aspirations to shed the derogatory stereotypes attached to ethnic Galatians. Or he may simply cite the formula as it was conventionally used, since the point he wishes to make concerns the constitution of the eschatological people of God, the heirs to the promise. This people is not to be characterized by any of the divisions of ethnicity, social status, or gender that typify the old creation (Martyn 1997, 382–83).

Chapter Four

Galatians 4

What I am saying is that as long as the heir is a child, even though he is [to be] master of everything, he is no different than a slave, but he is under guardians and stewards until the time set by his father. It is the same with us. When we were children, we were enslaved under the elemental forces of the cosmos; but when the fullness of time arrived, God sent his Son, born of a woman, born under the Law, to redeem those under the Law so that we might be adopted. Seeing that you are sons, God has sent the Spirit of his Son into our[1] hearts crying, "Abba, Father." So you are no longer a slave but a son; and if a son also an heir through God's choice.[2]

But you once were enslaved to gods who are not gods in reality because you did not know God; now that you know—or rather are known by God—how can you be turning again to the weak and impoverished elemental forces to whom you wish to be slaves all over again? You are observing days, months, special times, and years. I am concerned about you that somehow I have been laboring on your behalf in vain. (4:1–11)

Paul returns to analogies with human life (vv. 2–3; 3:15) in order to press home the distinction between the age of salvation that has begun with Christ and the previous situation of all believers, whether they were Jewish or Gentile.[3] The "heir" refers to every Christian, not to Christ (3:14a) or to Jews, previously subject to the Law as pedagogue (3:24–25; Williams 1988, 714–19).[4] The accuracy of Paul's analogy could be challenged. The "pedagogue" of 3:24–25 was a familiar childhood figure. However, his assertion that the heir was subject to *epitpropoi* and *oikonomoi* raises questions. An *epitropos* or guardian would come into play only if the son's father was deceased or absent for an extended period, perhaps due to military or governmental commission or exile. An *oikonomos*, the steward who supervised an estate, would not have charge of his master's family. Betz proposes that Paul's rhetorical focus on the comparison between the heir as child with a slave leads him to employ *oikonomos*, since the latter was in charge of slaves (Betz 1979, 203–204).[5]

Including all believers in his "we," the corresponding authorities who treated Abraham's heirs as "slaves" are not connected with the Law[6] but with cosmic forces, *stoicheia* (v. 3). The expression *stoicheia tou kosmou* ("elements" or "principles" of the cosmos) is problematic. Does it refer simply to the primal elements that constitute the universe? To their connection with astral forces that determine human fate or actions? Or, given the connection between the *stoicheia* and idols in 4:8–9, does the expression refer to demonic forces hostile to God (see Betz 1979, 204–205)? Without other semantic constraints, the phrase "elements of the world" would ordinarily be construed as the constituents of the material cosmos, earth and air, water and fire (Philo, *Congr.* 117; *Her.* 134–35, 146; Martyn 1995, 29–31). However, providing a plausible reading of "material elements" with the metaphor of slavery and freedom would require a dualism of spirit-self against matter or body that is not evident in Paul's theology. The semantic context seems to require an understanding of the phrase as some form of malevolent power (so Betz 1979, 205; Arnold 1996, 63–67).[7] But Paul's formulation of the antithesis shifts in vv. 6–7, along with alterations between the first person "we" and second person "you," to a contrast between the spirits that govern a person's life, that of slavery or the Spirit of God (Williams 1988, 718–19).

Insofar as the "we" involves both Paul and his Gentile converts, the experience of enslavement under the "elements" may be construed as an allusion to the material nature of the idols they had formerly served (Wis 7:17; 13:2; Philo, *Contempl.* 3; Dunn 1998, 108).[8] Paul has to argue that the coming of Christ has created the inheritance that includes both Jewish and non-Jewish believers on the same terms (Boers 1994, 69). So the "time of majority" set by a father becomes the time in salvation history fixed by God for the sending of his Son (v. 4). He uses a consistent pattern of fictive kinship relationships that derive from God as father of Jesus and extend through him to the adopted children of Abraham (Bossman 1996, 166–67).[9] The only other reference to the cosmos in Galatians occurs in Gal 6:14–15. The cross changes the believer's relationship to a cosmos that is marked by the division between circumcised and uncircumcised. What follows on the other side of that event is "new creation" (Martyn 1995, 28). Therefore whatever religious associations, astrology, idolatrous worship, mystery religions, or magic (Arnold 1996, 70–72) his audience may have attached to the phrase *stoicheia tou kosmou*, it also retains metaphorical overtones from its cosmological meaning.

Adams lists four motifs that link Paul's remarks about the *stoicheia* in Gal 4:3 and 9 with his reference to new creation in Gal 6:14–15: (a) believers once belonged to the *kosmos;* (b) Christ has separated them from the *kosmos;* (c) the Jewish religion[10] belongs to the old *kosmos;* and (d) assimilating to Judaism is equivalent to returning to the *kosmos* from which they were redeemed (Adams 2000, 229). The final assertion implies a theological evaluation of God's revelation in the Torah that is unacceptable not only to Jews but even to Paul himself. Paul's more extended discussion of the Law in Romans distinguishes between the Gentiles, who have been turned over to the sins that follow from their willful ignorance of God (Gaca 1999), and the Jews, who have failed to follow the light provided by the Torah (Rom 1:18–3:20). Did Paul change his theological understanding of Torah's relationship to righteousness through faith between the two letters? Many scholars conclude that he must have done so (e.g., Fitzmyer 1993, 131–35; Hübner, 1984, 55–65).[11] Or should we conclude that Paul holds a coherent theological understanding of the Law that is not explicated completely in Galatians (Dunn 1998, 131)?[12] This view focuses attention on the rhetorical agenda in Galatians. Martyn points to the antithetical pairs that govern Paul's argument: "when he speaks in 4:3 and 9 of the elements of the cosmos, Paul himself has in mind not earth, air, fire and water, but rather the elemental pairs of opposites listed in 3:28, emphatically the first pair Jew and Gentile, and thus the Law and the Not-Law" (Martyn 1997, 404).

Since the baptismal confession demonstrates that these oppositions are overcome in Christ, any return to the world marked by such divisions denies the effectiveness of salvation (Martyn 1997, 405). In his earlier reflection on the conflict with Peter at Antioch (Gal 2:15–21), Paul makes a similar point about Christians of Jewish origin. To insist upon using Torah to divide the assembly of believers between Jew and non-Jew constitutes a denial of Christ as the source of salvation (Dunn 1993, 135–47). If it constitutes apostasy from Christ to incorporate legal distinctions into the Christian assembly in that instance, then the Galatians' turn toward Torah observance reflects a similar spirit of apostasy.[13] To drive this point home, Paul returns to the heart of the gospel. God's plan for salvation has taken its decisive turn with the coming of Christ. The Son, heir to the promise made to Abraham, was a member of the Jewish people ("born of a woman, born under the Law," v. 4).[14] But his mission was not only to those children of Abraham. Rather Christ united Jew and non-Jew by making both heirs of the promise. Dunn (1993, 218) rightly cautions against interpreting Gal 4:5–6a as if "adoption" *(huiothesia)* preserved the distinction by incorporating the Gentiles into God's people on a different basis than the Jewish believers. The same term applies to Israel in Rom 9:4. Galatians 4:6–7 reminds Paul's audience of their reception of the Spirit in baptism as evidence for their new relationship to God (Kraus 1999. 132).

He describes that Spirit as "of God's Son," reminding the audience of their essential relationship to Christ (compare Rom 8:9; Fee 1994, 405–406). A subtle shift from the anticipated second-person plural "your" to the first-person plural "our" hearts[15] highlights the unity of all Christians in salvation. This shift immediately gives way to another, from first-person plural to second-person singular: "you (sg.) are no longer a slave but a son" (v. 7). For a brief moment, each believer is asked to consider her or his deepest identity in Christ. Ending the sentence with the word "God" reminds each person that God has energized the entire story of salvation that began with Abraham and reaches its goal in these heirs of the promise (Betz 1979, 212).

However, the stage is not set for further reflections on unity. Following the rapid emotional shifts characteristic of this letter,[16] Paul returns to his attack (Betz 1979, 213). What those who are considering adopting Jewish customs would do is nothing less than apostasy from the God who has called them (vv. 8–9; Dunn 1993, 225).

Whether Paul's view of Gentile idolatry assumes that their deities were projections of human heroes or demonic forces[17] hardly matters to the force of the argument. Paul wishes to establish his understanding of the gospel as the only possible choice open to those Gentiles who wish to exhibit their devotion to God. Thus he substitutes slavery to the "weak and beggarly *stoicheia*" for the actual choice facing his addressees (v. 9). By phrasing their choice in this manner, Paul makes the conclusion he wishes them to draw obvious. Now that they know God, they cannot return to the ignorance and slavery of their former life. Of course, that is not what they intend, as Paul well knows. He draws closer to the issues at hand in a subtle rhetorical shift in v. 10, introducing subservience to a religious calendar as evidence of slavery.[18] Though scholars have frequently appealed to the calendrical disputes evident in sectarian Jewish groups like the Essenes as evidence that Paul's Galatian opponents had linked Jewish observance and heavenly powers (Mussner 1974, 298–303), there is no evidence that Paul thinks his converts would move from observing a Jewish liturgical calendar to worshiping astral deities.[19] Nor is it necessary to find an equivalent item in the Jewish liturgical calendar for each of the items listed in v. 10.[20]

Paul deliberately masks the reference to Jewish observances, especially the Sabbath, with a generic list that conveys a negative impression. This catalogue would remind more culturally sophisticated listeners of philosophical and literary depictions of the superstitious person (Betz 1979, 217). Paul assumes that his audience finds the superstitious person a distasteful or ridiculous figure. They would not adopt behavior that could be so characterized.[21]

A tone of irony continues into v. 11 (Betz 1979, 219). If the Galatians remain superstitious, in fear of cosmic forces, then Paul's missionary efforts among them have been futile. Paul states this possibility tentatively, inviting the audience to prove him wrong (Dunn 1993, 230). They must treat the option of adopting Jewish customs as if it were a reversion to the superstitious idol worship of a pre-Christian past. If Paul's rhetoric has changed the emotional tone that the Galatians associated with adopting Jewish customs, then the arguments that follow serve to remove any lingering doubts about the truth of Paul's gospel. If not, they up the ante. No Gentile can be loyal to Christ and permit himself to be circumcised (Gal 5:2–3, 9; Thurén 2000, 71).

> You should be as I am, in that I am also like you are, brothers, I beg you. You did not injure me in any way; now you know that I first preached to you as the result of a physical illness[22] and you did not despise or spit out[23] your testing[24] by my illness[25] but you received me as an angel of God, as Christ Jesus. Where then is this happiness[26] of yours? For I can testify about you that had you been able to you would have dug out your eyes and given them to me. So now I have become your enemy by speaking truthfully to you.[27] They are not zealous for you in the right way, but they wish to shut you out so that you will be zealous for them; now it is always good to be zealous for what is good, and not only when I am present with you. My children, with whom I am again suffering labor pains until Christ is formed among[28] you; I just wish I was still present with you and could change my tone, because I am baffled by you. (4:12–20)

Paul initiates another appeal to the Galatians based on a shared friendship (v. 12ab; Betz 1979, 221; Martyn 1997, 419–20). Friendship presumes some respect in which the parties can be considered equal (Betz 1979, 222). Yet Paul's appeal, "become as I am" (v. 12a), is ambiguous. Galatians 2:14 indicates that the corresponding phrase, "and I also as you," must refer to apostles who are Jews setting aside ancestral tradition to live as if they were non-Jews. Therefore it would be reasonable for Paul's non-Jewish converts to conclude that reciprocity would favor adopting Jewish customs[29]—certainly not the conclusion that Paul wishes his audience to draw. The final phrase in v. 12, "you have not wronged me in any way," could be an attempt to shunt aside that inference. The "wrongdoing" would be failure of Paul's non-Jewish converts to accommodate to Jewish ways while they were hosting the apostle.[30] Paul argued that in Christ both Jews and non-Jews became God's adult children, free to live by faith, not under the guardian Law or the enslaving cosmic powers (Gal 3:21–4:11). The "like you" by which the apostle had lived when in Galatia was not an acculturation to the life of non-Jews who still worshiped gods and goddesses.[31] Paul is referring to the Gentiles who have become the "sons" in whom God's Spirit is at work (4:6).

An account of their previous relationship (4:13–15) supports the assertion that the Galatians were bound to the apostle by ties of friendship (Betz 1979, 224). Such relationships should not be viewed as merely a rhetorical convenience. Stark's sociological study of conversion demonstrates that the theology follows later. Individuals initially convert to a new religious movement because they have formed strong emotional attachments to others within the group (Stark 1996, 18–19). Paul never provides sufficient evidence to determine what he means by his "weakness of the flesh" (v. 13; 2 Cor 12:8–10).[32] For the ancient orator any form of bodily weakness could serve to discredit his message.[33] Paul renders the liability even more severe. His illness was so severe that people might have concluded that he was the object of a demonic attack. Spitting was a common response to ward off the evil that such persons bring into the community (Pliny, *Nat.* 28.36, 39; Theocritus, *Id.* 6.39; Longenecker 1999, 102; Dunn 1993, 234).[34] Having already hinted that the Galatians were subject to superstitions concerning the "evil eye" (3:1) and cosmic powers (4:9–10), Paul may have formulated this image to sharpen the contrast between what they would be expected to do and what they actually did. The Galatians did not drive the apostle away but received him as if he were an angel or Christ himself (v. 14b; Dunn 1993, 234–35).

Paul may have alluded to his own suffering as the public portrait of Christ crucified (3:1), which some sort of magic spell now obscures. Though he has not signaled the connection, Paul probably expects his audience to know that Abraham's hospitality to angels preceded the message that God would give him a son by Sarah (Gen 18:1–15).[35] Hospitality to an angelic visitor in disguise brings with it extraordinary blessings. The Galatians knew God's power when they first accepted the gospel, yet they now risk turning away what they received (v. 15; Gal 3:1–5; Dunn 1993, 235; Longenecker 1999, 103). In order to highlight the absurdity of what the Galatians are proposing to do, Paul describes the strength of their earlier feeling for him as similar to Oedipus ripping out his eyes (Betz 1979, 227–28). Once again, Paul has entered rhetorically treacherous ground. Those advocating circumcision might consider their proposal a more moderate sacrifice of solidarity and friendship than tearing out one's eyes. Paul clearly wishes his audience to view circumcision with something of the horror attendant upon dismembering one's body.[36] Indirectly Paul praises his audience for their initial enthusiasm (Betz 1979, 226). Had it been possible to aid the apostle by doing so, the Galatians would have expressed their gratitude for God's salvation with a gesture even more bloody and extreme than the castrated devotees of the local mother goddess cult. Yet something has gone amiss. The zeal they once expressed for Paul's gospel has been turned against him by persons advocating circumcision (vv. 16–17; Smith 1996).

Paul introduces this dilemma with another standard rhetorical topos, the distinction between the philosopher who boldly states the truth about his audience and the flatterer (v. 16; Betz 1979, 228).[37] The truth that has created enmity between these former friends cannot have been Paul's original preaching of the gospel. It must be his opposition to what they now propose as an appropriate consequence of their faith in Christ, accepting circumcision and other Jewish customs (Longenecker 1990, 193). Whether or not the Galatians could have anticipated that their proposal would elicit such a sharp rebuke from the apostle remains unclear. He asserts that those advocating circumcision do not have the welfare of believers at heart. Their zeal would not produce a closer bond between Gentile converts and Christ. Rather, like jealous lovers, the partisans of circumcision want exclusive control over the affections of the Galatians (v. 17; Smith 1996).[38] Or, taking the negative implications of the term "be zealous" in a political sense, the advocates of circumcision are attempting to win the Galatians over to one side in a partisan struggle. Such persons stand to strengthen their own position by drawing on this pool of Gentiles with Jewish leanings without any real benefit to the Galatians themselves. We cannot tell how the same issues of personal or group loyalty figured into the opponents' appeal in Galatia.[39]

Paul switches from the attack on partisan zeal that threatens to separate the Galatians from the apostle and his gospel to a positive meaning of "zeal," genuine concern for the welfare of the other.[40] Such friendship endures even when the parties are separated from each other (v. 18; Betz 1979, 232). Paul expects his converts to have sufficient discernment that they can persevere in fidelity to the gospel although he is not present to instruct them (cf. Phil 2:12–13). This expectation is a direct consequence of his view that God's Spirit causes believers to both desire and do what is appropriate to persons who belong in Christ (Engberg-Pedersen 2000, 122–23).

Another sudden shift in imagery—from the world of philosophers and rhetoricians, the apostle as a mother giving birth to children (v. 19)—has occasioned considerable discussion (see Gaventa 1990, 189–91). Paul combines similar motifs in 1 Thess 2:1–12 (see Malherbe 2000, 134–60). He is not the deceitful sophist aiming to take advantage of his converts but the divinely commissioned apostle whose concern reflects that of a father for his children (1 Thess 2:11) and whose gentleness resembles that of a woman nursing her child (1 Thess 2:7). Familial images of affection also figure in ancient treatments of friendship.[41] Since Paul regularly uses the father-child metaphor to characterize his relationship with converts (1 Thess 2:11; 1 Cor 4:15–17; Phlm 10), the Galatians probably were familiar with it. First Thessalonians 2:11 articulates an element in the philosophical use of the metaphor that Paul assumes his audience would recognize: the ability to adapt his teaching to the character and needs of individual children. In 1 Thess 2:7 and 11, Paul combines the gentle nurse with the concerned father as teacher and moral guide for his convert children (see Malherbe 2000, 150–51). The philosopher-father will vary his tone from harsh rebuke to gentle encouragement as the circumstances dictate.[42] We observe such rapid shifts in tone throughout this section. If the audience detected the topos, they might identify with children who need encouragement and distance themselves from those being rebuked.

However, the maternal image in Gal 4:19 does not evoke the vision of a nurturing mother. The verb ōdinein refers to suffering labor pains. Paul reminds his audience of the intense physical suffering that attended his initial preaching. But he does not continue with the earlier, "lest somehow in vain" (3:4). Instead Paul shifts to the consequences of such labor pains, a community in which Christ is made visible.[43] The moral exhortation that follows in Gal 5:13–6:10 spells out the positive requirements of this injunction (Engberg-Pedersen 2000, 132–36). Before turning to the positive description, Paul must demonstrate that the agenda of those advocating circumcision inhibits development of the image of Christ within the community.[44] Circumcision stands for a way of life that will enslave those whom Christ has set free (Engberg-Pedersen 2000, 134–35). Paul asserts that he is again experiencing the labor pains that attended the birth of the Galatian church. He does not assert that the Galatians are being born yet again, as commentators who find a conflict between vv. 13–15 and v. 19 assert (so Martyn 1997, 426). Rhetorically, Paul seeks to elicit a strong emotional response from his audience. The anguish he endures on their behalf separates the apostle from those advocating circumcision.

Scholars detect another register of meanings behind Paul's use of the verb ōdinein, found in Jewish texts that speak of the sufferings to come upon Israel when God judges the nation or upon God's elect in the last days (Mic 4:10; Isa 13:6, 8; Jer 6:24; 1 Enoch 62:4; 4 Ezra 4:42; cf. Mark 13:8; 1 Thess 5:3; Gaventa 1990, 193–94). As founder of a community that saw itself to be God's end-time remnant, the Essene Teacher of Righteousness is depicted as undergoing such torments (1 QH 11.6–12).[45] Paul uses the compound verb synōdinein ("suffer agony together") of creation's share in the suffering of the elect at Rom 8:22. Paul understands his apostolic sufferings as well as those of the believers who represent the new creation in Christ (Gal 3:27–28; 6:15) within an apocalyptic framework (Dunn 1993, 240–41; Martyn 1997, 429–30). God's Spirit is at work incorporating believers into Christ (Gaventa 1990, 197). This apocalyptic metaphor implies that God will destroy those who undermine the apostle's work. The choice facing the Galatians is not an optional alliance with Jewish interests and religious practice, as they may have thought. The choice is whether they are to be God's elect, since those advocating circumcision are endangering the Christ-likeness of the community (Longenecker 1999, 104).

Having presented this option in highly emotional language, Paul returns to the tone of a philosopher-father hoping to correct his children, using the language of persuasion rather than of rebuke (v. 20). If Paul could be present in person, it would be possible to change his tone. Ancient letters frequently refer to the author's separation from his addressees (Rom 1:11, 15:23–24; 1 Cor 16:7; Phil 2:26; 1 Thess

2:17; 3:6, 10; Betz 1979, 236). The imperfect tense of the verb indicates that Paul cannot be present in Galatia. Nor does he suggest any future plans to return to that region (Martyn 1997, 425–26). Instead he concludes this section with a note of perplexity (v. 20c). This note does not suggest that Paul is uncertain about how the Galatians should live.[46] Rhetorically it invites the audience to justify the change to a milder tone by proving that harsh speech is unnecessary. They are more likely to be positively disposed toward the apostle if his harsh words are not directly aimed at them (Betz 1979, 236). Since Paul's initial stay in Galatia was the unintended consequence of his illness, the region is not part of the mission territory that he and his associates are regularly covering. Consequently, he cannot incorporate the possibility of a future visit into his appeal (cf. Phlm 21–22; 2 Cor 13:1–10).[47] As v. 18b suggested, Christians in Galatia must be able to discern and act on the good, that is, following the lead of the Spirit in Christ-like community, without the apostle to direct them.

How is the audience to construe Paul's remark at the end of v. 20? The verb *aporoumai* indicates that the subject is uncertain or in doubt. Does Paul's uncertainty concerning his audience refer to what he has just said in v. 20? In that case, he intimates that the situation in Galatia is so disastrous that even if he were present Paul would have to use the same harsh tone that he has adopted in much of the letter.[48] Or does Paul's perplexity have a more benign interpretation? It could support Paul's earlier suggestion that the harsh tone of his letter would be easily changed to more moderate encouragement if he were present (Williams 1997, 124). In that case, Paul demonstrates a confidence in his audience that the present crisis has not destroyed. They may have some explanation to offer for what Paul has heard about them. In any case, Paul is confident that his epistolary reaffirmation of the gospel will "break the spell" that appears to have taken hold in Galatia (3:1). Rhetorically he invites the audience to stand with him against those who are falling away from the gospel.

Tell me, those of you who wish to be under the Law, do you not listen to the Law? For it is written that Abraham had two sons, one by a slave woman and one by a free woman. Now the son by the slave woman was begotten in the ordinary human way,[49] while the son by the free woman [was begotten] as a result of a promise. These things are allegorical; for they are two covenants, one from mount Sinai begotten for slavery which is Hagar. Now the Hagar is mount Sinai[50] in Arabia and corresponds to the present day Jerusalem, for she is enslaved with her children. And the heavenly Jerusalem is free, which is our[51] mother, for it is written: "Be glad, barren one who has not borne children; break out and shout, woman who has never been in labor, because the children of the barren one [will be] more than [those of] she who has a man."[52] And you,[53] brothers, are children of the promise according to Isaac. But just as in the past, the one born in the ordinary human way[54] persecuted the one born in accord with the Spirit, so it is now. And what does Scripture say: "Cast out the slave woman and her son; for the son of the slave woman will not inherit along with the son of the free woman."[55] Therefore, brothers, we are not children of the slave woman but of the free woman. (4:21–31)

Paul continues the invitation for the audience to identify with him by shifting the address from the community as a whole to those who actively advocate circumcision (v. 21; Betz 1979, 237). They will be refuted first by an appeal to Scripture (4:21–5:1), and then by Paul's personal testimony that the gospel excludes circumcision (5:2–6; Martin 1995, 450–52). The first argument returns to the theme of believers as heirs to God's promise to Abraham in Christ (3:6–9). Paul's allegory treats those who believe in Christ as descendants of Isaac and all other physical offspring of Abraham as children of the slave woman Hagar. This shocking denial of Jewish claims to be descended from Isaac results in the inference that Israel is not God's elect, a view that Paul clearly rejects in Romans (Rom 15:8; Klaus 1999, 20). Since Paul introduces the allegory as a contrast between a prior covenant and the new covenant, the allegory should not be seen as evidence that non-Jews (= Christians) have been substituted for Jews (= Israel) as God's chosen people.[56] Essene writings demonstrate that it was possible for members of a Jewish sect to claim that they were God's elect and participants in the new covenant over against the rest of Israel (Elliott 2000, 254–58).

However, despite considerable interest in the Hagar-Sarah story among Jewish writers of the period, no one identifies the slave woman Hagar and her offspring with the city of Jerusalem or with a particular group of Jews. The contrast between slave and free, which Paul also exploits in his allegory, does appear in contemporary Jewish material.[57] Paul's allegorical reversal takes it as given that Jerusalem, the city that gave first-century Jews their identity as *Ioudaioi*,[58] is enslaved (v. 25b).[59] By whom? Rome? Paul's other letters give no indication that he anticipated the violent overthrow of Roman domination as attendant upon Christ's coming in glory.[60] Or is Paul returning to the polemic against "false brothers," persons associated with the Jerusalem apostles who influenced Peter, Barnabas, and others to break fellowship with Gentile believers in Antioch (Gal 2:11–14; Esler 1998, 297)? This proposal fits a more general understanding of the allegory as crafted in response to arguments advanced by Judaizing missionaries who were preaching circumcision to Paul's converts (Longenecker 1990, 199; Martyn 1997, 433).

The division between an enslaved, earthly Jerusalem and the heavenly, freeborn Jerusalem becomes a code for two warring factions among the missionaries to the Gentiles.[61] The "false teachers" invited Gentiles to enter the Sinai covenant by accepting circumcision and Jewish observance. Paul countered their language by generating a conflict between the new covenant and Sinai. The Hagar story serves as an appropriate vehicle for sharpening the polemic[62] because there is no covenant with her in Gen 16–21. Paul creates the link between Hagar and the Sinai covenant in response to his adversaries' polemic. The participial phrase, "bearing children into slavery" (v. 24), indicates that Paul reads Genesis as a reference to the present state of affairs (Martyn 1997, 436–37; Dunn 1993, 250). He is not commenting upon the origins of persons born Jewish as though they were no longer of the line of Abraham, Isaac, and Jacob.[63] Paul's earlier reference to his apostolic labor pains (v. 19) introduced the connection between "being born" and conversion. Paul's own mission engendered heirs to the promise of Abraham who are freeborn, not slaves (4.:3–7). He is addressing some of those converts ("you who wish to be under the Law," v. 21), not official teachers dispatched from Jerusalem. The rhetoric of vv. 21–31 invites them to unite with the apostle in proclaiming that they are children of the free woman (v. 31) and to follow her example by expelling "the slave woman and her son" (v. 30, citing Gen 21:10 LXX; Betz 1979, 240–41).

The argument based on Abraham's two sons, slave and freeborn, becomes more complex as Paul introduces additional items on each side. Jerusalem and Sinai, central to the case for identifying with the Jewish people by receiving circumcision, are both attached to the slave woman Hagar. No Jew would associate the Sinai covenant with slavery. However, Paul's earlier arguments have implied that coming under the Law after the advent of God's Messiah is equivalent to a free person choosing slavery (3:21–25; 4:8–11). Commentators have sought to find sources for the links between Hagar, Sinai, and Arabia mentioned in vv. 24–25, without much success.[64] The textual variants in v. 25a show that early scribes had as much difficulty with the reference as modern scholars (Elliott 1999, 667). Elliott suggests that the combination of mothers, mountains, and slaves was not derived from the teaching of a Jerusalem-sponsored mission. She points to the native Anatolian cults of the mother goddess instead. Huge images of local mother goddesses could be seen carved into the facade of fortified mesas. The mother goddess was associated with enforcer deities who embodied her function as guardian of law (Elliott 1999, 672–75).[65] At this point, Paul is not addressing himself to an argument from Scripture formulated by opposing teachers. He is taking up the residual attraction of Anatolian cultic practices, which might strengthen the appeal of circumcision (Elliott 1999, 675–80).[66] Paul avoids a mountain identification for believers. Their Jerusalem is above, that is, over all such mountain deities (v. 26; Elliott 1999, 679).

Having described the Sinai covenant as a slave mother, "the Hagar mountain," producing children for slavery, one might expect a symmetrical treatment of the freeborn mother and her children. However, the "Jerusalem above" does not correspond to a mountain.[67] Nor to a woman as mother of her children. Although commentators routinely fill in "Sarah" when they list Paul's antitheses in this section (e.g., Betz 1979, 245; Martyn 1997, 439), Paul does not do so in Galatians.[68] He may intend that the audience supply another figure as "mother"—either the apostle himself (v. 19), or the Spirit (v. 6; Elliott 1999, 682). Verse 27 quotes Isa 54:1 LXX, which includes the verb ōdinein, previously used for Paul's relationship to his Galatian converts in v. 19. However, the citation makes the barren woman, one who has not suffered labor pains, the mother of God's elect. Therefore Paul does not appear to be substituting himself for the unnamed mother of believers. He probably intends the audience to infer that their birth is a consequence of God's action in the Spirit. Later Jewish sources explicitly equate the barren woman of Isa 54:1 with Jerusalem.[69] The connection is implied in the context of Isa 54, although Essene exegetes interpret this chapter of Isaiah as a reference to the founding of their community, the elect in the last days (4Q164; Dunn 1993, 255). Paul does not provide an interpretation of the passage. He may have read its reference to the children of the barren woman as evidence that Jewish parentage is not a necessary condition for inclusion in Christ.

The "we" in v. 26 asserted that the heavenly Jerusalem and the barren woman of Isa 54:1 are the mother of all who believe in God's Messiah, whether they are also *Ioudaioi* or not. With the "but you brothers" of v. 28, Paul returns to the issue at hand, persuading those who might still consider adopting a Jewish way of life to reject that option and its advocates. Paul began this section by dividing the audience between those who were considering coming under the Law and those already allied with him. He now addresses the audience as a whole. All believers are children of the promise made concerning Isaac (v. 28; 3:6–9, 14, 16–18, 29). Paul carefully avoids claiming that non-Jewish believers are physically descended from Isaac (Martyn 1997, 444);[70] otherwise, he might give credence to the move toward greater assimilation into the Jewish community. Jewish believers who are descended from Isaac may continue to circumcise their sons and follow Jewish customs as long as they are also willing to "live in a non-Jewish manner" when gathered with other believers in Christ (2:11–14).

The practical conclusion Paul wishes his audience to draw from listening to Scripture is stated indirectly as an application of Gen 21:9–10 to the present situation (vv. 29–30). Paul's shift from referring to Christians as "of the promise" (v. 23) to "of the Spirit" (v. 29) sets the stage for the next section of the epistle in which Spirit dominates the discussion of how those not bound by the Law are to live (5:5, 16–18, 22, 25; 6:8; Longenecker 1990, 216). Although Gen 21:9 does not speak of Ishmael "persecuting" Isaac, the motif appears in later Jewish writing and may have been familiar to Paul.[71] The difficulty lies in determining what Paul refers to in his present situation as an example of "the son begotten according to the flesh," that is, Ishmael as ancestor of those who demand circumcision, persecuting "the one born of the Spirit." If Paul expects his audience to remember the autobiographical section (1:13–14), then "persecute" refers to hostility toward believers in Christ on the part of other Jews (as in Rom 15:31; 2 Cor 11:24; 1 Thess 2:14; Schlier 1965, 227; Betz 1979, 250). But this reading has little connection to the issue at hand. Consequently, both persecutor(s) and victim(s) would appear to be within the Christian community (Martyn 1997, 444–45). Does Paul mean that he himself is the victim of persecution because of the gospel he preaches to the Gentiles? Or does he mean that outsiders have deliberately targeted his churches so that the churches can be said to experience persecution by those advocating circumcision? Galatians 5:11–12 could support either of these options. Both may be suggested, if one reads the stories of Paul's dealings with the "false brothers" from Jerusalem as part of a history that has now resulted in teachers sponsored by Jerusalem invading Paul's churches (Martyn 1997, 445, 459–65).

Paul leaves it to his audience to determine an appropriate response to this situation. He implies that all they have to do is follow the instruction contained in Scripture. Verse 30 cites Gen 21:10 LXX, with a slight addition by the apostle attaching "of the free woman" to "the son" at the end of the quotation (Betz 1979, 250). The action to be taken is clear: exclude the "son of the slave woman" from any association with the freeborn son. The latter clearly represents all believers in Christ. But who is the referent of the former? Jews opposed to the gospel as a matter of principle (so Betz 1979, 251)? Any Christian missionaries claiming allegiance to the "false brothers" in Jerusalem and preaching a message contrary to Paul's (Longenecker 1990, 217)? The anathemas in Gal 1:8–10 refer to such a situation (Martyn 1997, 446). If one abandons as unproven the hypothesis that an organized, anti-Paulinist mission with Jerusalem backing is responsible for the turmoil in Galatia, then the exclusion question looks somewhat different. Martyn has concluded that a significant group of teachers and firmly committed adherents are to be thrown out and pronounced anathema (1997, 446). However, one must take care not to confuse the drama of rhetoric with social realities on the ground.[72] The interest in circumcision and assimilation in a Jewish direction could arise from varied social and cultural factors that had nothing to do with bringing down the apostle and his gospel. Jewish-Christian visitors may have sparked local interest with their accounts of some of the events and churches to which Paul referred in the narrative. But, if the Galatians have not deserted their new faith *en masse*, then it is possible that no one will be expelled. Visitors whose views cause agitation in the community might be sent packing, but no one in Paul's audience need be.[73] As something of a rallying cry, v. 31 states the identity to which all members of the community should adhere, "children of the freeborn woman, not of the slave."

Chapter Five ———————————————————

Galatians 5

———————————————————————————

Christ has liberated us for freedom, therefore stand fast[1] and do not get tangled up in a yoke of slavery again! Look, I, Paul, am telling you that if you should have yourselves circumcised, Christ will not benefit you. I testify again to everyone who is circumcised that he is obligated to perform the whole Law. You have been cut off from Christ, those who are [trying to be][2] justified by the Law, you have fallen away from his[3] grace. For we have received the hope of righteousness in the Spirit which comes from faith. For in Christ Jesus neither circumcision nor lack of circumcision count for anything; only faith activated through love [counts].

You were progressing[4] well; who blocked you[5] from obeying the truth? Circumcision is not from the one who called you. A little yeast leavens the whole mass of dough. I am confident about you in the Lord that you will not think anything different; now the one who is disturbing you will bear his condemnation whoever he may be. But I, brothers, if I am still preaching circumcision, why am I still being persecuted? And those who are upsetting you ought to be castrated! (5:1–12)

The ringing summons to hold fast to their freedom in Christ (v. 1) draws on the affirmation of a common identity as children of the free-born woman in the previous verse (4.31). At the same time, it sets the agenda for the rest of the letter: how Christians should live in order to preserve their freedom in Christ (Betz 1979, 255).[6] Commentators differ over where to place the break between the theological argument in the letter and the shift to exhortation. Since 5:1 is picked up again in v. 13, one may either treat the exhortation as initiated with v. 1 (so

Betz 1979, 253) or with v. 13 (so Dunn 1993, 261). Paul's explicit command that Gentile converts not seek circumcision with its attendant obligation to observe Torah in 5:2–12 serves both as a conclusion to the theological argument and as a preliminary to the positive instructions concerning the Christian way of life.[7] The ethical exhortation in 5:13–6:10 reminds the Galatians of what they already know from Paul's initial preaching (Martin 1998, 458).[8]

Freedom should not be misconstrued in the modern political sense of individual liberties. Paul has played off the sociopolitical meaning of freedom in ancient society throughout his argument. Freedom is the antithesis of slavery. The legal, cultural, and social distinctions between persons who are offspring of freeborn parents and those born to slaves added powerful emotional resonance to the allegory of the two mothers (4:21–31) that goes undetected by twenty-first-century audiences.[9] Former slaves and children born to them after manumission, who were considered freeborn, were certainly determined not to become slaves again. Paul's appeal in v. 1 carries the weight of these social realities behind it. No one could imagine a voluntary return to slavery.

At the same time, Paul's call to maintain one's freedom can be heard in the context of ancient philosophical debates concerning virtue (Betz 1979, 257). Unlike the vast run of humanity driven by ignorance, passions, superstitious fears, and social conditioning, the wise are truly free. So stated, the various philosophical schools would agree that virtue secures freedom. Philosophical schools differ in the sociopolitical consequences that follow from this doctrine of freedom. Professing a radical Socratic independence of all social prejudices and constraints, the Cynics cast off the chains of social convention. They were known in the Roman period for shameless disregard for public decorum and boldness in speech that could be both obscene and inappropriate (Griffin 1996). Paul's blunt statement that those causing dissent in Galatia ought to be castrated (v. 12) exemplifies that style of speech. For Epicureans, withdrawal from the corruption and turmoil of social and political life and association with a philosophic circle of like-minded friends provided the best way of life. The wise are free from superstitious belief in the gods, from extreme agitation in mind or body (Diogenes Laertius, *Lives* 10.136; Erler and Schofield 1999, 644–69). Paul's allusions to the superstitiousness of the Galatians before their conversion (3:1; 4:9–10, 14) could be read in this vein. Christ has freed them from such false beliefs as well as from the agitation and fear they caused.[10]

Stoicism provides the most extensive analogies between ancient philosophical teaching and Paul's moral exhortation (Engberg-Pedersen 2000). Roman Stoics, outspoken in their criticism of the emperor, were exiled or executed under the late Julio-Claudians.[11] Freedom from fear of the consequences enables the philosopher to speak the truth even to the tyrant. The Stoic wise person expresses his or her freedom in actions that are appropriate to a human nature, which belongs to the larger, rationally ordered cosmos (Inwood and Donini 1999, 686–87). For Stoics the passions are symptoms of intellectual mistakes concerning what a virtuous person should choose, not irrational inner forces that overwhelm reason. Consequently, moral instruction provides the necessary corrective to erroneous judgments and to their resulting passions (Inwood and Donini 1999, 699–703).[12] Engberg-Pedersen argues for a structural similarity between Stoic moral pedagogy and Pauline paraenesis (Engberg-Pedersen 2000, 36–44). The audience is being reminded that their identification with Christ implies practice, that is, living according to normative ethical principles (Engberg-Pedersen, 2000, 138–39). Before Paul turns to a positive statement of this principle (5:13–6:10), he explicitly excludes circumcision and Torah observance from consideration (5:2–12).

Paul's opening salvo in v. 2 puts his personal oath behind the claim already defended in 2:15–21: Christ-belief excludes circumcision (Longenecker 1990, 225).[13] There cannot be dual sources of righteousness. Framing the exclusion with an eye toward the impending ethical discussion, it implies that there cannot be an alternative to Christ as the basis for a Christian life. Perhaps the Galatians considering circumcision thought the step was only indicative of a partial affiliation with Judaism, although non-Jews certainly considered persons who underwent the procedure to have defected (Dunn 1993, 264).[14] Rather than describe circumcision as the mark of belonging to God's covenant people, as advocates of the practice probably argued, Paul treats it as taking on all the commandments of the Torah (v. 3; 3:10 referring to Deut 27:28; 3:12 to Lev 18:5).[15] This emphasis would not sound strange to Jewish ears (e.g., 4 Macc 5:20–21; Dunn 1993, 266–67). Sectarian Jews like the Essenes might insist that only members of their group obey the whole Torah (e.g., 1 QS 1.1–20; Longenecker 1990, 227). With the rhetorical drama of an absolutist theology, Paul treats circumcision as the contaminating leaven that is cleared out in preparation for Passover (v. 9).[16] To consider circumcision is to desert Christ (v. 4), though Paul must admit that the "circumcised," that is, persons born Jews, are not excluded from Christ. His formulation in v. 6a is less absolutist: the mark of circumcision has no meaning in Christ (so Gal 3:27–28). Thurén (2000, 72) draws a further conclusion from the absolutism with which Paul expresses himself in Gal 5:2–9: there was no discernable difference in the practical way of life advocated by the two sides. Paul has to up the ante rhetorically so that the Galatians will perceive the fundamental theological issues at stake.

Buried in the negative slogans, Paul includes a positive argument. God has not required circumcision of the Gentiles. Righteousness is a consequence of faith in Christ (v. 5). Paul indicates that the righteousness to be achieved has an eschatological dimension. "Hope of righteousness" reminds the audience that God is the ultimate source of salvation (Betz 1979, 262). The way of life to which believers are obligated does not require the Law. "Faith energized through love" (v. 6b) is the principle that must inform their actions (Engberg-Pedersen 2000, 135, 177). Circumcision (= adherence to the Law) has no place "in Christ," whatever the ethnic origins of believers. Paul carefully inserts the first person plural "we" in v. 5 to make it clear that faith, Spirit, and righteousness come to all through Christ. The solidarity that unites believers with Christ, the apostle, and each other would be as surely broken by some non-Jewish Christians accepting circumcision and a way of life under the Law as it was broken when Peter and the others withdrew from fellowship with their non-Jewish brothers and sisters in Antioch (2:11–14).

Paul lessens the gulf between himself and his audience suggested by the charge in v. 4 when he questions the audience about the origin of their opinions (5:7–12).[17] Some scholars have seen the "you have been cut off from Christ, who think you are made righteous by the Law" in v. 4 as evidence that the majority are solidly in the camp of teachers advocating circumcision (especially Martyn 1997, 471). However, the shift in tone suggests that v. 4 is a dramatic statement of the consequences of an action that the audience is considering (Longenecker 1990, 228). The audience still has the option of taking instruction from the apostle. The crass proposal that castration would be a suitable punishment for whoever (pl.) is stirring up trouble in Galatia (v. 12) invites the audience to offload the anger and condemnation they may have felt was directed at themselves earlier onto these persons.[18]

Paul begins the questions with a third-person singular. Who is the person who cut in on the Galatians during the race? As did other moralists, Paul frequently used familiar athletic images to describe the Christian life (Gal 2:2; 1 Cor 9:24–27; Phil 3:14; De Vries 1975). This image shifts the blame away from the audience. They were running a good race until they were fouled. The obstruction had serious consequences. It appears to have put the Galatians off course, since they still are not "obeying the truth" (= the gospel).[19] Formal use of an indefinite third person in the diatribe genre introduces opinions or actions that the audience will reject. The track-and-field image of runners being fouled provides an emotional pitch to Paul's demand that advocates of circumcision be excluded (4:29–31). The concise statement in v. 8 refers the audience back to the argument that they have just heard concerning the truth of the gospel. Nothing in the gospel that Paul preached to the Galatians supports the conclusion that they should seek circumcision or assimilation to Judaism. They may have been deceived into thinking that coming under the Law was a logical expansion of their faith in Christ,[20] but the previous argument should have cleared away that confusion. The phrase "one who called you" reaches back to Gal 1:6. It has a double referent: the apostle, who preached the gospel, and God, whose Spirit awakened faith in their hearts.[21] Neither God nor God's predestined emissary to the Gentiles (Gal 1:11–17) is calling the non-Jews to become Israelites.[22]

Verse 9 is formulated as if it were a common proverb, although it only occurs in Paul (Betz 1979, 266).[23] Paul repeats it, with more extensive references to Christ as the Passover, in 1 Cor 5:6. That passage follows his demand that the Corinthians expel from the community a man who has contracted an incestuous marriage with his stepmother. In that context, the church is required to enforce a commonly held ethical precept because failure to do so would destroy its corporate identity in Christ (see Thiselton 2000, 401–407). Although the expulsion argument has been more indirectly stated to this point, Paul probably intends his audience to draw the same conclusion from the proverb. It also serves to bolster Paul's contention that advocating circumcision for Gentile Christians is not a matter of indifference.[24] The stereotypical confidence expression in v. 10ab introduces a strange note into the argument. Have the previous suggestions that the Galatians are deserting the apostle and his gospel been forgotten (Betz 1979, 267)? Hardly. The statement of firm assurance that the audience will see the matter as he does has theological roots in Paul's conviction that his gospel is from God, not merely a human creation (Dunn 1993, 276).[25] At the same time, this change of tone serves as a rhetorical invitation to the audience to side with the apostle. Their earlier bonds of friendship can still win out over the flattery of false suitors (4:12–20).

Harsh language returns as Paul directs his attention toward those responsible for the confusion in Galatia (5:10c, 12). He shifts from condemning a single individual (v. 10c) to the plural (v. 12). In either case, the person(s) responsible are depicted as interlopers, persons who come into a community from the outside in order to stir up turmoil.[26] Introduction of foreign religious cults into an ancient city often spawned charges of fomenting discord and resulted in persecution or expulsion of those responsible.[27] Paul himself was the victim of such actions on several occasions.[28] He presumes that his audience is familiar with the sufferings he undergoes while preaching the gospel (v. 11).[29] But Paul's formulation of the appeal to persecution as evidence for his character and for the credibility of his message takes an odd turn in v. 11. He implies that preaching circumcision would be a means of avoiding the suffering attendant upon preaching the gospel. The cross would cease to be a stumbling block (cf. 2:18–3:1). The word *eti* ("still") in v. 11a suggests that there was a time when Paul could have been described as "preaching circumcision." The expression "preach circumcision" is presumably Paul's own shorthand for advocating adherence to the Jewish way of life. It is formally similar to Paul's "preach Christ" (e.g., 1 Cor 1:23, 15:11; 2 Cor 4:5; Phil 4:5; Betz 1979, 269). It may refer to Paul's enthusiasm for ancestral traditions as a young man or to his own persecution of the church (1:13). However, the context of an intra-Christian conflict makes it appear that Paul refers to some element in his earlier activity as a Christian missionary.[30] He admits to adopting the way of life appropriate to those among whom he wishes to preach, to live as a Jew among Jews in order to win them over to the gospel (1 Cor 9:20). Those advocating circumcision may have had such examples from Paul's own past with which to bolster their case.[31]

If there was such an ambiguity concerning Paul's missionary preaching elsewhere, then the anathema formula at Gal 1:8–9 would seem to resolve the issue from the beginning.[32] There can be no other gospel than the one that Paul has preached and will set forth in the letter. Paul's narrative of the past facts concerning his call and early mission among the Gentiles (Gal 1:11–2.14) was crafted to show that he consistently carried out the task entrusted to him by God. The case of Titus at the Jerusalem meeting shows that non-Jews were never required to undergo circumcision in order to be fully accepted as followers of Christ (Gal 2:3).

Paul does not make it clear how "preaching circumcision" would lessen the persecution that he suffers. Possibly he refers only to the hostility of the Christians who advocate it against himself and his churches (4:29), which continues a series of episodes that go back to his struggles against false brothers in Jerusalem and Antioch (2:1–14; Martyn 1997, 476–77). Hostile Roman authors considered circumcision the mark by which Jews identified fellow members of a sinister and antisocial group. Proselytes learn to despise the city's gods, traditions, and their own relatives (Tacitus, *Hist.* 5.5.1–2; Juvenal, *Sat.* 14.96–106).[33] A mission to the Gentiles that "preached circumcision," that is, was proselytizing, would not lessen tension with civic authorities. Furthermore, the authorities could be expected to intervene if preaching the gospel caused turmoil within the Jewish communities of the Diaspora. Consequently, Jewish leaders might police their own boundaries against persons whose activities caused dissent.[34] Had Paul's approach to the Gentiles required that they consider becoming proselytes, or at least enter a relationship of patronage and partisanship toward Jews, it might have been less controversial in

Jewish circles. Lacking further details, we cannot decode the message that Paul intends to convey with any certainty.

The severe words about what will or should happen to the person or persons causing trouble in Galatia may be Paul's reaction to calumnies against himself and his mission. However, they could also be a rhetorical gesture intended to solidify the identification of the audience with the apostle. Verse 10c announces judgment against the person responsible. The judgment in question certainly implies divine sanctions against anyone who would destroy God's work among the Galatians (1:8–9; so Martyn 1997, 475). However, Paul has intimated that the Galatians should exclude such persons from the community; therefore, the statement that whoever is responsible will get what he deserves contains the hint that the community should pass its own judgment (Williams 1997, 140). Paul's wish for the opponents of the gospel in v. 12 is an even more crass suggestion that divine retribution might take the form of an accident. The knife they would use to circumcise others could cut them off. Most commentators hold that the phrase refers to castration, perhaps even wishing that such persons would be included among the devotees of the mother goddess (Martyn 1997, 478). Williams points to a different allusion, the severed penis (Deut 23:2 LXX). According to Deut 23:2, no one whose testicles are crushed or whose penis has been cut off can be admitted to the community of the Lord (Williams 1997, 142; also Dunn 1993, 282–83). In either case, the "judgment" would exclude the agitators from the very community that requires the "cutting" of circumcision. Their operating instrument could exclude them from the Jewish community just as Paul asserts that they are using it to exclude Gentiles from Christ (Dunn 1993, 283).

> For you were called to freedom, brothers; only not freedom as an opportunity for the passions;[35] but rather be slaves to each other through love. For the whole Law is fulfilled in one saying, namely: "Love your neighbor as yourself."[36] And if you bite and eat up each other, watch out that you are not destroyed by each other.
>
> And I say: Walk by the Spirit and you will not satisfy human passion.[37] For passion[38] lusts against the Spirit, and the Spirit

against passion,[39] for these are opposed to one another with the
result that you do things that you do not wish to. And if you are
led by the Spirit, you are not under the Law. Now acts dictated
by passions[40] are obvious, they are: sexual immorality, impurity,
indecency, idolatry, sorcery, quarrels, rivalry, jealousy, outbursts
of anger, selfish ambitions, dissensions, factions, envies,[41] drink-
ing bouts, orgies, and things like these, which I warn you, as I
said earlier, people who do such things will not inherit the kingdom of God.

Now the fruit of the Spirit is love, joy, peace, patience, kindness, goodness, faith, gentleness, self-control; there is no Law
against such things. Those who belong to Christ Jesus[42] have crucified the flesh with its passions and desires. If we live by the
Spirit, then we follow the Spirit. Let us not be conceited, provoking one another, envying one another. (5:13–26)

Verse 13a picks up the call to stand fast in the freedom given
through Christ from v. 1a. However, the "yoke of slavery" that was the
Law in v. 1b has been replaced by a double injunction: freedom is not
"opportunity for the flesh" (v. 13b) but the occasion to "serve one
another in love" (v. 13c). Betz (1979, 272) understands the first
expression, "opportunity for the flesh," as a crucial clue to the
Galatian interest in the Law. Advocates of adopting the Law (5:3)
probably held it up as the solution to problems of immorality that
had emerged within the community (also Esler 1998, 229). Martyn
picks a specialized reading for the term *aphormē* ("opportunity") that
is found in military contexts. It can mean a base from which to launch
a military operation. Therefore he translates it "a base of military
operations" and suggests that Paul wishes his audience to see themselves engaged in the end-time conflict. The "flesh" is the base from
which attacks can be launched against freedom in the Spirit (Martyn
1998, 481–85).[43]

Most interpreters follow the lead forged by Rudolf Bultmann's use
of existentialist philosophy in understanding what Paul means when
he speaks of "the flesh" as a negative power in human life that is
opposed to the Spirit (Dunn 1998, 62–70). The term *sarx* ("flesh")
takes on a wide range of meanings in Paul's usage. It can simply mean

the physical body or a human being. It can refer to humans in the weakness or fragility that embodiment implies. Or, as here, it can refer to a hostile moral power that undermines even the best human efforts (see Dunn 1998, 64–65).[44] Engberg-Pedersen uses the structural similarity that he detects between Paul and Stoic moralists to clarify the issues encoded in Paul's terse formulation. Flesh and Spirit are codes for mental attitudes, which will be specified in the lists of virtues and vices that follow in 5:16–24. The attitudes that follow upon the Spirit are directed toward relationships within the community as certainly as those that follow "desires of the flesh" destroy communal harmony (Engberg-Pedersen 2000, 160–61). This emphasis would remind Paul's audience that those advocating circumcision are to be excluded because they have "disturbed you" (vv. 10, 12), that is, created discord within the community.[45] Thus Paul has crafted the elements of ethical exhortation in this section to the specific problems posed by advocates of circumcision.[46]

The positive formulation "through love be slaves of one another" (v. 13c) forms the antithesis to the misuse of freedom.[47] The noun "love" appeared for the first time in v. 6. The exhortation will spell out what "faith active through love" means for the community.[48] But a surprise in this exhortation escapes modern readers accustomed to praising any appearance of egalitarianism.[49] It lies in the characterization of love as enslaving oneself to others. Throughout the earlier argument, Paul has played off the social abhorrence for being enslaved. Don't be enslaved to superstitions, elemental powers of the universe, the Law. Don't seek to join the children born to a slave woman. Suddenly he pulls a positive slave term out of the hat, slavery to one another. Even that must have sounded a bit strange. Slavery is not an egalitarian institution. It encodes the severity of hierarchical order in ancient society (Esler 1998, 224).[50]

Paul introduces a passage from the Law in support of his positive admonition (Lev 19:18).[51] The introduction to this quotation, "all the Law is fulfilled in one word," continues to generate heated exegetical debate. Many scholars presume that Paul seeks to separate a positive use of the Law in Christian moral reflection from its use to force Gentiles to assimilate to Jewish customs (Dunn 1993, 289–91). The love command sums up the legitimate demand of the Law that remains intact for Christians. Further, Dunn argues that Paul expected his audiences in Galatia (5:14) and Rome (Rom 13:8–10) to understand that Jesus had set them an example of what such other-regarding love implies (Dunn 1996, 77–80). The exegetical view that Paul considers Lev 19:18 to encapsulate the positive meaning of the Law apparently led the translators of the NRSV to translate the verb *peplērōtai* ("been fulfilled," perfect tense) as "summed up." Linguistically the verb does not refer to a summary of something but to filling up, satisfying, completing, or perfecting its object. The NRSV translation has substituted Rom 13:8–10, where Paul refers to Lev 19:18 as "summing up" *(anakephalaiein),* for what he says in Gal 5:14.[52]

Other scholars underline the resulting contradiction. Paul adamantly rejects circumcision of his Gentile converts because they would be obligated "to do the whole *(holos)* Law" (v. 3). He cannot then be offering them a "condensed version," a way to fulfill "all *(pas)* the Law," in v. 14 (Martyn 1996). Instead, Martyn highlights the disjunctive rhetoric that Paul has used in the earlier argument. The Law speaks with two voices: one that cursed Christ crucified (3:10–14); another that promised salvation to the seed of Abraham (3:6–9; Martyn 1997, 506–13). Christ has brought the Law's curse to an end (3:13; 4:5; 5:1; Martyn 1996, 51–53). The same deed that freed believers (5:1, 13) establishes Lev 19:18 as the guiding imperative for the daily life of the church (Martyn 1996, 60). Esler (1998, 184, 203–204) makes a similar argument against treating Gal 5:14 as preserving a place for ethical instruction through the Law. He points out that the gifts that unite members of the community stem from the Spirit. Those led by the Spirit act according to love. They are not under the Law (Esler 1998, 203). Paul's rhetorical emphasis on separating his converts from any association with the Law makes a discontinuity between the Law and the love command a more plausible reading of this passage. However, Esler's recognition that "be slaves to one another" is likely to strike the ears of the audience as odd or objectionable provides a simpler explanation for this citation. Verses 14 and 15 take up the clauses attached to "you have been called to freedom" (v. 13a) in reverse order. The appeal to a word that completes the Law (v. 14a) is a proof by authority for the demand, "be slaves to one another."[53]

Verse 15 exemplifies the consequences of misused freedom, social disintegration. The metaphor is deliberately shocking: "brothers" chewing one another up like wild animals.[54] Such sarcasm continues the elements of the diatribe genre employed by the apostle (Betz 1979, 276). Although such images have wide currency in ancient moralists, this admonition must refer to conditions in the Galatian community (Martyn 1997, 491 n. 63). Paul has warned that those who adopt the Law will be cut off from Christ (5:4). This warning suggests that the communal dissent that has been stirred up by advocates of circumcision could result in destroying all parties to the fight (Esler 1998, 226). Recognizing the possibility that this imagery would suggest savage political divisions, Dunn concludes that love of neighbor is to restrain the ugly possibilities of freedom. He assumes that "the call for neighbour-love was also a call for love towards those who 'savagely' disagreed with Paul!" (Dunn 1993, 293). Our analysis of the rhetorical progression of the argument requires that this suggestion be revised. Paul is adamant in requiring that the person or persons responsible for stirring up dissent be excluded. He has subtly but consistently applied pressure to the emotional sensitivities of his audience. They are to shift to Paul's side against persons who knocked them out of the good race they were running (5:7). The only persons who may experience "love" from others in the community are those who once disagreed but are now persuaded by the apostle.

Verse 16 provides a solution to the dilemma posed by what Paul refers to as "desire of the flesh" *(epithumia sarkos),* following the dictates of the Spirit. Paul's affirmative statement, "walk by the Spirit and you will not[55] fulfill the desire of the flesh," sets out the fundamental principle of his ethical vision (Betz 1979, 277).[56] This certainty that moral perfection represents a definitive change from one mode of action to another is analogous to Stoic moral psychology (Engberg-Pedersen 2000, 161).[57] However, the antithetical pair "flesh vs. spirit," which Paul uses to formulate his understanding of how Christ has transformed the believer's moral life,[58] cannot be derived from philosophical speculation.[59] The phrase that Paul uses as code for negative moral actions, "desire of the flesh," seems to derive from Palestinian Jewish sources. The expression, *rwh bśr* ("spirit of flesh"), turns up in wisdom texts found at Qumran (4 Q416–418) and was used in sectarian writings (1 QS 11.11–12; Frey 1999, 55–62). This "spirit of flesh" generates disobedience to God. It will be destroyed at the end-time judgment. For the Essene sectaries, the "sons of Truth," God's Spirit supports their way of life in opposition to the lies and disobedience of those outside the sect. Their solution to the false spirit at work in the world does not reject the Law as effective power. A renewed and intensified obedience to God's Law is key to salvation in the sect (Frey 1999, 73).

The contrast in part reflects the circumstances of Paul's experiences with his congregations of Gentile converts.[60] However, the antithesis between flesh and Spirit as Paul uses it depends upon the central theological insight that the "Spirit" in which Christians participate is the sign that God's new age was initiated with the death of Christ (e.g., Rom 8:2–4; Dunn 1998, 644–46). This eschatological perspective emerges with more explicitly apocalyptic overtones in v. 17. Paul draws up battle lines: "desire of flesh" on the one side, against the Spirit on the other (Martyn 1997, 493–94). This engagement is not a reflection on principles within human nature, such as Jewish traditions concerning the good and evil spirits battling for the human heart since creation (e.g., 1 QS 4.15–16);[61] it is the consequence of the presence of the time of salvation in a world that remains subjected to the "elemental powers" of the old age. The end-time battle was not declared by the cosmic powers, but by Spirit, which has been let loose among those once subject to them (Martyn 1997, 493). Paul has invited his audience to understand the concrete struggles within their community as a reflection of this cosmic dynamic that is God's plan of salvation.[62]

This new perspective enables Paul to draw a conclusion in v. 17c that initially seems contrary to the promise made in v. 16: "so that what you do not wish, these things you do." Some interpreters resolve the apparent difficulty of leaving believers subject to "desire of the flesh" by concluding that the power that moves in and compels their action is the Spirit (so Barclay 1988, 112–16). Since v. 17ab describes a state of mutual warfare between "desire of the flesh" and "Spirit," the possible compulsion must come from either side (so Longenecker 1990, 246; Dunn 1993, 299). Dunn represents the line of interpretation that treats this passage as a reflection on the anthropological problem of individuals: "Believers (Paul states it as a general truth) experience in themselves a real unwillingness and antagonism against the Spirit as much as against the flesh. . . . That is why the call to 'walk by the Spirit' is so important: there must be that inward resolution and determined discipline to side with the Spirit *against oneself* in what is an ongoing and inescapable inner warfare" (1993, 299; similarly, Schlier 1965, 250).[63] But this shift to a psychology of individual moral conflict must face two serious objections: (a) its contradiction of Paul's explicit statement in v. 16, and (b) the communal orientation of the discussion to this point. The divisions and turmoil are not within individuals but between persons, as v. 15 states.

The first objection could be resolved with only a slight modification. Dunn's modern view that persons never transcend inner moral conflict could be replaced by the ancient stoic understanding of moral progress. Then v. 16 describes the "wise," the person who has achieved the goal of moral pedagogy. Verse 17c, on the other hand, represents those who still require instruction. Paul is not describing a permanent state of being a Christian. He is reporting to the Galatians the reason for their lack of moral certitude and stability, which they might otherwise have taken to be an objection against the promise in v. 16.[64] However, the communal orientation coupled with the hints that they are involved in a war between two powers presents a difficulty for this solution as well. Paul elsewhere assumes that divisions within the community can be a manifestation of end-time distress and testing (e.g., 1 Cor 11:19). This observation is a more concise and apparently extreme conclusion. Persons caught in a war find themselves compelled to do what they do not wish and would not do in other circumstances. Actions performed under such constraints do not reflect the moral character of individual soldiers. This analogy assumes that Paul is referring only to morally evil or ambiguous actions. Martyn (1997, 494–95) suggests that he has in mind the lack of integrity among those who side with the opposing teachers. Thus Paul's explanation shifts the burden of blame for what has occurred from his audience to the war in which they have been caught. This move makes it possible for those who might be wavering to move back to the apostle's side.

Verse 18 explicitly returns to the controversy over circumcision. Those who are in the Spirit are not under the Law. The parallelism

108 Abraham's Divided Children

between this verse and v. 13 evokes an odd conclusion. The Law is associated with "opportunity for the flesh"! As we have seen, proponents of circumcision may have been advocating that the Law would enable Christians to restrain the "desires of the flesh" (Esler 1998, 229).[65] So having made this statement, Paul excludes all such actions from the Christian life (vv. 19–21). Lists of vices and virtues were a familiar feature of ancient moralizing (Betz 1979, 281–83; Dunn 1998, 662–65; Longenecker 1990, 249–52). Paul employs this cataloguing technique to shape his depiction of the Christian life. Vices exclude believers from God's reign (vv. 19–21). Virtues demonstrate the working of the Spirit among those who identify with the crucified Christ (vv. 22–24). Analyses of Paul's use of such catalogues in his epistles indicate that he does not simply repeat a preformed tradition. His selections of virtues and vices are relevant to the particular contexts in which they appear (Dunn 1998, 665). The vice catalogue in vv. 19b–21a includes a number of items in the plural rather than the singular: "sexual immorality *(porneia)*, impurity *(akatharsia)*, licentiousness *(aselgeia)*,[66] hostilities *(ecthrai)*, strife *(eris)*, jealousy *(zēlos)*, rages *(thymoi)*, dissensions *(dichostasiai)*, factions *(haireseis)*, grudges *(phthonoi)*,[67] drunken episodes *(methai)*, revels *(kōmoi)*,[68] and such things." This technique may be intended to suggest the chaotic moral disorder caused by "the desire of the flesh" (Betz 1979, 283). However, the selection of vices is hardly random. Sexual immorality, idolatry, and superstition reflect back on the pre-Christian past of Paul's non-Jewish converts. The remaining vices all describe forms of conflict, hatred, and disordered behavior in the community (Martyn 1997, 497). Paul follows this list with a reminder that none of this teaching should be news to the Galatians. They had been instructed from the beginning that persons who do such things will not be among God's elect (v. 21b). This comment may be directed against the suggestion of others that Paul's evangelization failed to provide an adequate moral foundation, hence the need to introduce obedience to the Law (Martyn 1997, 497).

Unlike the chaotic impression of the vice list, the virtues are treated as a unified whole, the singular fruit of the Spirit (v. 22; Betz 1979, 287).[69] The list is shorter: love *(agapē)*, joy *(chara)*, peace *(eirēnē)*, patience *(makrothumia)*, kindness *(chrēstotēs)*, goodness *(agathōsunē)*, faith *(pistis)*, gentleness *(prautēs)*, self-control *(egkrateia)*. After "love," a principle that Paul has already introduced (vv. 6 [along with faith], 14), the selection may have been intended as a counter to the divisiveness of the previous group. Paul's comment, "against such things there is no Law" (v. 23b), calls the audience back to the issue at hand (v. 18). However, the formulation is somewhat awkward. Commentators generally read the phrase as if Paul intended *"kata tōn toioutōn"* to mean simply that the Law cannot or does not concern itself with such virtues (so Engberg-Pedersen 2000, 165).[70] That reading puts Paul in the position of contradicting the quotation of Lev 19:18 in v. 14, where the Law certainly does commend love of neighbor. Others conclude that Paul intends to indicate that the Law does not produce these states of mind because it can only deal with actions (Engberg-Pedersen 2000, 166). That Paul certainly does imply, since the Spirit whose fruit is represented by these virtues came to believers on the basis of faith, apart from the Law (3:1–5). Campbell (1996) proposes to resolve the dilemma by treating the genitive plural, *tōn toioutōn*, as a reference to persons, not to the items in the list. Paul's point would be that the Law does not condemn persons who act in this way. Therefore, contrary to what they have been hearing, the Galatians do not have to fear that living according to the Spirit will result in their exclusion from God's elect. Paul would certainly concur with this conclusion. However, had he intended a reference to persons rather than to deeds, one would expect a variant of the phrase that follows the list of vices, "those who do these things." The reference to persons comes at the beginning of v. 24, "those who are of Christ." This verse contrasts the situation of believers with that of the battle-plagued in v. 17c.[71] Assimilation to Christ crucified ends the regime of flesh along with the passions and desires that derive from it. This statement affirms the soteriological vision that Paul has articulated earlier in the letter. "[C]rucified with Christ" (2:19–20) and "putting on Christ" (3:27) are not just metaphors for belief in Christ. They are actively reflected in the freedom of an ethical life that walks by the Spirit with which Christians are endowed (4:6; Betz 1979, 289).

Verses 25–26 can be understood as a summary statement of the previous section (Longenecker 1990, 265). Or they can be considered a return to the fundamental principle, living in the Spirit, and an introduction to the final set of moral maxims (6:1–10; Betz 1979, 293–94; Martyn 1997, 541). Paul gathers his audience to his side. The verb *stoichein* ("stand in line" or "walk straight") has a military overtone, to stand in the battle line. The apostle may expect his audience to hear more in this sentence than the summons to a moral life in accord with the Spirit. As he has done throughout the earlier argument, Paul indirectly calls them to take sides, specifically to line up with the apostle under the Spirit. In order to be successful, closing ranks requires an end to the communal disturbance that the conflict in Galatia has caused. Paul has dealt with this issue repeatedly in ch. 5. He suggests exclusion of those most responsible. He has shifted most of the blame for the state of affairs off the shoulders of those in his audience, first onto the agitators and secondly onto the war between the "desire of the flesh" and the Spirit. We have seen that the vices and virtues in his lists have been crafted with these problems in mind. So v. 26 returns to warn against socially divisive behavior once again (Martyn 1997, 545). As our discussion of v. 13 suggested, those who would be "slaves to one another" must surrender self-centered views of personal honor that were deeply ingrained in ancient society. The warning against vainglory *(kenodoxos)* speaks to such competition for honor. Those against provoking or challenging others *(prokalein)* and grudging envy of them *(phthonein)* refer directly to the vices in vv. 20–21a. Unified as a group by these common resolutions, Paul turns to a series of maxims that can order the life of the community (Martyn 1997, 542).

Chapter Six

Galatians 6

Brothers [and sisters], if someone is discovered committing some transgression, those of you who are spiritual should bring him [or her] back to their senses with a gentle form of correction,[1] watching out for yourself[2] that you are not tested as well. Bear one another's burdens and so you will fulfill the Law of Christ. For if someone is held in esteem though he is nothing, he deludes himself. Let each person examine his [or her] activity[3] and then he [or, she] will have reason to boast in only what he [or she] has accomplished,[4] and not what is meant for another. For each one should carry his own burden. Let the person who is taught the word share all goods with the teacher. Do not be deceived. God is not mocked, for whatever a person sows, he [or she] will reap it: so the one who sows in his [or her] passions[5] will reap decay[6] from the passions, while the person who sows in the Spirit will reap eternal life. Let us not grow tired of doing good, for we will reap a harvest at the proper time provided we do not slack off. Now then, since we have an opportunity, let us do good for all people, and especially for those who belong to the household of faith. (6:1–10)

Paul concludes his moral exhortation with specific advice for the churches in Galatia. He has no plans to visit the region again, so the apostle must ensure that they are able to regulate their own life in Christ. Given his argument against assimilation to Judaism, Paul cannot take the steps one might expect of a leader faced with an immature and disorderly group. Paul cannot propose a new set of rules and regulations (Murphy-O'Connor 1996, 156). This refusal may have a philosophical attraction in addition to the decisive theological argument

111

that Paul has just given. Ancient philosophical traditions held that the person who was mature in virtue did not need written codes of law. Such persons had a clear vision of truth and justice, an "unwritten law," to guide their actions (Philo, *Virt.* 194; *Mos.* 1.162).[7] The shift remains somewhat surprising given the picture of the Galatians that has been painted up to this point. Despite the powerful manifestations of God's Spirit when they were converted (3:1–5) and the genuine bonds of friendship established with the apostle at that time (4:12–20), they are wavering, immature, in danger of deserting the gospel and even Christ himself. How can Paul expect them to exhibit the Christian maturity his maxims require? Were his opponents correct in thinking that such persons would be better off under the Law?

Solutions to such difficulties include treating the ethical material as preformed tradition that was not addressed to the situation presupposed in Paul's letters[8] or dissociating the ethical problems in Galatia from those advocating circumcision, assuming that Paul faced two different fronts (so Longenecker 1990, 271, 283–84). However, we have seen that the letter advocates a consistent position with no suggestion of a second front. The exhortation in the previous section also addresses those concerns. Should Paul's address to some as *pneumatikoi* ("spiritual persons") be treated as irony (so Schlier 1965, 270)? Irony would undermine the rhetorical solidarity that Paul has established with the audience (5:25–26). Therefore, this shift in tone indicates confidence in his audience. They will exclude the persons responsible for the recent disturbances and return to their former relationship with the apostle. The procedure proposed in v. 1 provides for dealing with future difficulties by explaining how to correct those who fall victim to the "flesh" (5:17) and restore them to the community (Barclay 1988, 174; Martyn 1997, 546–47).

The opening *adelphoi* ("brothers")[9] signals that what follows is a matter of critical importance (Betz 1979, 295). Paul continues to dichotomize the Christian experience of evil to suggest that Christians are unwilling actors, as in the warfare between "desire of the flesh" and Spirit in 5:17. Here the subject is not explicitly identified as a fellow Christian, although that would be implied by the context of communal correction. Instead, the indefinite *anthrōpos* ("man," "human being") is the subject of the passive verb, *prolēmphthē* ("be overtaken," "seized unawares," "trapped").[10] The prepositional phrase "in some transgression" has a double referent. It can indicate the activity in which the subject has been caught by someone else.[11] However, the preposition *en* with the dative case is also used to designate the instrument or means; that is, transgression has caught the person unawares. Were Paul to continue the battle metaphor, the point would be that sin had managed to overtake the individual by surprise (so Longenecker 1990, 272). This second reading accommodates a stoic reading of moral error as a lapse in appropriate judgment, as well as the dualistic imagery of an apocalyptic battle initiated by the Spirit's entry into the age dominated by the "desire of the flesh."[12] Betz observes that Gal 6:1 is the only explicit reference to transgression by a Christian in the letter (Betz 1979, 296). However, the language that Paul uses is both indefinite and dichotomizing to such a degree one might even say that he avoids attributing sin to the Christian as such.

Paul's audience may have previously heard one or both of the messages conveyed by v. 1a. Although "surprised" or "trapped by transgression" has much to commend it, we have chosen "discovered in transgression" as the primary referent, for two reasons. First, the opening address, *adelphoi*, focuses attention on the persons who will engage in correction (so Betz 1979, 296), not on the sinner.[13] Second, the comparable advice on how to treat erring members of the Essene sect also presumes that the individual has been observed by others. Verse 1b speaks to those who undertake correction. The verb *katartizein* can mean to repair or restore, which is the goal of the activity proposed. It can also refer to settling a dispute by mediation. In either case, the "spiritual persons" are not acting as watchdogs or moral police hunting for moral deviants. The earlier vice catalogue highlighted precisely those sins that destroy the community; therefore, those who intervene are acting as mediators. They must repair what has been broken so that the person in question returns to his or her true identity in Christ. Such activities could easily have the opposite effect, disrupting and dividing the community even further; therefore, the way in which those involved conduct themselves is crucial. Paul's call for "a spirit of gentleness" (cf. 5:23) has a close parallel in the Essene rule: "They shall rebuke one another in truth, humility, and charity. Let no one address his [erring] companion with anger" (1 QS 5.24–25; Martyn 1997, 546).[14]

The stipulation to undertake correction in a spirit that would not divide the community has an additional note attached, "watching out for yourself" (v. 1c).[15] Paul continues to be indefinite in his statements with "lest you be tempted." He does not indicate the source of such tempting. Galatians 5:24 would appear to exclude it from the identity of a Christian. If "spiritual persons" had a hold on virtue analogous to that of the Stoic wise, they would not need to be cautioned against falling away from it. On the assumption that Paul admits that all Christians are continually subject to temptations that derive from the "desire of the flesh" (5:17a; Martyn 1997, 547), this injunction reflects the moral immaturity of Christians in Galatia.[16] The shift to the second person singular in v. 1c could reflect the origins of this comment in an ancient proverb (Betz 1979, 298). Or, as in Paul's shift from plural to singular in 5:7, it may be another way of distancing the problem from those being addressed. Although there are a group of persons who qualify as "spiritual ones," only occasional individuals are envisaged as liable to temptation.

The second half of v. 2 has drawn considerable critical discussion because Paul introduces a new expression, "law of Christ." Has he capitulated to the language of his opponents by providing a sense in which Christians might be said to obey "Law"? Betz (1979, 300) concludes that Paul has taken this phrase from the opposition in part to defend his teaching against the charge of lawlessness. It is not fundamental to his theology, or he would have incorporated it earlier in the letter (Betz 1979, 301). If the appeal to Lev 19:18 were an instance of summarizing the Torah that Paul assumes derives from Jesus himself, then "law of Christ" might serve as code for such teaching.[17] Others assume that Paul uses the Greek word *nomos* ("law") without connection to the Jewish law in this verse (Esler 1998, 181).[18] However, such a shift away from the consistent use of the term *nomos* is only credible if this material is discrete from the rest of the letter, which we have seen to be implausible (Winger 2000, 538).

Therefore, the phrase must be seen as some form of shorthand for earlier stages in the argument. This "law of Christ" is something that

Christians can "bring to completion" *(anaplērōsete)*, a phrase analogous to that used of the "word," Lev 19:18, in 5:14 *(peplērōtai)*. What Christians now do is a consequence of what happened to the Law as a consequence of Christ's death (Rom 8:2; Martyn 1996, 59). There can be no distinction between "walking by the Spirit" (5:22–23) and "fulfilling the Law of Christ"(Winger 2000, 538–39). Such a correlation requires that the opening injunction, "bear one another's burdens" (v. 2a), represents an alternative formulation of 5:13c, "through love be slaves to each other" (Winger 2000, 539; Murphy-O'Connor 1996, 157). Although exegetes frequently assume that the "burdens" *(ta barē)* in question are a consequence of the transgressions referred to in the previous verse (so Longenecker 1990, 274; Martyn 1979, 547), the term more commonly suggests physical or other burdens. Friendship traditions emphasize the mutual assistance that true friends provide for each other (so Betz 1979, 299). However, if this phrase alludes directly back to 5:13c, the actual, physical sense of carrying heavy burdens may be intended. It was the slave's task to carry heavy loads.

Verses 3–5 turn to another problem that could have divisive effects on a community, an inflated self-promotion.[19] In that context, v. 5 comes to a conclusion that appears contrary to v. 2a: "for each person will bear his [or her] own load *(phortion)*." Why the shift? One solution takes v. 5 as a popular proverb that Paul has quoted without alteration (Betz 1979, 303; Longenecker 1990, 278). Betz associates the maxim with a philosophical tradition on self-sufficiency. The philosopher may eschew the struggles for wealth or honor pursued by others and adopt a lowly form of life in order to preserve his self-sufficiency. The maxim is a warning to watch out what one takes on (Betz 1979, 304).[20] The "for" and the "each" at the opening of v. 5 link the maxim back to the discussion in vv. 3–4. How does it address the competitive boasting and struggle for honor in those verses? Is it merely tacked on for rhetorical emphasis (so Longenecker 1990, 278)? Perhaps. However, Gal 5:26 introduced the issue of vainglory and a divisive, envy-producing competition for honor. Warnings against inflated self-importance, such as one finds in v. 3, crop up frequently in Paul's letters (Rom 11:20, 25; 12:3, 16; 1 Cor 1:30; 4:8; 8:1–2; 12:21; 2 Cor 12:11; Phil 2:3; Dunn 1993, 324).[21] It would appear to be a commonplace appropriate to any communal setting that might tempt individuals to engage in partisan conflicts for honor and status.[22] The suggestion that persons should lay claim only to what is their own work *(ergon)* so as not to boast of what in fact belongs to another (v. 4) hints at another source of honor in ancient society, alliance with a powerful patron or family.[23] Even slaves might engage in status comparisons and competition with each other and with freeborn persons of low status if they could assert personal ties to a powerful owner (Martin, 1990, 55–65). Perhaps Paul is engaged in an indirect attack on the motive that some persons had for seeking circumcision and assimilation to Judaism, alliance with a socially prominent patron or a group perceived as such. Alternatively, perhaps Paul is taking another indirect swipe at those advocating circumcision. He suggested in 5:2 that his audience had not been told that being circumcised implied taking on obligations to observe the whole Law. Those who are stirring up trouble in Galatia could be indirectly accused. They seek to gain honor and credit from a "work" that is not their own, fidelity to God's Law. Paul will say as much about them explicitly in Gal 6:13.

Verse 6 rather abruptly shifts the focus from general advice on communal relationships to a specific item: appropriate support for those who instruct others in the gospel.[24] Whether instructing pupils to support those who instruct them merely affirms an established practice in Galatia (so Betz 1979, 306) or aims to correct or restore a relationship that had been broken by the turmoil in Galatia (so Martyn 1997, 552), the context does not indicate. Such teachers will be crucial to the survival of these churches, since Galatia is not on the regular routes that would bring Paul or his associates back to the region.[25]

Paul introduces an eschatological warning (vv. 7–8), which intensifies the significance of his instruction. Such eschatological notes frequently occur at the conclusion of the body of the letter in Paul (Longenecker 1990, cvi).[26] After the warning, "do not be deceived," v. 7 has been patched together from two proverbial statements: "God is not mocked"[27] and "what a person sows, he [or she] will reap" (Jas 5:7–8; Prov 22:8; *Testament of Levi* 13:6; Dunn 1993, 329; Betz 1979, 306; Longenecker 1990, 279). For Paul and his Christian audience, that reaping comes with the end-time judgment of God (e.g.,

Rom 14:10; 1 Cor 3:12–17; 4:4; 6:9–11; 9:24–27; 2 Cor 5:10; 11:15; Phil 2:12; Betz 1979, 307). Paul incorporates these general warnings into the dichotomy of "flesh" against "Spirit" that he employed in 5:13–26. Mortality and liability to decay is a fundamental characteristic associated with "flesh" in both the Hebrew Bible and Hellenistic philosophy. So whatever is sown there will suffer the same fate. The earlier exhortation to live according to the Spirit (5:16, 18, 25) clearly refers to God's Spirit, not to an anthropological dualism between the corruptible material body and an eternal soul such as one might find in the philosophers. Consequently, the eternal life that is the reward for "sowing in the Spirit" is God's gift, not a human attribute (Dunn 1993, 330 31). At the same time, Paul's audience will not have forgotten the real issue concerning the flesh that is the occasion for the letter, those who advocate circumcising the flesh. That form of "sowing in the flesh" will not produce eternal life either (3:3; 4:23, 29; 5:2; Dunn 1993, 330). Indeed, if circumcision and other Jewish customs were being promoted as the cure for the "desire of the flesh" that is the source of immorality, it could be as dangerous as the "occasion for the flesh" that might result from freedom (5:13; Barclay 1988, 212; Martyn 1997, 553).

The final maxims (vv. 9–10) are linked by the catchword *kairos* ("right time," "critical moment") and the exhortation to good deeds ("do the good," *to kalon poiein*; "work the good," *ergazein to agathon*). Verse 9 employs an eschatological promise to promote endurance in doing what is good. A variant of the exhortation to zealous pursuit of the good appears in 4:18, where possible loss of enthusiasm follows from the apostle's absence rather than from delayed judgment.[28] Verse 10 shifts from using the word *kairos* to designate the hour of judgment in the future to the present. The word *kairos* refers to the opportunity available to the faithful before the judgment.[29] The addition of "especially toward those from the household of faith" (v. 10b) need not be taken as a limitation on the obligation to do good toward all persons (cf. 1 Thess 4:12 and 5:11; Rom 12:9–18); rather, it returns to the concrete situation at hand, the need to restore communal solidarity. The love command applies to fellow Christians in 5:13–14 (Betz 1979, 311). Paul may have an additional reason for this sequence. If persons in Galatia were considering circumcision based on familial or patronage ties to non-Christians, then the apostle must remind his audience that obligations to those "in Christ" supersede all other relationships (Gal 3:28).[30]

> Look at the big letters I have written with my own hand. Whoever wishes to show off a physical attribute,[31] they try to compel you to be circumcised, only so that they would not be persecuted for the cross of Christ. For those who are circumcised themselves do not keep the Law, but they want you to be circumcised so that they can boast in your flesh. As for me, let me never boast except in the cross of our Lord Jesus Christ, through whom the world has been crucified to me, and I to the world. For circumcision is not[32] anything, nor is lack of circumcision, but [only] new creation. And whoever stays in line with this rule, peace and mercy upon them and upon the Israel of God.
>   As for the rest, let no one cause troubles for me, for I bear the marks of Jesus on my body.
>   The grace of our Lord Jesus Christ be with your spirit, brothers [and sisters]. Amen. (6:11–17)

The closing of the letter begins with the apostle's autograph (cf. Phlm 19), a common element in epistolography (Betz 1979, 312; Longenecker 1990, cviii). The apostle's large and unpracticed letters would have been easily distinguished from those of the scribe who transcribed the rest of the epistle (Longenecker 1990, lviii–lx, 289). Longenecker (1990, 289) suggests that the verbal signal that the handwriting is changed reflects the fact that Paul's letters were delivered orally to gathered congregations (1 Thess 5:27; Col 4:16). However, the gesture may also be connected with the formal peculiarity of this letter's closing. Only the final blessing (v. 18) follows the usual conventions of Paul's other letters (cf. Phlm 25; Phil 4:23; 1 Thess 5:28; Longenecker 1990, 300).

It is not unusual to find an author making a final disposition of the business of the letter in the conclusion. One would anticipate the phrase, *tou loipou* ("in addition" or "finally")[33] in v. 17 to introduce such a conclusion. A harsh rebuke follows. Who does Paul mean when he says, "let no one supply sufferings *(kopous)* for me"? The middle form of the verb *parechō* indicates offering or producing something out of one's own means. In a legal setting, it can be used for bringing forward someone as a witness. The noun *kopos* can refer to work, toil, any kind of hardship or suffering, even to beatings received. Paul uses it for the toil of evangelizing (1 Cor 3:8; 1 Thess 2:9, 3:5). It figures in his catalogue of apostolic hardships (2 Cor 6:5; 11:23, 27), where it is associated with such physical afflictions as beatings, imprisonments, hunger, and shipwreck. Therefore, this phrase suggests somewhat more than mental anguish or personal affront.[34] It indicates an intention to inflict physical, bodily harm upon the apostle. The rejoinder in v. 17b, "for I bear the marks *(stigmata)* of Jesus on my body," draws together a number of motifs sounded earlier in the letter. A *stigma* was the mark used in branding slaves. Paul presumably means that the scars and bodily disfigurement that have resulted from years of harsh conditions in preaching the gospel are his brand. The debilitating illness that led to his first preaching in Galatia figures in the mix (4:13–15; Longenecker 1990, 300). Paul may even have pointed to himself when he reminded the Galatians that they had seen Christ crucified publicly portrayed (3:1).[35] In his case, the injunction to "crucify the flesh with its passions and desires" (5:24) has been carried out on his own body. This image is the one that Paul leaves in the minds of his audience.

Its emotional power is undeniable. Its reference to the concrete issue, whether or not Gentile Christians should mark their bodies with the sign of the covenant, circumcision, is also clear. Paul's body was circumcised, but in Christ that counts for nothing (Gal 2:19–21, 3:28). In fact, he has redefined that mark from being a sign of freedom to being a sign of the slave-born descendants of Abraham (4:21–5:1). If the Galatians seek to mark their flesh for religious reasons, they should imitate the apostle, not his detractors. Still, to jump from this dramatic salvo directly to the final greeting makes a very odd ending for a conventional letter. There is nothing personal here. No names of persons to be greeted; no practical arrangements for future travel plans; no news about persons known to the recipients whom Paul has recently seen; no recommendation of persons who will be coming to Galatia. These peculiarities lead Trobish to place the subscript to Galatians in a separate category. It is not to be considered private correspondence, but as a conclusion appropriate to a legal proceeding (Trobish 1994, 87).[36]

This observation leads one to expect something other than an ordinary ending to the letter in vv. 12–16. As we have just seen, Paul frames these verses with two demands that his audience look at something: in v. 11, the large letters made by the apostle's own hand; in v. 17, the "marks of Jesus" on his body. In between these examples of tangible evidence, Paul once again engages in a condensed argument against those who advocate circumcision and assimilation to a Jewish way of life. The unstated premise throughout much of the epistle has been that there must have been an advantage to be gained from adopting Jewish customs. Paul opens this argument by attributing a motive to the opposition: desire to avoid persecution "for the cross of Christ"(v. 12; Esler 1998, 73). One must be careful about building a historical scenario on this verse, since its rhetorical point is to instill in the audience a negative reaction to the opposition (Betz 1979, 314). First, Paul charges those persons with wishing to boast in "flesh"—an accusation whose negative overtones are highlighted by the previous ethical exhortations. Whose "flesh" are they interested in? Paul makes sure that his audience recognizes with some horror that it is theirs (vv. 12–13).

Scholars have tried to figure out a scenario in which compelling non-Jews to adopt circumcision would ward off persecution rather than increase it.[37] Perhaps Paul is referring to an inner-Jewish quarrel opposed to Jewish Christians who are sharing table fellowship with Gentile believers, along the lines of the Antioch episode (Gal 2:15–21; so Esler 1998, 74). While such an inner-Jewish conflict makes sense for a city like Antioch, with a prominent Jewish community that had ties to Jerusalem, its relevance to churches in Galatia is not self-evident. Therefore, Betz (1979, 315) suggests that "avoid persecution for Christ" is not a historical fact, but Paul's conclusion about the motive of his opposition. The apostle's self-presentation in v. 17 highlights the base nature of persons who will not imitate the crucified Jesus in suffering. Paul launches another *ad hominem* attack. He charges the opposition with being circumcised but not Law observant (v. 13a). There may be some factual basis for that accusation.

He informed the Galatians that persons who were circumcised were obligated to "the whole Law" in 5:3. That view is coherent with Paul's own zeal for ancestral traditions before his conversion (1:13), but it does not reflect the practice of all Jews living in the Diaspora. Even among Palestinian Jews, charges of failing to observe the Law were the stock-in-trade of intrasectarian rivalry, as the Essene writings demonstrate.[38] There is no reason to construct a rationale for Paul's "they wish you to be circumcised, so that they may boast in your flesh" (v. 13b), as though the numbers of Gentile foreskins were some sort of war trophy. He wishes the audience to react with disgust (Betz 1979, 317). He has just reminded them that boasting in what is not one's own is morally reprehensible (6:3–5).

A somewhat awkward transition allows Paul to move the argument from illegitimate boasting in the circumcised flesh of others to boasting in the cross (v. 14). Ancient readers would have been familiar with discussions of appropriate and inappropriate boasting (Betz 1979, 317). Paul's self-identification with the cross runs throughout the letter:[39]

(a) indirectly, the Son whom God revealed to the apostle must be the crucified (1:16);

(b) he participates in the life of the Son by being "crucified with Christ" (2:20);

(c) he made Christ crucified publicly visible in evangelizing the Galatians (3:1);

(d) on the cross, Christ was cursed by the Law and brought us out of slavery to it (3:12–14);

(e) indirectly, the reception given the afflicted apostle mirrors the faith the Galatians showed in the crucified Son of God (4:12–15);

(f) indirectly, the appeals to exhibit "faith working through love" (5:6c, 13c, 14) refer to the cross;

(g) were the apostle to advocate circumcision, he would be negating the cross (5:11) as his opponents do, because they are unwilling to suffer persecution (6:12);

(h) Christians have crucified the "desire of the flesh" (5:24); and

(i) as Paul will say in summing up, the apostle's own body is marked by the cross.

In short, the cross is the background story that emerges at every turn in this epistle (Hays 1987).

By this point in the argument, Paul has established the credentials to back up the claim that he boasts in nothing but the "cross of our Lord Jesus Christ" (v. 14a), a claim that—he has been careful to indicate—sets him apart from those advocating circumcision (Dunn 1993, 337).

Paul attaches a tag to the end of this statement, "through whom the world has been crucified to me and I to the world" (v. 14b). For the apostle to be "crucified to the world" evokes several items from the previous list. The term "world" could be substituted for "Law" in 2:19, "I died to the Law that I might live to God." Or it could substitute for "the flesh with its desires and passions" in 5:24, which is the consequence of life in the Spirit. Insofar as Christ's death on the cross was the condition for believers' freedom from the custodial Law (for Jews, Gal 3:24–25) or superstitious fear of elemental forces of the world (for non-Jews, Gal 4:8–9), "the world" stands for everything that Paul has included under the category of slavery.[40] Whether the negative pole is a social, religious, or moral mode of self-identification, it has been rejected in the move to life in Christ.[41] "Crucified to" is analogous to "dying to" or "being freed from." Persons are no longer determined by these powers, just as the religious (Jew/Greek), status (slave/free), and gender (male/female) markers do not determine existence in Christ.

As code for the complex processes at work in changing one's identity from all its past determinates to that of believer in Christ, "crucified to the world" suggests a permanent state of what some anthropologists have referred to as liminality. The new reality into which persons are being incorporated does not have its own, socially accepted set of boundaries and rituals. It is not a clearly defined ethnic, social, or religious entity. Baptism is the entry point to this "crucifixion to the world" (Strecker 1999, 253–79). But the community that Paul insists should see itself as having passed this divide remains very much part of "the world," as Paul's ethical exhortation in Gal 5:13–6:10 indicates. Does the apostle's first-person singular distinguish his mode of living Christ (Gal 2:20) from that of his audience? It would not if those being addressed had achieved a fixed state of living in the Spirit, if what began with their evangelization were not in danger of being abandoned for elements associated with "the flesh" (3:1–5). But in the present situation, Paul's Galatian converts are still wavering and immature. The preferred cure would be Paul's personal presence (4:18–20). Then, like the students of a truly wise philosopher, the Galatians could not only hear teaching about living in the Spirit, they could see it embodied.[42]

These connections explain the human, social, and religious dimensions of the "crucified to the world" code, but Paul has another phrase tucked in the same clause, "through whom [= Christ] the world is crucified to me." Is this just fancy rhetorical compression for the fact that all the attributes of Christian life in the Spirit are received as gracious gifts, thanks to the death of Christ (2:20–21)? That until Christ came, what was promised could not be realized (4:4–7)? The cross has to end the custodial functions of the Law and break the imprisoning elemental forces of the cosmos before the Spirit can begin working in the freeborn children of God. To speak in this fashion of God's action, disrupting or putting to death hostile powers in the world so that God's elect people can be freed from the constraints of an evil age, is to evoke symbols and myths of apocalypse. Martyn has pursued such allusions throughout Galatians (Martyn 1997, 393–406, 530–31, 564–71). Paul carries the apocalyptic metaphor over into the conclusion of the next verse. God does not break up imprisoning, hostile powers simply because of the suffering and evil they have caused. God intervenes to bring about the new creation in which these powers are no longer operative (*Jubilees* 4:26; 1 *Enoch* 72:1).[43] Paul's declaration that circumcision and uncircumcision are indifferent, that they do not count for anything in the new creation, parallels the baptismal affirmation in 3:28, "neither Jew nor Greek, . . . you are one in Christ Jesus." The difference signaled by circumcision and its attendant obligation to the Law would matter if Christians were not in some sense participating in the new creation (Adams 2000, 227). Granted the old age has not completely disappeared, but Paul insists that the cross has initiated a transformation that belongs to the new age.[44] He has answered the potential objection that the powers of the evil age can still do plenty of damage, damage that the Law is enacted to control, by declaring circumcision and uncircumcision indifferent now that a new ethical power has arrived on the scene, "faith working through love" (5:6).

Since Paul has just invoked the "new creation" to negate the dichotomy, circumcision or uncircumcision, which divided the old creation from a Jewish perspective, one might expect another statement of unity. But v. 16 delivers something less. One suspects that the apostle knows he cannot win the day. The Galatians will not expel a few agitators and then rally to Paul's gospel. So he pronounces what Betz describes as a "conditional blessing"—a blessing for those who toe the line he has laid down—and an implied threat against those who persist in agitating for circumcision (Betz 1979, 321). The threat is the curse with which the argument opened (1:8–9).

The formulation of the benediction also poses problems, since it is unlike those Paul uses elsewhere. It may reflect an ancient Jewish formula, since it has similarities to later Jewish benedictions: "bestow peace, happiness and blessing, grace and loving-kindness and mercy upon us and upon all Israel your people" (Betz 1979, 321). Paul has chopped up the liturgical flow of the language in order to insert a qualification. The benediction is not addressed to "us," the speaker and his entire congregation. It only applies to those who accept the authority of what Paul has said. On analogy with the Jewish formula, one would expect those who actually receive the blessing ("us," "those who adhere to this rule") to be a subset of the larger community that God is also to bless ("all Israel your people," "the Israel of God"). Can Paul, who has just concluded a blistering attack on circumcision, really consider those who accept his ruling in the matter "the Israel of God"? Betz concludes that in light of the fact that Christianity was not clearly distinct from Judaism at this time, Paul might easily use the expression for Jewish Christians who accepted his position concerning the Gentiles (Betz 1979, 323). Martyn agrees that Paul must be speaking about Christians in both clauses—not suddenly tossing in a kind word for Jews. But based on the way in which Paul speaks of Abraham and Christ in Gal 3:15–29, he must be using this formula for the Galatians, Gentiles who thought they needed to be circumcised to gain entry into God's promises. He would not have used the awkward expression "Israel of God" for Galatian believers if the opposition had not been speaking about Israel (Martyn 1997, 574–77).

Were this formula the closing benediction, Martyn's solution would seem the most probable. However, Paul is using liturgical-sounding language to make a point: that their decision is not an indifferent matter. To receive God's blessing, the Galatians must line up with the principles of the new creation. He also takes one more dig at those who will remain his opponents in the concluding salvo (v. 17). Paul has accused them of not being devoted to observance of the whole Law. By the suggestion that God may have mercy on "real Jews,"[45] he implies that what the advocates of circumcision offer is less than real incorporation into Israel. Cohen's study demonstrates that, looking from within the Jewish community out, the non-Jew never became an Israelite, even if he was circumcised and lived a life that appeared Jewish to others (Cohen 1999, 152–53). Therefore, Paul is using this benediction formula to draw a sharp division through the mix of Jews, Jews who believe in Jesus as Messiah, Jews who believe in Jesus and also associate with Gentile believers, and Gentile believers. Only two groups receive God's blessing: Christ-believers, both Jew and non-Jew, who accept Paul's gospel, and Law-observant Israelites who do not believe in Jesus. Paul can make that affirmation about the latter without compromising his argument, because those assimilating to Judaism can never be "Israel." Nor is he involved with nonbelieving Jews. God sent him as apostle to the Gentiles (1:16–17), a commission that Paul has obeyed since the first days, almost twenty years before Galatians was written.

Conclusion

The new Roman order shifted the commercial and civic power in the province of Galatia to the cities along the *Via Sebaste* in the southern part of the province. The populace in the cities along the older northern route through Pessinus may have found social, political, and religious allegiances up for grabs as the region lost its importance to the new rulers. Those whom Paul addressed as "Galatians" did not belong to the Greek or Roman aristocracy. The formula "neither Jew nor Greek" (Gal 3:28) does not include them. Social and historical studies of Jewish identity in the Greco-Roman Diaspora indicate that "to Judaize" does not mean that the persons in question were proselytes. Therefore we cannot be certain what elements of social, political, or civic allegiance were at stake when these new Christians considered allying themselves with Jews. Certainly they perceived some advantage in the move. Paul's sharply honed rhetoric converts their legitimate concerns into the distasteful consequences of "being taken advantage of" by persons devoted to stirring up civic discord (Gal 6:12–13).

Unfortunately, we lack evidence concerning Jewish communities in much of Asia Minor. The tensions between Jews and "Greeks" over the aspirations of the assimilated Jewish community in Alexandria or problems encountered by Jews in Rome itself may have been peculiar to those settings. For a colonized "gallic" population, "Jews" may have been considered well-placed patrons with ties to the Roman rulers. Or the possibility of assimilating Jewish forms of life could have been driven by more pragmatic local ties, such as marriage. The Letter to the Galatians is such a finely crafted rhetorical piece that elaborate "mirror reading" reconstructions of the theology of Paul's opponents only reflect what the apostle would have the audience conclude.

Despite Paul's efforts to solidify the perception that he had been victorious in forging a common agreement in Jerusalem (2:1–10), the actual situation was fraught with tension and latent conflict (Esler 1995, 292–94).

Paul's references to his former zeal for ancestral tradition (1:14), to his persecution of the nascent Christian movement (1:13), and to "preaching circumcision" (5:11), point to a pattern of identity formation grounded in exclusion. What is "other" or only ambiguously "Jewish" was consistently rejected. Further, Paul's anticircumcision rhetoric in Galatians persists in excluding the "other" from assimilation toward or existence on the fringes of Jewish community (6:13). Jewish believers can be required to "live in a Gentile manner" for the sake of the new fellowship with non-Jewish believers in Christ (2:11–14), but no movement in the other direction is permitted. Paul pulls out all the rhetorical stops to condemn that possibility, "spies out to compromise freedom" (2:4), "hypocrisy" (2:13), "making Christ a cause of sin" (2:17), "friendship turned to enmity" (4:12–20). The consequences of his position are clear. Although believers have become God's children and heirs to the promise God made to Abraham (3:6–4:7), they are neither "Jews" nor allies, supporters, or patrons of those whose civic and religious home is Jerusalem (4:21–31).

Binary oppositions force the issue. Identity means exclusion of the "other." In part, the traditional Jewish antipathy toward idolatry and non-Jewish cult surfaces when Paul warns the Galatians that assimilation to Jewish customs would be a return to slavery under cosmic powers (4:8–11). Perhaps this offensive rhetorical identification of "a Jewish-like way of life" among Gentile believers and a relapse into paganism echoes the concrete religious situation in Galatia. Devotion to the mother goddess exhibited in self-castrated priests and evident in monumental cliff sculptures might find analogues in some elements of Jewishness. Paul himself plays off satirical disgust with circumcision as pseudo-castration (5:12). The God of Sinai/Zion dwells in glory on a Temple mount. Hence, Paul shockingly reduces Sinai to a place of slavery, the earthly Jerusalem (4:21–27), and cites Scripture to demonstrate an abiding hostility between "the Jews"—that is, persons whose identity is grounded in Jerusalem—and "believers," Sarah's descendants! How can we rescue the apostle from the historical and theological consequences of this rhetoric of identity politics? Scholars often appeal to the more irenic treatment of Israel and Christ-believers in Rom 9–11. However, nothing in Romans indicates that Paul has changed his opposition to non-Jewish believers assimilating to a Jewish pattern of life. Troy Martin (1995) resorts to a rhetorical solution, concluding that Paul is not speaking about assimilation to Jewishness at all. The Galatians really were in danger of lapsing back into paganism. That hypothesis removes the offensive suggestion that partisanship for Jews or a Jewish way of life would be equivalent to idolatry. However, it cannot be sustained throughout the argument in Galatians.

Paul's understanding of Jewish identity depends upon the conviction that there can be no "ambiguous Jews," hangers-on from the Gentile side. Nothing in Galatians supports the view that he had engaged in attempts to convert non-Jews prior to his conversion. His "obligated to the whole Torah" (6:13a) coheres with a more orthodox, exclusivist understanding of Judaism than with the movements toward assimilation among the educated elite of ancient Alexandria, for example. In some civic contexts, social and religious isolation may have served the Jewish community better than the open boundaries and moves toward civic assimilation of Alexandria. Elsewhere Paul evidences an affinity for social quietism as a strategy for reducing the persecution to which Christians might be subject (1 Thess 4:11). His concluding moral maxim, "as we have opportunity, let us do good to all, especially the household of faith" (6:10), exhibits the same spirit. Perhaps Paul does have reason to fear that "Judaizing" would generate civic discord, but he does not say so explicitly.

The rationale for the apparent equivalence of adopting Jewish customs and outright apostasy by returning to former idolatry is theological, not social pragmatism. Paul does not assert that the religious status of Jews who remain faithful to Torah observance is equivalent to that of non-Jews. Although both can be said to remain enslaved to sin until the death of God's Messiah establishes righteousness through faith (2:15–21; 3:21–28), the Jew knows the God who promised salvation. The non-believing Gentile does not. Only the Jew has the Law as slave guardian, watching over and disciplining the future son and heir (3:23–25; 4:1–3). With the coming of God's Messiah, the times have changed for all humanity. Both "under the Law" (3:23) and "slaves to weak and impoverished *stoicheia*" (4:9) describe life prior to the coming of the Messiah. Faith as trust in God's salvation through Christ was not possible for anyone. When Paul ascribes faith to Abraham, its recipients are not Abraham's genetic offspring through Isaac. The "offspring" in question is Christ (3:6–14). Faith only becomes possible for those who have become Abraham's descendants in Christ, whatever their religious and ethnic origin (Gal 3:26–28).

The Paul of Galatians cannot be enlisted in support of postmodern religious pluralism and toleration. Nor should his treatment of Abraham, faith, and the Law as *paidagōgos* be treated as a historical development into Christ. No formal pattern of history, whether continuous, dialectic, or evolutionary, fits the apocalyptic schemata of Pauline theology, as Martyn has forcefully demonstrated (1985a). The apocalyptic event of the coming of God's Messiah eradicated the cursing voice of the Law and enabled its Abrahamic promise. It also established the root intentionality of the Law to guide the life of the community of believers in Christ (5:13–14; Martyn 1996, 58–59). Paul even speaks of believers bringing to completion the "law of Christ" (6:2) in a way of life that imitates Christ's deed (Martyn 1996, 59 n. 25, 61 n. 29).

This theological conviction rests on an apocalyptic understanding of God's dealing with the world. Christ's death and resurrection mark the emergence of a new age, different in kind from the prior story, which Paul elsewhere begins with Adam (Rom 5:12–21). Martyn takes this apocalyptic break as the governing structure that generates the antinomies that Paul uses throughout the letter. Every statement must be tagged as "then" or "in Christ." From this perspective, it becomes evident that Paul's "Israel of God" (6:16) has nothing to do with an attachment to "the Jews" (Martyn 1997, 348–52). Paul refers to "Israel" here as the community of believers gathered on the basis of faith. Adams's study of the antithesis that Paul draws between "world" and "new creation" (6:14–15) reaches a similar conclusion: "Judaism (cf. 1:13–14), as a social, cultural and religious entity, belongs along with paganism to the dying *kosmos*. To assimilate to Judaism, therefore, is to alienate oneself from the new creation" (Adams 2000, 228).

Paul, the zealous Pharisee, saw humanity divided between those who were devoted to Torah according to a particular halachah and the "wicked," who compromised the identity of God's people. His activities as persecutor indicate that he considered the emerging movement of Jesus believers among "the wicked." Paul, the apostle, has a no less dualistic view of identity politics among the children of God. The apocalyptic foundations of his theology divide the descendants of Abraham even more sharply than the old categories of Torah observance because there is no "transition zone" or mediating term between "the world" and the "new creation," between Sinai/Zion and the heavenly Jerusalem. Paul has forged a radical rereading of Scripture out of his revelatory experience. The Messiah who came under the Torah's curse established the "Israel of God" by his sacrifice. Paul's conviction that this theological perspective coheres with God's revealed truth not only echoes through his words, it is written on the apostle's physical body (6:17).

Did the Letter to the Galatians carry the day? As a forceful and coherent rhetorical argument for Paul's theological understanding of the situation, one can hardly imagine it failing. Yet some modern scholars have constructed a picture of Paul's overall mission that presumes that he lost that battle. We have no evidence to establish a firm conclusion. Paul's copy of the epistle may be the source for its inclusion in the Pauline letter collections (Trobisch 1994). The more troubling question for twenty-first-century readers does not lie in the immediate reception of Paul's argument but in the subsequent tale of apocalyptic dualism and identity politics. Paul may be excused for assuming that the full emergence of God's "new creation," which would resolve the tensions and suffering of the world not yet recreated (Rom 8:18–39), was immanent. God would somehow gather others with the suffering remnant believers into the glory of the risen Christ. But can an apocalyptic vision ground theological reflection when the "end of days" stretches out to cosmic scales? Can the apostle be absolved for the social, political, and religious hostilities among the children of Abraham legitimated by the value judgments embedded in his apocalyptic antinomies?

On the one hand, understanding the apostle's words as rhetorical appeal directed toward a particular situation in the first century C.E. would seem to inhibit such universal conclusions. On the other, for Christians, Galatians has the authority of revealed Scripture. Even if

Paul himself did not envisage setting his letter alongside the texts he refers to as Scripture, he does make strong claims to divine truth for his understanding of the gospel. His particular exegetical moves in reading Scripture support the truth of that gospel. It may be a fairly easy matter for Christians to say that Paul's apocalyptic timetable was off. It becomes more problematic to dismantle the entire framework that supports the proclamation of righteousness for all people through faith in Christ. Not surprisingly, perhaps, Christians have privileged inclusive statements like Gal 3:26–28 over the rhetoric of exclusion. However, the twenty-first century must now grapple with the legacy of anti-Semitism along with increasing anti-Islamic attitudes that attach like barnacles to the submerged negations concerning Abraham's other children.

Galatians 5:13–6:10 presents another possibility. Although Paul uses the ethical dualism "flesh" vs. "spirit" to great effect in arguing against circumcising the flesh, the vice and virtue lists are not coded to "others" vs. "believers in Jesus." They are aimed at building up communal solidarity in imitation of the sacrificial self-offering of Christ. If the "law of Christ" means bearing the burdens of the "other" (6:2), then in the twenty-first century those burdens must include the evils, suffering, and opprobrium heaped on nonbelievers in the centuries of Christian political and cultural domination. In the end, a praxis that can stand the judgment of the cross was also Paul's claim for his gospel (Gal 6:11–17).

Notes

Chapter One: Galatians 1

1. Literally, "brothers." This translation assumes that Paul is referring to all the Christians, male and female, in the church from which he is writing, rather than to a more limited group of his male missionary associates.

2. A number of manuscripts (p[46] p[51vid] B D G H Byzantine vg syr cop[sa]) read "our Father and Lord" instead of "our Father and the Lord" (so ℵ A 33 81 256 it[ar. b], vg[mss] et al.). Less well-attested readings omit the pronoun "our" completely or include it twice.

3. The reading of *huper* (p[51] B H 33 TR); the implication of "on behalf of" is preferred to *peri* (p[46vid] ℵ* A D G), "for, concerning" because it coheres with other creedal formulae in Paul (see Gal 3:13; 1 Cor 15:3). In Koine Greek the two prepositions are often interchangeable.

4. The phrase "unto the ages of ages" reflects the LXX "unto the age of the age" (e.g., Ps 40:14 LXX), that is, "forever and ever." This translation preserves the repetition of the word *aiōn*, "age," from the previous verse.

5. For a discussion of Paul's activities in the Hellenistic context of persons who "found cults" by introducing new deities and rites by gathering cult associations in Greco-Roman cities, see Betz (1994a, 242–54).

6. This assertion must be distinguished from the claim that a human Jesus only achieved that relationship after his death and resurrection, on the one hand, and the full development of Trinitarian theology, on the other. Fitzmyer puts it concisely in his note on Rom 1:4: "The title 'Son of God' is being used in a messianic sense . . . nothing is intimated in the text about Jesus' anointed status or agency, and no OT background relates 'son of god' to 'Messiah.' . . . Moreover, Paul is not thinking here of an inner-trinitarian relationship of Father and Son, but only of the unique relation of Jesus Christ as Son to God, the Father in the salvific process. For Paul the resurrection made a difference in that process, but it did not *make* Christ, the Son of God" (Fitzmyer 1993, 235–36).

7. *Thaumazō* expresses surprise or astonishment, but when used in a letter may also carry overtones of rebuke (see Mullins 1972, 385), hence the rendering "shocked" in this translation.

8. With most manuscripts (p[51] ℵ A B Fc Y 075 150 6 33 et al.). The genitive phrase is omitted in some other witnesses (p[46vid] F* G l 1178 it[ar, b, g, o]).

9. See the detailed discussion of cursing in Betz 1979, 49–53. He includes the practice of cursing the "outsider" or what is profane in religious cults as a possible background for Paul's use of the term anathema. Personal forms of cursing involved magic used to gain a love object, unseat an opponent, or win in legal proceedings (see the examples in Gager 1992). Angels are sometimes summoned to carry out the wishes of the magician as in the opening, "I invoke you, holy angels and holy names, join forces with this binding spell and bind, tie up, block, strike, overthrow, harm, destroy, kill and shatter Eucherios the charioteer and all his horses tomorrow in the arena at Rome" (Gager 1992, 74). Listeners acquainted with this type of spell must have found Paul's reference to cursing an angel (v. 8) somewhat bizarre. Martyn's elaborate reconstruction of the opponent's speech, which appealed to the angelic mediation of the Mosaic law to account for this reference to an angel, is unnecessarily speculative (Martyn 1997, 113).

10. For *gnōrizō* as part of a common disclosure formula in Hellenistic letters, see Longenecker (1990, cv–cvii, 22).

11. Betz 1979 (16) recognizes that v. 11 introduces the shift to the *narratio* that follows, but to account for v. 10 attaches it to the latter to create an unnecessary transitional section.

12. On this verse as a "demonstrative enthymeme" in the sense of Aristotelian logic, see Cook (1996, 95 n. 27). Paul need not have studied Aristotle to employ this type of rhetorical logic.

13. Reading *gar* with some witnesses (ℵ1 B D* F G 0150 33 it[ar, d, f, g] vg cop[sa]) rather than the more ordinary narrative continuation *de* in other manuscripts (p[46] ℵ*, 2 A D[1] Y 075 0261). *Gar* is being used to bind together successive verses (10, 11, 12, and 13).

14. Although "brothers" may refer simply to all Christians regardless of gender as in v. 2, this translation retains the masculine reference on the assumption that the concrete issue at stake in the letter and the persons engaged in the controversy were male Christians. Only male converts would be in the position of undergoing circumcision.

15. Supplying a phrase to fill out Paul's elliptical expression that embraces both of the previous verbs.

16. Literally, "of my former way of life in Judaism *(Ioudaismus)*." This translation avoids modern reification of Judaism and tries to retain both the social and religious implications of the term *Ioudaismus* for the sum total of what persons in antiquity thought characterized Jews as an *ethnos* (see Cohen 1999, 7–8, who proposes the translation "Jewishness").

17. Or "in Jewishness"; see n. 16.

18. A number of witnesses supply *Theos*, "God," as antecedent for this long relative clause (¿ A D Y 075 6 33 et al). For its omission (p[46] B F G 0150 it[ar, b, f, g, o] vg et al.).

19. Treating the prepositional phrase *en emoi* as a simple dative (cf. 1 Cor 14:11). However, the preposition may have its usual locative sense in which case it should be translated "in me," implying an interior form of revelation.

20. Smith 1999, 207–208. On Matt 23:15, which is frequently cited as evidence for Pharisees seeking proselytes in the Diaspora, see Davies and Allison (1997, 288–89). Davies and Allison are uneasy with the consensus that Jews were not engaged in proselytizing activity, so see the appeal to Galatians as evidence for a policy of turning those who were "God fearers," fellow travelers with Jews, into full converts.

21. Contrary to Martyn 1997 (155), who argues that this information must be derived from the opposing teachers since Paul would not have spoken of his pre-Christian life to the Gentiles. Martyn concludes that the audience would identify Paul's zealous devotion to tradition with the attitude of those encouraging them to adopt circumcision.

22. Davies 1999 (683) points out that the verbs *diôkein* ("persecute") and *porthein* ("destroy") cannot refer to a literal campaign of attempting to execute Christians or to a policy organized by Jewish officials as Acts presumes. Paul was subject to persecution (see Gal 5:11) without being executed. Paul must be exaggerating a campaign of verbal harassment. However, Paul's words imply that persecution was a habitual way of acting that enjoyed some success (so Murphy-O'Connor 1996, 67). Private individuals could not order punishments such as flogging, but they could denounce Christians to the authorities and confront them in the synagogues (idem, 68).

23. Murphy-O'Connor 1996, 60–61. He points out that Josephus speaks of the zeal of the Pharisees in imposing oral traditions, "from the tradition of the fathers not written in the Law of Moses (Josephus, *Ant.* 13.297) and priding themselves on exact interpretation (*Ant.* 17.41; idem, 56). Hengel and Schwemer 1997 (37–38) argue that although Paul was not known to the Christian churches in Judea (1:22), the persecutions to which he referred must have occurred in Jerusalem .

24. Hengel and Schwemer 1997 (45) caution against trying to derive Paul's pre-Christian views by "mirror reading" his later Christology, though some elements of the argument in Galatians do appear to derive from his pre-Christian polemic, as we shall see.

25. Bowersock 1983 (68) doubts that Aretas really had control of Damascus. He proposes that he was "king" only of the Nabatean population in the city.

26. Paul's trade would have involved both provision of tents and awnings made of cloth like linen or canvas and of various forms of leatherwork.

Contrary to the usual view that Paul had learned his trade as a youth, Murphy-O'Connor presumes that he picked it up after his conversion as a means to support his missionary activity (1996, 86–88).

27. For this meaning of the verb *historeo*, see Josephus, *War* 6.81; Plutarch, *Thes.* 30; Pomp. 40; *Luc.* 2; *Curios.* 2; Epictetus, *Diatr.* 2.14.28; 3.7.1.

28. Aramaic *kephā*, "rock" or "stone" with a Greek ending; Cephas is Paul's regular name for the apostle better known as Peter (John 1:42 indicates that "Peter" is the translation of the nickname "Cephas" that Jesus had given to Simon). The Western and Syrian manuscript traditions substitute the more familiar name.

29. For the adjectival use of the phrase *en Christō* in Paul, see 1 Thess 2:14, "the churches of God which are in Judea in Christ." Martyn 1997, 176, proposes retaining the locative expression "in Christ" on the assumption that Paul intends to substitute the more important theological location, "in Christ," for the geographical one, "Judea."

30. So Dunn (1993, 73), who also admits that forging a personal relationship with Peter was also involved in the visit. Martyn 1997 (171) argues that Paul would never have chosen a verb that could imply that he required information from Peter without destroying the case that he is attempting to build.

31. Acts 7:58 and 9:4 reports the Semitic form of his name to have been Saul.

32. Gal 2:8 has "Peter," an indication that Paul is familiar with the Greek form of Simon's nickname. There is no reason to attribute that shift to a source that contained it as part of the Jerusalem agreement, although Paul may be using "officialese" at this point (see discussion in Longenecker 1990, 55–56).

33. Paul includes such an introduction for the deacon Phoebe in Rom 16:1–2. On the genre in general, see Kim (1972) and White (1986, sec. 71, 77–79).

34. Not least because there is no clear legal evidence that would give Jewish authorities in Jerusalem the power to seek out offenders in other regions, as Luke's narrative implies (see Murphy-O'Connor 1996, 65–67).

35. 1 Thess 2:14–16, assuming that it is Paul's and not a later interpolation, asks a Gentile congregation in Thessalonika to imitate the churches in Judea when facing their own persecutions (Bruce 1988,103). Thus Paul assumes that Gentile churches will consider the churches of Judea witnesses to the authentic Christian faith.

36. Martyn 1997 (176) concludes that the unusual pileup of phrases, "churches of Judea which are in Christ" in Gal 1:22 and 1 Thess 2:14, has further implications. By placing "in Christ" in a strong position at the end

of the sentence, Paul intends to replace the geographical location of the churches with their true spiritual location "in Christ": "He thinks of Christ as the new realm God is now establishing in the world. Thus, while the churches are geographically located in Judea, they are more importantly located in Christ" (176). While "in Christ" can serve such a unifying function as it does in Gal 3:28, for example, the rhetorical emphasis of this section does not favor the claim that Paul is out to override geography here. Paul's polemic requires that he underline the geographical division that separates his mission from that of the Jerusalem apostles.

Chapter Two: Galatians 2

1. "Important people" translates the dative plural masculine participle of *dokeō*, "seem, have the appearance; be influential, recognized as something." There is no reason to assume that Paul's use of the verb implies that the persons in question do not deserve the influential standing they have among Christians in Jerusalem. Other translations insert an ironic sense, "reputed to be important" (see Longenecker 1990, 48).

2. Literally "am running or had run," an athletic metaphor that Paul frequently uses for strenuous exertion as a Christian (Gal 5:7; Phil 3:14) and for his missionary efforts (1 Cor 9:24–27; Phil 2:16). This translation highlights the effort involved at the expense of the metaphor.

3. Translation adds "in any way" to capture the force of opening the whole clause with *all' oude*, "but not." The phrase remains ambiguous. The idea of forced circumcision may be introduced from the dispute in Galatia. Paul's point is that there was no pressure put on Titus at all by those in Jerusalem.

4. This sentence lacks a main verb clause. Paul may imply that while the important people did not pressure Titus to be circumcised, another group who had somehow infiltrated the meeting did so.

5. The Western text; Irenaeus (*Haer.* 3.13.3) and Tertullian (*Marc.* 5.3.3) know this passage without the phrase *hois oude*, hence they conclude that Paul had yielded to the opposition.

6. Literally, "entrusted with the gospel of uncircumcision as Peter of the circumcision," which might suggest that the content of the gospel being preached was different. This translation assumes that Paul refers to groups of persons.

7. A guess; the phrase lacks a verb.

8. Words added to fill out an elliptical phrase.

9. The reference point adopted has consequences for Pauline chronology. Assuming that fourteen years separate the two visits to Jerusalem requires that the Jerusalem Council occur later than would be the case if Paul is referring back to his conversion. Scholars who hold that view assume that Paul had preached in Asia Minor and Greece prior to the Jerusalem Council

(so Murphy-O'Connor 1996, 24–28, who dates the Council in October of 51 after Paul's expulsion from Corinth under Gallio). However, a somewhat less complex view places the Council prior to Paul's missionary work in Galatia and Greece, sometime in 47 or 48 C.E. (see the discussion of these problems in Barrett 1998, lviii–lxi).

10. At least for the first section of Acts (15:3–12), in which it is agreed that Gentile converts are not obligated to circumcision or to the Mosaic law. The subsequent decree dealing with dietary matters (Acts 15:13–33) may have been derived from a different source and introduced into the account of the Jerusalem Council by Luke (so Fitzmyer 1998, 544, 551–54).

11. The present tense "which I preach" in v. 2 underlines the consistency and continuity of what Paul preaches. One cannot imagine that Paul would have modified his preaching if the Jerusalem leaders had disapproved (Bruce 1988, 109).

12. This dismissive tone may be designed to undercut the claims made about the Jerusalem authorities by Paul's opponents and need not represent Paul's personal attitude toward them or their role in the Jerusalem church (so Longenecker 1990, 48).

13. Referring to their status as associates of Jesus (Bruce 1988, 118; Smiles 1998, 44). This parenthesis suggests a challenge to Paul's freedom as an apostle (Bruce, 117).

14. Deut 10:17; Sir 35:12–13 LXX (Smiles 1998, 45).

15. Some interpreters treat the expression "not compelled to be circumcised" in v. 3a as a suggestion that Titus voluntarily underwent the operation. As Esler points out, that inference would undermine Paul's entire argument (explicitly opposed to circumcision of Gentiles, 2:5, 21b; 5:2, 11a). Paul uses the verb *anagkazein* with "to live like Jews" as a charge against Peter in 2:14 and with "to be circumcised" against his Galatian opponents in 6:12. Gal 2:3 directly reports a fact that did not happen in such a way as to parallel the contrary demand being made for the Galatians to adopt circumcision (Esler 1995, 295).

16. Bruce 1988 (115–16) takes vv. 3–5 as a digression and suggests that Paul has collapsed a later intrusion, perhaps into Antioch, into his account of the Jerusalem meeting. Murphy-O'Connor 1996 (113) considers the intrusion to be the Antioch episode before the Jerusalem meeting. However, the function of the digression in vv. 3–5 is to account for claims being advanced about the Jerusalem apostles; therefore, the infiltrators have to be associated with Jerusalem (Esler 1995, 296).

17. For a discussion of the historical implausibility of such a group, see Barrett 1998, 704–70. Fitzmyer 1998 (545) accepts the possibility that these persons may be identified with the false brothers of Gal 2:4, without comment on the historical question.

18. For a contemporary account of the Caligula crisis, see Philo, *Legat.* 188, 198–348; Claudius's edict to Alexandrian Jews can be conveniently found in White 1986, sec. 88.

19. The social and political prudence of James's decision to strengthen ties with the Antioch church would have borne fruit with the outbreak of the rebellion. Painter 1997 (72) points out that Christian refugees from that conflict probably fled to the city, bringing with them the Christian Jewish traditions that were incorporated into Matthew's gospel.

20. Paul's collection appeal in 2 Cor (8:14–15; 9:6–14) addresses the abundance/lack of asymmetry by stipulating an equality of benefits between the two parties, material on the side of the Gentiles, spiritual on the side of the Christian Jews, and placing the wealthy Corinthians under obligation to a greater benefactor, God, the source of their prosperity.

21. Dunn's reference to the agreement as a "ruling" (1993, 105) suggests a binding, legal, or constitutional authority that goes well beyond the contentious, semiprivate arrangement suggested in Paul's account.

22. Given the unusual phrases found in vv. 7–8, Martyn agrees that the formula or an earlier agreement between Peter and Paul has been incorporated into this passage. V. 9 represents the acceptance of that earlier formula by those present in Jerusalem. He emphasizes the apparent shift in leadership from Peter to James in the interim (1997, 212).

23. On power relationships implied by the collection that would make the Jerusalem Christians *clientes* of the contributing Gentile churches, see Holmberg 1978, 55–56.

24. Without alluding to the military metaphor, Martyn hypothesizes that the opposing teachers in Galatia had introduced the Law as God's vehicle for liberating believers (Martyn 1997, 219).

25. In defense of the view that the same collection is referred to throughout, see Dunn 1993, 113–14. Dunn remarks that Paul's understanding of the collection effort may have developed considerably between the initial agreement and his delivery to Jerusalem several years later.

26. Phrase added to fill out the meaning of the verb. Cephas was not condemned by a court, but *kategnōsmenos* is also used of persons condemned by their deeds or publicly expressed opinions (so BGAD, 409).

27. A minority of witnesses (p[46] it[d. g2, r] Irenaeuslat) have the singular, *tina*, probably to accommodate the tradition that has a singular verb in v. 12b.

28. Following A C D[2] H Y 075 0150 6 81 et al.; a number of early witnesses have the singular verb *ēlthen* (p[46] א B D* F G 33 1175 et al.).

29. Literally, "those from the circumcision," which could refer to Jews generally, as "the circumcision" does in 2:8 where it describes those to whom Peter is an apostle. Here Paul has shifted to speaking about a subgroup or party within the Jewish-Christian churches of Judea.

30. Given the participation of prominent Christians like Barnabas, Paul appears to be using *Ioudaioi*, "the Jews," to mean Jewish members of the church community at Antioch, not persons from Judea, from the Jerusalem church, or Jews in general.

31. *Ioudaizein*, "to Judaize," has a wide range of meanings, from adopting Jewish customs to simply siding with Jews to being politically helpful to the Jewish community (Cohen 1999, 180–97).

32. For a description of the ancient city, see Kondoleon 2000; on the Jewish community in Antioch, see Smallwood, 1999, 187–90. It was the crossroads between the Euphrates in the East and Mediterranean ports to the West, as well as the land route between Jerusalem to the South and Ephesus in Asia Minor to the North (Kondoleon 2000, 4).

33. Other episodes of anti-Jewish violence between 67 and 71 C.E. originate with an apostate Jew who had acquired citizenship and municipal office, turning against his father, a Jewish community official, and the Jewish community generally. Charges of arson were lodged that spearheaded efforts to deprive the Jewish community of its rights to be an organized political group. Titus refused such appeals when he visited the city in 71 C.E. (Smallwood 1999, 189–90; against Longenecker's assumption of a persistent anti-Jewish violence in the city from the time of Caligula on [1990, 69]).

34. Historians are sharply divided over the question of whether or not Jews would share meals with non-Jews. Their reputation among Gentiles for being unwilling to do so is often indistinguishable from Jewish antipathy toward pagan religious practices, as Diodorus Siculus (first century B.C.) remarks: "[H]aving organized the nation of the Jews and had made their hatred of mankind into a tradition, and on this account had introduced utterly outlandish laws: not to break bread with any other people, nor to show them any good will at all" (*Hist.* 35.1, 2, quoted in Schäfer 1997, 22).

35. Holmberg 1998 (405) thinks that given the large number of God-fearers in Antioch, Gentiles who shared table fellowship with Jews are likely to have made such arrangements.

36. Short of the Gentile Christians becoming Jews, presumably. Holmberg 1998 (407) points out that Paul never suggests that had the Gentiles been stricter in observing Jewish food rules, these Christians would have eaten with them.

37. So Perkins 1994, 117–20. However, the situation of a Gentile eating with Jewish hosts does not pose the same problems of religious observance for the Jew as that of a Jew eating at a Gentile's table.

38. The contrast draws on rhetorical topoi that condemn those who play to the crowd, a motif that Paul introduced in 1:10 as evidence of his own integrity. Dodd rightly sees this contrast between Paul and Peter as a model posed for the Galatians. They should imitate Paul in resisting advocates of

circumcision: "Paul is the slave of Christ who stands against any who oppose the gospel he has proclaimed" (Dodd 1996, 102). Ancient readers might also pick up the unusual juxtaposition of "slave of Christ" and bold speech, since slaves were commonly depicted as prone or even compelled to flattery and other vices by their circumstances (Bradley 1994, 122–24, 143).

39. For a brief survey of the ancient reactions to this episode from its use in anti-Christian polemic (Origen, *Cels.* 5.64) to those like Jerome who suggest that it was staged by Peter and Paul in order to effectively condemn the Judaizers (Jerome, *Comm. Gal.* on 2:11), see Longenecker 1990, 64–65.

40. And it only gets worse when Paul begins to make his argument. Gal 2:17 suggests that Christian Jews who hold to these customs are sinners (Holmberg 1998, 415).

41. Paul's opposition to non-Jewish Christians being circumcised could be particularly awkward if such a man wished to marry into a Jewish or Christian-Jewish family where circumcision might be required of a prospective son-in-law, although that would imply that the Gentile Christian is thought of as more "Jewish" than Gentile. Otherwise, the Jewish woman marrying a Gentile would be assumed to adopt his family religion. Gentile women marrying Jews were presumed to become "Jewish" upon marriage (see Cohen 1999, 156).

42. Even proselytes, who were members of the Jewish polity, were not "Jews" in the same sense as those born Jewish (Cohen 1999, 160–61).

43. For examples of the latter, see Schäfer 1997, 96–102. Paul comes even closer to the Latin satirists in his persistent use of "the circumcision" to refer both to Jews as opposed to Gentiles (2:8) and to Christian Jews (2:12). Schäfer observes: "those who use circumcision almost as a stereotype to characterize Jews are the Latin satirists" (99).

44. The phrase "fulfilling stipulations of the Law" attempts to render the meaning of Paul's *erga nomou*. The expression refers to concrete deeds commanded by the Law. It appears in Jewish sectarian texts found at Qumran (4Q398 Fr. 14–17 *col* II, 3 = 4QMMT C 29; also see 4QFlor I.7 and 1 QS 5.21; 6.18; Fitzmyer 1993, 338). "Deeds of the law" in this sectarian Jewish context refers to precise stipulations of Torah as interpreted by members of the sect. Fitzmyer translates Paul's phrase "deeds prescribed by the Law."

45. Treating the genitive *pistis Christou* as objective, referring to the content of the believer's faith, rather than subjective, referring to the faithful conduct of Christ.

46. Literally, "not . . . all flesh," an echo of Ps 143:2.

47. Literally, "in Christ"; translation presumes the instrumental use of the preposition *en* plus the dative. Others treat all uses of "in Christ" as examples of the close personal relationship between the believer and Christ (see Dunn 1998, 396–401; BGF, 259).

48. Greek: *diakonos*, also "servant, deacon"; "agent" captures the implication that Christ is "serving up" sin, if fulfilling prescriptions of the Law remains necessary to be upright before God.

49. Literally, "in flesh" *(en sarki)*, an expression that often denotes the weakness, mortality, and vulnerability to sin of human beings (Dunn 1998, 64–65). However, *sarx* can also denote created existence in contrast with God, the Creator, as in v. 16. The translation assumes that Paul is referring to the ongoing conditions of life as a human being.

50. "Son of God" is supported by ℵ A C D^c et al. The reading *Theou kai Christou*, "God and Christ," found in p^{46} D˙ F G it$^{(b), d, g}$ Victorinus-Rome must be a scribal error.

51. A guess. The clause lacks a verb.

52. Dunn treats vv. 15–21 as Paul's summary of the argument that he had presented against Peter at Antioch. He must do so because he cannot point to a triumphant victory over Peter and the others as he could do in the Jerusalem episode (Dunn 1993, 132–50).

53. For a detailed logical analysis of the interrelationships between the statements in Gal 2:15–21, see Bachmann 1992, 59.

54. "Sinner" can be applied to Gentiles by virtue of their idolatry and its associated immorality (Wis 13:1–9), as Paul's argument in Rom 1:18–32 indicates. He is engaging in ethnic name-calling, not making a claim about whether or not Jews are also sinners (so Rom 2:17–24) or have rites to deal with sin that Gentiles lack.

55. T. Martin's attempt to use formalist rhetorical categories to demonstrate that the Galatians were apostatizing back to paganism, not Judaism (1998), completely misses Paul's rhetorical play on ethnic identity in Galatians.

56. For a survey of recent discussion, see Dunn 1998, 128–61. Winger 1992 provides a linguistic approach to Paul's use of the word "law" that demonstrates that he almost always has the Mosaic law in mind.

57. Bruce 1988 (141) questions the modern Greek text editions that have this particle, *âra*, that is not used elsewhere in Paul. He prefers the inferential particle, *âra*, "in that case," but retains the interrogative. The first option seems preferable, since Paul needs to break into the awkward construction of the *protasis* to signal the absurdity of its conclusion.

58. See Longenecker 1990, 88–90, who advocates an even more complex theory based on the assumption that Paul is opposing both Judaizing and a tendency to libertinism in Galatia.

59. Williams 1997 (71) argues that the price is paid on one side only because the very fact of calling the Gentiles into Christ requires loosening or dissolution of the Law. Dunn 1999 concludes that Paul would not have described himself as "Jewish" at this point in his life.

Chapter Three: Galatians 3

1. Alludes to the goal of ancient orators to make the audience "see" the events about which the orator is speaking (Aristotle, *Rhet* 3.11; 1411b).

2. See Neyrey 1988 for an anthropological description of witchcraft charges and countercharges. This rhetorical topos does not imply that the advocates of circumcision had actually engaged in magical practices to capture the hearts of their opponents (contrary to Schlier 1965, 119).

3. Compare Paul's statement that in his preaching he was determined to know nothing but Christ crucified in 1 Cor 2:2 (Bruce 1988, 148).

4. Belief that persons might be victims of the "evil eye" *(baskainein)* was so prevalent in antiquity that a first-century audience would have entertained the charge as a real possibility. Persons who used magical spells were often described as covetous or envious of their victims (Plutarch, *Quaest. Conv.* 681A–683A). Therefore, Longenecker suggests that Paul wishes to convey to the audience the sense that they have been injured by the envy of those agitating for circumcision. The opposing teachers may even have pointed to Paul's physical weaknesses as evidence that the apostle was "cursed" (Longenecker 1999, 93–96).

5. The risk of this strategy backfiring and further alienating the Galatians from the apostle is lessened if they recognize the rhetorical form for what it is (Longenecker 1990, 99). In that case, the Galatians are not really the uncultured dullards of the popular ethnic slur.

6. Rabens 1999 makes a strong case against Horn's view that statements about the Spirit are theological claims based on early Christian eschatology: the elect community of the end-time must be endowed with God's Spirit. Horn 1992 insists that such claims do not imply an experiential element. Esler 1998 (52–53) substitutes a sociological analysis of the role of claims to the Spirit in subordinate groups for the theological version of early Christian appeals to the Spirit. Spirit claims improve the sense of identification within the group by redefining challenges to that identity as goods.

7. Elliott 2000 (416) remarks: "The negative side of this association of pneumatology with soteriological dualism is the *attribution of the inspiration of the opponents to Belial or demons.* The idea that Israel could harden itself against the Spirit of God was previously known in Israelite tradition (cf., e.g., Zech 7:12), but this notion was carried to extremes in the scrolls." Paul's assumption that the opposition has been practicing magic may reflect a similarly dualistic view of their activities.

8. O'Neill 1998 (70–79) advocates a more positive reading of "works of the Law" in Paul's usage based on the link between "works" and "life" in the Qumran material. This proposal flounders on the rhetorical use of dualistic categories to force mutually exclusive options in Galatians.

9. Paul uses *enarchomai* ("begin") and *epiteleô* ("end" or "complete") for the beginning of the Christian life up to its completion with the second coming in Phil 1:6 (Bruce 1988, 150).

10. An inference from the present tense of the verbs (Bruce 1988, 151).

11. Gen 15:6 LXX without the name "Abraham" after "he believed."

12. Gen 12:3 LXX has *phulai tēs gēs*, "tribes of the earth," as recipients of the blessing. Gen 18:18 LXX has *panta ta ethnē*, "all the nations" (or: Gentiles).

13. Deut 27:26 LXX[A] but omitting "man" after "everyone" and the preposition *en* before "all things" and substituting "written in the book of the Law" for "words of the Law." Paul may be quoting from memory or from a version that is not extant.

14. Hab 2:4 LXX[A] , omitting the possessive pronoun "my" [= God's] after "righteous person"; another tradition, Hab 2:4 LXX[B] has "the righteous one shall live on the basis of my [= God's] faithfulness."

15. Lev 18:5 LXX, omitting the word "man" as the subject of the verb "to do."

16. A rendering of Deut 21:23 LXX that does not correspond to any known version.

17. With ; A B C D[2] Y 0150 6 33 et al.; a few witnesses repeat *eulogia* from the previous clause (p[46] D˙ F G it[b, d, g] vg et al.).

18. For further discussion of these traditions, see Nickelsburg 1998 and Gaca 1999.

19. Martyn 1997 (290–94) attributes to the teachers advocating circumcision a double reference to the "flesh": the physical sign of the covenant and the spiritual over passions and impulsive desires associated with the evil impulse. This metaphoric use of circumcision occurs in Essene texts (1 QS 5.5), which also attribute victory over the evil impulse to Abraham (CD 3.2–3).

20. Scholars tend to assume that the expression "sons of Abraham" is a polemical appropriation of the terminology used by those advocating circumcision (e.g., Longenecker 1990, 114). However, Betz 1979 (138) rightly identifies the form of v. 7 as an exegetical thesis; therefore, we understand it as Paul's comment on the Abraham story referring to Isaac in contrast to the other descendants of Abraham mentioned in Scripture.

21. Paul's use of Abraham, children through faith, and blessing on the nations here does not force his audience to conclude that Torah observance is excluded (despite Betz 1979, 143).

22. Blessings and curses formed a significant part of the covenant renewal ceremony among the sectarian Jews at Qumran (1 QS 1.16–2.18). For an extensive discussion of the use of this Deuteronomic scenario of blessings and curses in sectarian Judaism of the period, see Elliott 2000, 290–96.

23. Reinbold 2000 (97–98) argues against the scholarly tendency to assume that Paul is demonizing the Law itself.

24. We prefer to elucidate Paul's logic here by appealing to the convictions about the universal sinfulness of humanity that he later elaborates in Rom 1:18–3:20, which preserves the Law as testimony to God's righteousness, instead of speaking about the Law's curse falling on observant as well as nonobservant, as Martyn has done (1997, 312).

25. Young 1998 proposes an even more specific setting for the need to pronounce Jews free from the Law in order for Gentiles to be included. They cannot be under its curse when they abandon requirements such as circumcision and holy days in their association with non-Jewish believers. While this interpretation gets at practical issues faced by churches like that in Antioch, it too easily sidesteps the collision between the Law and faith in Christ that Paul's argument creates.

26. Martyn 1997 takes this hypothesis too far when he comments: "In short, then, the pronouns of vv. 13–14 point to one of the central facets of Paul's thought in Galatians: In essence the human race was a monolith prior to Christ's advent, and it is the human race as a whole that Christ has liberated. . . . He will not accept, however, the teachers' insistence on the basic difference between Jews and Gentiles" (317–18). As we have already indicated, Paul is unwilling to separate the two in the church, but he certainly plays identity politics. A Jew may cross or blur the boundaries to "live in a Gentile manner," but a Gentile may not engage in similar behavior vis-à-vis Jewish practices.

27. This translation presumes that "Scripture" is the subject. Others take "God" as the implied subject of the verb because God is the subject of "ratify earlier" in v. 17; see Longenecker 1990, 131.

28. Gen 12:7 LXX.

29. Though not sufficient to erase the overall effect of Paul's consistent use of standard rhetorical techniques to vilify an opponent, which render his statements about Torah observance a hostile caricature with no evidentiary value for the actual content of either the opponents' views or the practice of first-century Judaism (Thurén 2000, 66–68). "Speaking of the views of his opponents, Paul does not actually attribute to them the overstated legalistic soteriology which he is discussing. On the contrary, they are said *not* to fulfil the law, and are alleged to be interested in circumcision *not* in order to gain salvation but to avoid persecution because of Christ (6, 12–13). If Paul sought to imply that his opponents agreed with the position which is presented in the Letter as an antithesis to his own theology, he would hardly describe them in this way" (68–69).

30. Jewish texts also refer to the singular descendant of Abraham, namely Isaac, as ancestor of the righteous, so attaching an exegetical identification to

"seed" as singular should not be overemphasized as a Pauline innovation (Bruce 1988, 173).

31. A reference to Exod 12:40, which uses the figure for the period of Israel's captivity in Egypt. Josephus (*Ant.* 2.318) knows this number as the period from Abraham's entry into Canaan and the Exodus from Egypt. Paul is probably relying on popular tradition for the number (so Longenecker 1990, 133).

32. Dunn 1993 (187) points out that the key word "promise," used nine times in this chapter, has no equivalent in the Hebrew Bible and is only widely used in Greek beginning in the second century C.E. In Jewish circles it is ordinarily integrated with Torah, God's promise is kept with the observant (2 Macc 2:17–18; *Psalms of Solomon* 17:6; *Sib. Or.* 3.768–9; *2 Baruch* 14:12–13; 57:2).

33. For a linguistic argument demonstrating that when Paul uses "law" he intends "Mosaic law," see Winger 1992.

34. Martyn 1997 (353) points out that what Paul has said previously also presses the question of why the Law was given: the Law pronounces a curse that falls on both observant and nonobservant (3:10, 13); no one becomes righteous through the Law (v. 11); the Law is not connected with faith (v. 12) or with receiving the inheritance of Abraham (v. 18).

35. The ambiguous Hebrew phrase, *ēšdāt lāmô,* "with a fiery law," was translated into Greek, "angels from his right hand were with him" (Longenecker 1990, 139).

36. Greek *paidagogos* refers to a slave charged with looking after and disciplining young boys in the family. It does not have the connotations of "teacher" associated with the modern English word "pedagogue" (see Longenecker 1990, 146–48).

37. Martyn 1997 introduces the category of "antinomy" for the contrasting categories that Paul employs. Unlike an "antithesis," which presumes an ontological opposition between items in a pair, the "antinomy" is an apocalyptic opposition that is dynamic. Some antinomies are overcome with the coming of the Messiah, such as the opposition of Jew and non-Jew. Others are the consequence of the new creative act by which God's Spirit is now active in the lives of believers (570–73).

38. Paul must know that his view runs counter to an understanding of the purpose of the Law as a source of life with God (Betz 1997, 174).

39. The proposal that the prison metaphor be treated as "protective" custody in view of v. 24 (Longenecker 1990, 146; Dunn 1993, 197) ignores the parallelism between vv. 22 and 23. "Protective custody" might work as applied to the Law—although the verb is clearly used of persons locked up in jail—but it could not be applied to the consequences of sin.

40. This section does not contain the more developed association between the baptismal rite and participation in the death of Christ that one

finds in Rom 6:3 and so on, although all of the elements of Paul's theological understanding in Romans are already present in Galatians (see Betz 1994, 261–71).

41. See Betz 1979 (188–89), who suggests that the eschatological sense might be picked up by Paul's reference to Christians as the new creation in Gal 6:15.

42. Glancy 1998 (500–501) points out that this advice is particularly problematic for slaves, because the use of both male and female slaves as prostitutes makes it impossible for them to avoid the sexual immorality that Paul depicts as polluting the body of Christ (1 Cor 6:12–20). Although the baptismal formula declared the barrier between slave and free abolished, Christian slaves might encounter considerable barriers to their participation in the church.

Chapter Four: Galatians 4

1. With p⁴⁶ ℵ A B C D˙ et al.; some witnesses have corrected to *humōn* ("you," pl.), in agreement with the verb in the previous clause (D² Y 075 0150 6 33 et al.).

2. Literally, "through God" (p⁴⁶ ℵ˙ A B C˙ 33 et al.); numerous variants to the phrase occur in the manuscripts: reading an accusative *dia theon* denoting efficient cause rather than the genitive of agency (F G 1881); "through Christ" or "through Jesus Christ" (81 2464 et al.); omitting the preposition "through" (1962 arm); combining the genitive *theou* modifying "heir" with a following prepositional phrase, "through Jesus Christ" (P 6 263 et al.).

3. Contrary to the apocalyptic understanding of the shift of the ages, which we presume to underlie this transition (Martyn 1997, 389–90, uses the dramatic language of redemption as invasion), White 1999 (153–56) argues for a teleological interpretation. Human maturation is guided by God as Creator.

4. Thurén 2000 (77–79) observes that shifts in the pronoun "we" and "you" in chs. 3 and 4 deliberately obscure the distinction between Jew and Gentile because "we" serves to unite the speaker with the audience. With regard to the Law after Christ, both are in the same situation. However, in this section v. 5 refers specifically to Jews who had been under the Law. The inclusive "we" of vv. 1–3 includes Jews with Gentiles as subject to the *stoicheia* of the cosmos.

5. Betz 1979 (204) notes that our only evidence for paternal determination of the date at which his son reaches his maturity stems from the provinces. Paul may have been familiar with provincial custom rather than with the more ordinary situation in which the age of maturity was determined by civic authorities.

6. Contrary to what the pedagogue analogy has often led readers to presume (see Thurén 2000, 78).

7. Longenecker's attempt to force a consistent reference to "principles of the Mosaic law" into this reference (1990, 165–66), while agreeing that Paul intends a negative overtone, strains the interpretation of his repetition of the term *stoicheia* for powers worshipped by Gentile idolaters in 4:9.

8. The tendency of commentators has been to work the Law into this argument as a manifestation of some form of enslaving principle (see survey in Arnold 1996, 67–70), as in Dunn's remark, "It is important for the flow of Paul's thought from iii.19 on to appreciate the fact that he clearly understood the law to be functioning in effect as one of those forces" (1993, 213). However, Paul has made rhetorical shift away from identification with "us" (= Jews) over against "you" (= Gentiles) to identification with his audience of Gentile converts in Galatia, even though he continues to distinguish Jews who had been "under the Law" (vv. 4–5) from Gentile idol-worshippers (vv. 8–9). This shift becomes explicit in 4:12.

9. Bossman 1996 (169) observes that Gal 1:3–3:5 implies that Paul is acting as the broker in this kinship system. God as "father" engenders the new family of Abraham through the gift of life. Paul as "father" refers to his nurturing and instructing role with respect to his churches, a function often performed by maternal uncles (166).

10. "Jewish religion" is Adams's expression (2000, 229). We would prefer Torah observance, since it is not evident that Paul intends to distinguish something called "Christian religion" from something called "Jewish religion." For a treatment that suggests Paul should be understood as having a theory about the eschatological transition to what would later be considered "Christian religion," see Betz (1994b).

11. The more extreme position, that Paul was simply inconsistent and that scholars should not try to patch the flawed logic in his theology, has been forcefully argued by Räisänen 1983 (9–15). However, we concur with the majority in holding that the conceptual coherence of Paul's thought supports the assumption that he held theologically consistent positions (see the argument in Beker 1988).

12. Dunn 1998 (130) agrees that the sharp antithesis between the Law associated with the *stoicheia* and the gospel found in Gal 3:10–13 and 4:8–10 played a key role in Reformation theology.

13. The rhetorical parallelism between the two situations makes apostasy return to the divisions of humanity prior to Christ, although "under the Law" is not equivalent to non-Jewish idol worship "under the *stoicheia*" from the pre-Christian perspective. Martin's attempt to discover another rhetorical model that would support the conclusion that the Galatians actually were on the verge of returning to idolatry (1998) has not been persuasive.

14. Dunn 1993 (215–16), relying on the equivalence of the phrase "born of a woman" and "being human" in Jewish texts (Job 14:1; 15:14; 25:4; 1 QS 11.21; 1 QH 13.14; 18.12–13), finds a reference to Adam Christology in this formulation.

15. Textual variations show that scribes substituted the expected second-person plural in this context.

16. Thurén 2000 (70) points out that exegesis of Galatians must consider its dramatic, agonizing style in evaluating its argument: "Paul meets the exigency with oppressive rhetoric, polarizing and dramatizing the situation. He paints a stark picture and forces a choice between the alternatives. This requires him to alienate the addressees from the antagonists as effectively as possible."

17. See the evidence for both possibilities in Betz (1979, 214–15). Arnold has argued that the *stoicheia* are demonic powers, given their depiction as enslaving as well as the adjectives "weak and beggarly" (cf. 1 Cor 10:20; *Jubilees* 11:4–5; *Testament of Judah* 23:1) and Jewish accusations that Gentiles worship the elements as gods (Wis 7:17, 13:2; Philo, *Contempl.* 3–4; Arnold 1996, 70–71).

18. Sampley 1995 (40–52) has identified this tactic in Rom 14:1–15:13. Paul uses a figure of indirect speech, in this case "days" for "Sabbath" and "vegetables" for kosher, so that his audience can all identify with "strong Christians" and then apply the exhortation concerning mutual tolerance to their relationships.

19. Arnold 1996 (73–75) agrees that the role of astral phenomena in apocalyptic and Essene texts permits Paul's shift to the festal calendar. However, the purpose of the whole is not to debate over calendar or possible astral deities in charge of it, but to demonize the choice being proposed to the Galatians.

20. Jewish observance of the Sabbath was well known among Gentiles (Philo, *Mos.* 2.21; Josephus, *C. Ap.* 2.282; Juvenal, *Sat.* 14.96). Dunn 1993 (227–28) suggests the following correspondences: "days" and Sabbaths; "month" and new moons (Num 10:10, 28:11; Ps 81:3; Ezek 46:3–7; most likely associated with *stoicheia*); "years" and annual feasts, perhaps the New Year festival, which appears to have been disputed at Qumran (1 QS 10.6).

21. Nor is Paul making any claim at all about keeping the Sabbath or about the observance of other holy days in the Jewish liturgical calendar. Jewish followers of Jesus must have continued to observe the religious calendar and Sabbath customs of family, friends, and associates. When the various gatherings for prayer and the Lord's Supper referred to in Paul's letters occurred (1 Cor 11:2–34; 14:1–40) is not stated. Martyn 1997 (414–18) has hypothesized an even more elaborate theology by which Paul's opponents had taught that the Galatians were giving proper reverence to God's created

astral powers in observing the Jewish calendar. He has Paul adapt the so-called teachers' terminology to the creation account of Gen 1:14 in order to support the assertion that all forms of ritual calendar are reflections of the old creation, not the new creation in Christ. Paul is not anti-Judaic because his apocalyptic theology leads him to reject all forms of religious distinction between holy and profane days (418).

22. Literally, "weakness of the flesh."

23. A magical or superstitious gesture to ward off evil. Other translators adopt a metaphorical translation, "disdain."

24. With ℵ* A B C² D* F G 33 itb, d, f, g, o, r vg et al. Others read "my testing" (p⁴⁶ Cᵛⁱᵈ D² Y 075 0150 et al.).

25. Literally, "by my flesh."

26. Greek *makarismos* could also be translated "blessing."

27. The Greek does not indicate whether this sentence is a statement or a further question to the audience.

28. Translating the preposition *en* as "among" (BDAG, 258) rather than "in," since Paul is speaking about social relationships rather than individual conformity to Christ.

29. Paul consistently opposes the possibility of Gentiles following Jewish customs. Even in Romans 14:1–15:13, where Paul indirectly admits that different house churches among the Roman Christians will have different customs, there is no suggestion that the "strong" actually participate in the food or calendar concerns of the weak. Rather each group is to accept the other without criticism. On the rhetoric of this passage in Romans, see Sampley 1995.

30. This reading assumes that there is a failure in "justice" as the reciprocity among friends to which the Galatians have become sensitive, rather than a period of solidarity with the apostle marked by a sudden shift to animosity, as Martyn proposes (1997, 420).

31. As Dunn's description of the ambiguity of Paul's identity that emerges from his engagement with Gentiles and relativizing of ancestral customs indicates, Paul never accommodates to Gentile idolatry and immorality (1999, 191–92).

32. This reference makes it clear that the "weakness" is a physical condition, probably chronic, and not a personal, spiritual suffering or the opposition to Paul's mission as some interpreters of 2 Cor 12:8–10 have proposed (see the discussion of the various interpretations of 2 Cor 12:8 in Thrall 2000, 809–18).

33. Paul faced challenges on these grounds in Corinth (2 Cor 10:11; D. Martin 1995, 53). Plutarch, *Tu. san.* 130F–131A, recounts the story of a sophist, Niger, who died in Galatia. Rather than yield to a newcomer, Niger persisted in giving a public performance with a fish bone lodged in his

throat. Suffering a painful and chronic inflammation of the throat, Niger underwent surgery to remove the bone only to die from the subsequent infection (reference from a lecture by Robert Renehan, Boston College, 9 September 1999).

34. There is no reason to assume that people would have taken the person afflicted by a demonic spirit thanks to the activity of a magician as also a magician. The victim's presence introduces evil forces into the community of itself (contrary to Martyn 1997, 421).

35. Even if the audience did not pick up the association on first hearing, the reference to Abraham's two sons in v. 22 would bring it to mind.

36. Betz (1979, 228) appeals to Lucian, *Tox.* 40–41, in which a person with nothing else to give sacrifices his eyes to ransom a friend, who then reciprocates by blinding himself. Assuming that this gesture was a standard topos in friendship literature sidesteps the rhetorical question of whether Paul intended his words to carry a negative emotional impact.

37. Some editors and translators punctuate v. 16 as a question, despite the lack of an interrogative particle. However, the *hōste* ("so that") clause generally states the consequences of what the speaker has just said (see discussion in Longenecker 1990, 193).

38. Paul returns to the charge that those advocating circumcision act only out of self-interest in Gal 6:12–13 (Longenecker 1999, 105). "Self-interest" violates a fundamental principle of both philosophical and Pauline understanding of ethical conversion. Virtue requires that persons shift from an identity based on individual self-interest to identification with a power beyond those self-interests and to incorporation into a larger community (Engberg-Pedersen, 2000, 33–40).

39. Martyn (1997, 422–23) suggests an emotional appeal in which the advocates of circumcision sought to benefit the Gentile Christians by bringing them the blessings of Abraham through observance of the Law.

40. BDAG3, 427 translates v. 18ab: "it is fine to be zealously courted at all times in what is fine." The expression *to kalon*, "what is fine," can refer to the beautiful, the noble, or the good. We have taken the phrase as a reference to Paul's concern for the good of his converts in contrast to the implied flattery or deceit of the opposing position, since he continues speaking about his personal efforts on their behalf in vv. 19–20. Compare Martyn's rendering, "to be courted by someone who is concerned for your welfare is in every instance a good thing" (1997, 423). However, since these phrases have the appearance of established aphorisms (Betz 1979, 231), they may not be formulated to fit Paul's argument. The maxim may be directed at a lack of discernment among the Galatians. They should be able to recognize *to kalon* ("the good") and therefore the difference between true apostles like Paul and false teachers.

41. Betz (1979, 233) cites such passages as Plato, *Lysis* 207E; Aristotle, *Eth. nic.* 1155a15–20; 1159c28–34; and Cicero, *Amic.* 27 to illustrate the use of maternal affection in such treatises.

42. Malherbe (2000 151) cites Dio Chrysostom, *Or.* 77/78.38, as an example.

43. The prepositional phrase *en hūmin* refers to the community, "among you (pl.)," rather than to an internal, individual transformation (Schlier 1965, 214).

44. For the idea of a process by which the community is transformed into the image of Christ, see Martyn 1997, 424–25; 2 Cor 3:18.

45. In the older numbering of the Hodayoth, 1 QH 3.6–12.

46. Contrary to Martyn 1997, 426, who thinks that Paul is genuinely at a loss and fears that this letter will be a failure: "[I]n the immediate political sense the letter may very well have failed as thoroughly as did Paul's speech to Peter in the Antioch church (2:11–14). As he dictates it Paul is painfully aware of that possibility."

47. As Martyn 1997 (425) argues that concern for the mission territory in which Paul is active explains the lack of reference to visits by Paul or associates such as one finds in the other letters. This feature does not demonstrate that Galatians was written close to the time of Romans, when Paul had decided to abandon that region and shift to the western part of the empire (Rom 15:22–29).

48. As Martyn's reconstruction of the debate with the teachers implies, since he holds that Paul is contemplating the failure of the letter (1997, 426). Longenecker (1990, 196) also suggests that Paul conveys a certain pessimism about the situation at this point, but misses the rhetorical significance of changing one's tone. He treats the latter as a simple preference for face-to-face communication over the use of a letter.

49. Literally, "according to the flesh."

50. Versions vary on whether the connecting particle is *de* or *gar* without difference in meaning. This translation assumes the text reading *gar* [or *de*] *Hagar Sina* "for Hagar is Sinai" (A B D Y 062 075 0150 6 33 et al.) is to be preferred as more difficult. Other witnesses have *gar* [or *de Sina* "for Sinai is" (p[46] ℵ C F G 1241 it[ar, b, f, g, or, r] vg et al.).

51. With p[46] ℵ* B C˙ D F G Y 062[vid] 6 33 et al. Some witnesses have *panton humōn*, "of all of us" (ℵ[2] A C[3] 075 0150 et al.).

52. A woman's *anēr* would ordinarily be her husband. However, the context requires a reference to offspring, so "man" would refer to a grown son. The citation is from Isa 54:1 LXX.

53. With p[46] B D˙ F G 0261[vid] 6 33 et al.; other witnesses have "we . . . are" (ℵ A C D[2] Y 062 075 0150 et al.).

54. Literally, "according to the flesh."

55. Gen 21:10 LXX. Paul has changed the speaker from Sarah to Scripture and shifts the designation "my son Isaac" to "the son of the free woman."

56. Against such an anachronistic division, Brändle and Stegemann 1996, 121–25, propose referring to Christianity as "Christ-faith." They comment, "The immediate context in which early Christianity in general, can be situated historically is the 'diffusion' of Diaspora Jews within a society dominated by a non-Jewish majority" (121).

57. See the detailed survey of Jewish exegesis in Longenecker 1990, 200–206.

58. For the persistence of *Ioudaios* as an ethnic, geographic term by which even Diaspora Jews were viewed as "citizens" of Judea or the city-state Jerusalem, see Cohen 1999, 72–81.

59. John 8:31–33 suggests familiarity with a similar polemic between followers of Jesus and *Ioudaioi*, seed of Abraham, who claim never to have been enslaved, but the evangelist interprets "enslaved" allegorically as sin and disbelief in God's Son. For the slave woman Hagar as emblematic of preliminary studies that are to be cast out once true virtue is achieved, see Philo *Cher.* 9; *Leg.* 3.244; Longenecker 1990, 204.

60. Contrast anticipation of an eschatological war in which even the "wicked" Jews will be aligned with the evil imperial powers depicted in Essene texts (Collins 1997, 91–109). The eschatology of the Qumran sectaries may have envisaged an end-time conversion of "all Israel" to the group prior to the outbreak of that conflict. On the *Kittim* as Romans who have oppressed Jerusalem, see the pesher on Nah 2:12b (4 Q169 3–4.i.2–3; Lim 2000, 470).

61. Martyn's section devoted to Gal 4:21–5:1 is entitled "Two Gentile Missions" (1997, 431–66). Although his commentary elsewhere suggests that the teachers had made significant inroads among the Galatians, he paraphrases Paul's message in this section as a contrast between the relatively insignificant Law-observant mission, with its vocal supporters in the Jerusalem church, and the much more successful "liberating circumcision-free" mission conducted independently of Jerusalem by Paul (433).

62. There is no reason to extend the principle of "mirror reading" to the point of asserting that those advocating circumcision were accusing Paul's Gentile converts of being nothing but descendants of Ishmael (contrary to Longenecker 1990, 218, who speaks of their opposition to Paul's "Ishmaelian" gospel).

63. Davies 1999 (720–21) presumes that "sons of Hagar" must refer to persons of Jewish descent, whether they are Jews who do not believe in Christ or Jewish Christians. Since Paul speaks only of a heavenly Jerusalem (v. 26) and a "new creation" (6:15) in Galatians, he cannot be said to envisage the eschatological reconstitution of Israel.

64. Hengel and Schwemer 1997 (113–17) propose an elaborate connection with Nabatean Arabia, which was referred to in some ancient sources as Hagra or Hegra (Ptolemy, 6.7, 29; H[a]egra, Pliny, *Nat.* 6.157) and the tradition reported in Josephus, *Ant.* 1.220–21, that the Nabateans were named after the eldest son of Ishmael, Nabaioth. Betz (1979, 245) treats the possibility of an Arabic designation, *hddjar*, for the rocky mountains around Sinai as the source, as no more than a guess. Longenecker 1990 (211–12) concurs with the view that Paul has picked up this tradition in Nabatea.

65. The northern Galatian city of Pessinus was a renowned center of this cult (Elliott 1979, 74).

66. Elliott's references to local, religious iconography explains the use of the verb *sustoichein* in v. 25 as a reference to something standing in a line, that is, carved upright on a cliff face, as well as its use among logicians and grammarians for tables of categories.

67. Paul avoids identifying the eschatological Jerusalem with Zion (for "mother Zion" see Ps 87:5 LXX; Isa 1:1, 51:18; Jer 1:12; Hos 4:5; Dunn 1993, 254), not to mention the tradition that God showed Jerusalem to Moses on Sinai (*2 Baruch* 4.2–6; Dunn 1993, 253).

68. Sarah is mentioned in Rom 4:19 and 9:9 (= Gen 18:10, 14).

69. *Tg. Isa.* 54.1 (Longenecker 1990, 215). Longenecker assumes that Paul intends Sarah as the subject throughout, as does Martyn 1997 (441). Both rely heavily on a later tradition that depicts Sarah/Jerusalem providing her milk to Gentiles at Abraham's request (*Pesiq. Rab Kah.* 22.1).

70. Martyn (1997) speaks of Paul's understanding of God's deeds of salvation as *punctiliar*. The birth of Isaac and the birth of the Galatian church correspond without being linked by a "line extending through the centuries from Abraham, Isaac, and Jacob (444). This interpretation of Pauline theology not only undermines Christian talk of "salvation history," it challenges the legitimacy of any Christian claim to the narratives of the Scripture between these punctiliar events, a view that Paul's use of Scripture elsewhere does not support (e.g., 1 Cor 10:1–13; 2 Cor 3:7–18).

71. *Gen. Rab.* 53:11; *Tg. Ps.-J.* Gen 21:10 (Martyn 1997, 444; Longenecker 1990, 217).

72. Or with a dogmatic statement, excluding Jews faithful to the Torah from salvation, as Dunn correctly observes (1993, 258).

73. Dunn (1993, 259) rightly observes that the harsh tone in v. 30 is moderated to some extent by the "warmth of personal address" in vv. 28 and 31.

Chapter Five: Galatians 5

1. With א* A B D* (omit: *oun*) P 33 et al. The manuscripts exhibit a wide range of variations in the rendering of this passage, especially in attaching an

article and/or relative clause to the word "freedom," providing the sense: "stand fast in the freedom for which Christ freed us" (so D 075 et al.). The variants seek to resolve the awkward dative, "for/with respect to freedom," as attached to the verb "set us free," and the lack of transition between 4:31 and 5:1. See the discussion in Longenecker 1990, 220.

2. Assuming that Paul is using the present tense in the conative sense, "are trying to," not as a simple statement of what is the case.

3. Taking the article as possessive, referring to Christ.

4. Literally, "running." Paul has returned to the athletic metaphor that he used of his own mission earlier (Gal 2:2).

5. Possibly a continuation of the metaphor. Someone has put a stumbling block in the runner's way to cause a fall or failure to win the race.

6. V. 1 marks a transition between 4:31 and 5:2 that is an effective oral device. The numerous textual variants show that ancient scribes tried to formulate a smoother written transition. Modern editions of the Greek text sometimes attach 5:1 to 4:31 and begin a new paragraph at 5:2 (so UBS[4]) or print the verse as a separate interjection (so NA[27]). The latter is more appropriate to its rhetorical function.

7. Engberg-Pedersen (2000, 135) makes a strong case for the interrelationship of these sections with the rest of the letter. Gal 5:2–12 picks up the question of opponents as a conclusive determination of the earlier argument. Vv. 2–6 state the consequences of the argument advanced in 2:14–4:11 and vv. 7–12 invoke the anathema of 1:6–9. At the same time, Paul will return yet again to the attack on those who advocate circumcision in 6:11–13. The intervening ethical material specifies what it means to live out Christian freedom in love (5:1, 6a).

8. Martin (1998, 446) is less persuasive in arguing that vv. 11–12 also belong to Paul's original preaching in Galatia.

9. The issue of slave, freed man or woman, or freeborn parents may have had personal significance to Paul himself. If he did possess the Roman citizenship that Acts attributes to him (Acts 16:37–38, 25:10–11, 26:32), he likely inherited it from a father or grandfather who had been freed by a Roman owner (Murphy-O'Connor 1996, 40–41).

10. A closer analogy to Epicurean quietism appears in 1 Thess 4:9–12: United in mutual love, Christians should live quietly, mind their own affairs, avoid dependence on others, and conduct themselves honorably toward outsiders. Malherbe 2000 (244–60) agrees that Paul's language has Epicurean overtones in v. 11, but argues that Paul is opposed to the possibility of Christians withdrawing into Epicurean quietism.

11. Nero's successor Galba recalled Musonius Rufus and Demetrius the Cynic, exiled in 65–66 on charges of treason. Tension between the *princeps* and Stoic philosophers continued under Vespasian (Griffin 2000, 41–42).

12. The Stoics recognized that feelings arise within a person. The wise refuse to assent to impulses that would violate their convictions about what is good, appropriate, or necessary for human life. Inwood observes: "The passionless wise man is not someone who never feels. But he remains clear-headed about what he feels, distinguishing what makes a difference to happiness from what does not. By keeping this difference firmly in view, he prevents the transient upsets of life from gaining the momentum that would turn them into passions" (Inwood and Donini 1999, 705).

13. Paul has not explicitly excluded the possibility of Jewish Christ-believers continuing to observe Torah for cultural and social reasons. 1 Cor 7:17–24 instructs believers not to alter the situation in which they were called (Longenecker 1990, 226).

14. Epictetus, *Diatr.* 2.9, 20–21, describes a person wavering as distinct from one who undergoes conversion in characteristically Stoic fashion, differentiating between the mental attitudes of the persons in question: "whenever we see a man hesitating between two faiths, we are in the habit of saying, 'He is not a Jew. He is only acting the part.' But when he adopts the attitude of mind of the man who has undergone the washing and has made his choice, then he both is a Jew and in fact is also called one." Schäfer 1997 (97–98) rightly sees "washing" as a reference to circumcision as well as other requirements for proselytes. He misses the Stoic moral epistemology behind Epictetus's discussion of attitude of mind, making a choice, and applying professed principles.

15. These assertions do not depend upon an unstated premise that persons cannot fulfill the Law, but that Gentiles who take it on become permanently indebted to the Law (Martyn 1997, 470–71). If one treats the debt language as signing on to be "client" of a powerful patron, then the sharp division between the Law and Christ follows. Although it is possible to owe debts to more than one person, only the most powerful patron will command the life of the client.

16. Thurén (2000, 71) treats the extreme formulation as rhetorically designed to exclude a deviation from Paul's view of Christianity. Paul has a more moderate formulation in his *peroratio* (6:15). In Stoic moral categories, circumcision would be an "indifferent thing."

17. Betz (1979, 264–65) identifies elements of the diatribe style typical of philosophical school instruction in this section. Paul takes the role of the teacher instructing still-immature students about the truth.

18. Betz (1979, 270) notes the use of sarcasm in diatribe. Paul expects the audience to react with contempt, ridicule, or disgust at this point; not with admiration for castration as a sign of devotion to the mother goddess.

19. Betz (1979, 265) suggests that the phrase may exploit a common proverb concerning the absurdity of not doing the truth that one knows.

However, if Paul is drawing upon a Stoic idea of moral pedagogy as Engberg-Pedersen 2000 has suggested, then the verb *peithesthai* may not be intended in the sense of "obey," that is, to put into action a truth that one knows, but in the sense of "be persuaded," that is, the Galatians lack cognitive certainty concerning the truth of the gospel.

20. Paul's earlier references to the Galatians as "bewitched" (3:1) serve to resolve the epistemological dilemma of how persons who initially knew the truth came to adopt or waver in the direction of false opinions.

21. Martyn (1997, 475) translates the phrase "God who called you," thus specifying one party to the process. However, the indefinite third person singular in v. 7 focuses attention on human actors. The "who fouled you?" leads to a denial that the apostle is responsible for their false opinions. Consequently, one pole of "not from one who called you" answers that query, "certainly not me!"

22. Despite the contemporary emphasis on Paul's loyalty to his Jewish heritage and his perception that God has had a single plan of salvation from the beginning, this refusal to concede that God could call non-Jews to identify with or assimilate to Judaism through their faith in Christ does set the groundwork for a religious division between Christianity and Judaism (so rightly, Betz 1994b).

23. Leaven as an image of what is corrupting or negative is not limited to Jewish writers familiar with the Passover tradition of cleansing the house of all leaven (e.g., Philo, *Spec.* 1.293, 2.184–85; *Q. Exod* 1.15). It was generally thought to operate by causing rot or corruption (so Plutarch, *Quaest. Rom.* 289F; Betz 1979, 266).

24. Dunn (1993, 276) rightly points out that since Paul does not apply the proverb to the situation in Galatia, one cannot use it as information about events there. Presumably, the "little corrupts the whole" image best fits a context in which the issue of circumcision has only recently begun to gain its adherents.

25. Dunn (1993, 277) argues that neither Paul's rhetoric nor his theological confidence can be taken to indicate that he is no longer fearful about the outcome of the situation in Galatia. Similarly, Martyn (1997) remarks: "This confidence has not arisen, however, because he has received encouraging reports about the Galatians. . . . it is the confidence of an apocalyptic theologian who, equipped with bifocal lenses, sees that the power of Christ is 'much more' than the power of the Teachers' false gospel" (475).

26. The verb *tarassō* not only refers to mental confusion or agitation as stipulated for this passage in BDAG[3] 990, it also designates political or social turmoil. The latter was regularly attacked in rhetorical appeals for civic harmony. Within the framework of Stoic ethical pedagogy, the former would cause persons still progressing toward virtue to fall away and experience the

ill effects of passions and other vices. Paul likely intends the audience to hear both meanings in his use of the verb.

27. As in the expulsion of persons from the Jewish community in Rome for rioting over "Chrestus" under Claudius (Suetonius, *Claud.* 25.4; Acts 18:2) ca. 48 C.E. Murphy-O'Connor (1996, 9–10) opts for an earlier date of 41 C.E. In either case, civic discord, probably in only a single synagogue of the city (so Murphy-O'Connor 1996, 333), caused the expulsion of the persons held responsible for it.

28. He is smuggled out of Damascus to avoid persecution under Aretas IV (2 Cor 11:32–33) ca. 37 C.E. (Murphy-O'Connor 1996, 90); run out of Philippi (1 Thess 2:2; Acts 16:38–40), and presumably later out of Thessalonika (1 Thess 2:17–20; Acts 17:1–10).

29. Compare 1 Thess 2:2, where reference to his suffering at Philippi serves to underline the boldness with which Paul preached in Thessalonika (Malherbe 2000, 136).

30. Paul's treatment of circumcision as indifferent in 3:28, 5:6, and 6:15 could be invoked on either side of the issue (Schlier 1965, 238).

31. Or Paul may be responding to some form of slander. The text does not permit us to draw any certain conclusion about what Paul is referring to (Betz 1979, 269; Dunn 1993, 278–80).

32. Martyn (1997, 168) rejects the possibility of factual reports that Paul had once preached circumcision to non-Jews. Any report that Paul actually preached circumcision must be slander or, in Martyn's rendering, a false report that some persons had made in Galatia (476–77). A minimal basis for such a rumor could have been an occasion on which one of Paul's Gentile converts was circumcised, as Acts 16:1–3 reports about Timothy (477).

33. Cohen (1999, 42–45) observes that the situation may have been different in the eastern provinces where other groups were known to practice circumcision. While no proselytes would have been uncircumcised, Gentiles might be considered "Jews" by other Gentiles if they destroyed household gods, declared exclusive loyalty to the God of the Jews, and followed other Jewish practices (Cohen 1999, 150–53).

34. Paul reports suffering punishment at the hands of synagogue authorities (2 Cor 11:24–25).

35. Literally, "flesh." In an ethical context, Paul uses "flesh" for the passions or desires (see Dunn 1998, 67).

36. Lev 19:18 LXX.

37. Literally, "desire of flesh."

38. Literally, "the flesh."

39. Literally, "the flesh."

40. Literally, "the works of the flesh."

41. With p⁴⁶ ℵ B 38 81 et al. Others add "murders" (*phonoi*; A C D F G Y 075 0122 et al.).

42. With ℵ² A B C P Y 075 et al.; others omit "Jesus," p⁴⁶ D F G 0122ᶜ 6 81 et al.

43. Paul does inject military metaphors into his ethical exhortation, as 1 Thess 5:8 and 2 Cor 10:4–5 indicate, but there weapons and siege tactics are explicitly mentioned. *Aphormē* is not restricted to military operations, so it can hardly carry the metaphor by itself. Martyn 1997 (550) sees the whole theology of Galatians as built upon an apocalyptic understanding of God's intervention in the world to establish God's righteousness by means of the cosmic war that defeats evil.

44. Dunn (1998, 64) points out that the antithesis "flesh" against Spirit should not be understood as a dualism that opposes matter to reason or consciousness. Hence translators have tried to find another option in English, such as "nature," "human nature," "sinful nature," etc. (see Dunn 1998, 63 n. 59).

45. Esler (1998, 207–30) also highlights the appeal for communal concord that is fundamental to Gal 5:16–26. He suggests (230) that Paul's view of harmonious life in community, which is the consequence of following the Spirit, would form a serious challenge to his audience. The competitive and honor-sensitive ethos of ancient Mediterranean males would not be receptive to subordinating oneself to others.

46. So Dunn 1993, 285–86. There is no reason to hypothesize a separate ethical problem or "libertine tendencies" as the occasion for Paul's shift to paraenesis (as does Longenecker 1990, 238–39).

47. Unlike the shifting meanings that Paul attaches to some of his theological code words, such as "flesh" or "faith," he consistently uses "love" whether that of God or of humans, as an unqualified positive attribute (Boers 1997, 696–97).

48. Esler 1998, 206, points to 1 Thess 5:8 as evidence that the combination of faith and love was characteristic of Paul's exhortation.

49. By contrast, the ancients typically saw democratic freedom and equality as a quick route to demagoguery, divisive partisan struggles, and decay of civic concord (Dunn 1993, 285).

50. The positive overtones of claiming to be "slave of a deity"—or in Paul's case, "slave of Christ" (1:10)—does not violate this social hierarchy, since the slave takes the positive identity from the exalted status of his owner.

51. Also introduced as the meaning of the Law/Decalogue in Rom 13:8–10.

52. Dunn (1993, 289) argues for the equivalence of meaning in the two passages. However, "law" is not one of the theological terms that Paul uses with the same range of meanings in all cases, so one should be careful about substituting meanings between letters (Boers 1997, 706–13).

53. Compare Paul's introduction to the allegory of Abraham's two sons in 4:21: "[Y]ou who wish to be under the Law, do you not hear the Law?"

54. Esler 1998, 225–26. Esler points out that Plutarch describes behavior like wild animals as something to be avoided by brothers (*Frat. amor.* 486b).

55. The future tense can be understood to be an imperative (so RSV, NRSV), with v. 16 picking up the tone of command from v. 13. Betz (1979, 278) refers to the future tense as a promise dependent upon the imperative "walk by the Spirit." Longenecker 1990, 245, sees the present-tense imperative "walk" as a description of an action that is in progress, since the Galatians have experienced the presence of the Spirit.

56. This affirmation that the Spirit determines Christian ethical life or, as Paul commented in the statements about love (5:6b, 13c, 14), inspires an other-regarding treatment of others modeled on the example of Christ, does not imply a naïve trust in individual claims to be moved by the Spirit (Rabens 1999).

57. When Paul asserts that those who live "in Christ" no longer desire to do deeds of the flesh (5:24), he presumes that moral actions follow from a transformed understanding. He is not describing "will" or desires that arise spontaneously as individuals interact with the world (Engberg-Pedersen 2000, 165–69).

58. Although the structure of Paul's thought has parallels in the moralists of his day, his understanding of Christian ethics depends upon his soteriological and eschatological vision. God's saving act in Christ ("you have been called to freedom," 5:1) is necessary to this ethic, not the natural powers of human reason (Dunn 1998, 626–31).

59. Attempts to argue for a derivation from Hellenistic Jewish sources influenced by philosophical speculation have also proved unsatisfactory (Frey 1999).

60. Frey (1999, 71–73) argues that Paul created the antithesis flesh-spirit in response to the situation in Galatia, since the antithetical pair does not appear in Paul's earliest letter, 1 Thess. Originally, "flesh" as a negative moral force was derived from Palestinian Jewish sources. "Spirit" represented the new life with God.

61. Despite Betz, who treats this section as evidence for Paul's anthropology (1979, 272–80). He recognizes that Paul moves beyond the dualism of Gal 5:17 in Rom 7:15–24.

62. To speak of this shift as apocalyptic mythologizing as Frey does (1999, 75) seems inappropriate, because Paul does not present a scenario of end-time demonic, human, and angelic actors.

63. Dunn himself points to the parallel between his analysis of this passage and Rom 7:14–8:30 (1993, 300). This analysis is another example of the scholarly tendency to read Galatians as if Paul intended to write Romans.

64. Engberg-Pedersen (2000, 163) does not engage in sufficient discussion of Stoic teaching about moral progress to make this point clearly. He does point out that the "for" (*gar*) in v. 17 makes what follows an explanation of v. 16b, and therefore concludes that the battle cannot be within the soul.

65. Esler (1998, 229) suggests that Paul has formulated the phrase "works of the flesh" in v. 19a as an ironic parallel to the expression "works of the Law."

66. Esler (1998, 227) notes other meanings for this term that would be a better fit with Paul's earlier comments about the situation in Galatia, "wanton violence," "insolence." However, since the next terms in the list are idolatry and sorcery, the sexual meaning seems preferable. The first five items reflect the standard Jewish view of Gentiles as sexually immoral idolaters. Martyn (1997, 496) suggests the possibility that the sexual immorality would have been taken as an allusion to behavior of devotees of the Cybele cult.

67. Refers to envy that begrudges the good fortune of others and may evoke attempts to employ the "evil eye" against the possessor of those goods (Esler 1998, 228).

68. Can be a band of drunken revelers disrupting the city streets during a religious festival (Esler 1998, 228).

69. Using a singular "fruit of the Spirit" prior to the list may also reflect a common Stoic moral conviction concerning the unity of virtue. Engberg-Pedersen (2000, 164) takes it to represent a distinction between the Law, which deals with "act-types," and the Spirit, which creates a state of mind.

70. This reading would have been easier had Paul used an accusative noun after the preposition *kata* to give the reading "concerning such things." With the genitive, *kata* implies opposition. The legal context also suggests opposition.

71. The goal for believers is not permanent internal warfare with the "desire of the flesh," but what Paul refers to in Phil 2:5 as "thinking [about practice] yourselves as Christ Jesus" and in Gal 5:13 as "being slaves to one another through faith," a state of mind that permanently identifies with the crucified Christ (Engberg-Pedersen 2000, 165).

Chapter Six: Galatians 6

1. Literally, "spirit of gentleness."
2. Paul shifts from "you" pl. to the sg., addressing the individual who undertakes correcting another.
3. Literally, "work."
4. Literally, "in himself alone."
5. Literally, "flesh."
6. Some translators prefer "destruction" for *phthopa* to generate an allusion to condemnation at God's judgment as the contrast to eternal life.

7. That Paul is aware of such traditions is evident in his reference to the topos of the self-sufficient wise man, who is judged or evaluated by no one in 1 Cor 2:14–16. Thiselton 2000 (271–86) thinks that Paul has adopted the motif from the Corinthians, adding his own proviso in v. 16c that those who claim to make such judgments must have the mind of Christ. He assumes, as I do, that Galatians was written earlier than 1 Corinthians and that the problem with immature persons claiming to be *pneumatikoi* ("spiritual people") in Gal 6:1 indicates that Paul may have been responsible for introducing that category in his churches. In any case, the Corinthians appear to have preferred the term *teleioi* ("perfect," "mature").

8. See the summary of such views in Longenecker 1990, 269–70.

9. Most modern translations treat the masculine plural "brothers" as a generic reference to both men and women members of the congregation. Gal 3:28 negates gender differentiation "in Christ." Rom 16:1–16 greets a number of women among those who have been active in missionary efforts and commends a woman, Phoebe, "our sister," as deacon of the church in Cenchrea. Therefore, it is entirely possible that Paul intends to include both men and women as "spiritual persons," able to correct fellow Christians. However, both circumcision and the vices of civic discord and competition for honor dealt with in the letter are gender-specific. Consequently, one cannot presume that Paul or his audience heard this advice as gender-neutral. Paul may have been addressing issues that were only relevant to the male members of the Galatian churches.

10. Longenecker (1990, 272) notes that some manuscripts render the indefinite use of the word by substituting *tis* ("someone").

11. The issue of how members of the Essene sect are to deal with observed transgressions of the Law and community rule involves several stages, including private correction and finally communal action (1 QS 5.24–6.1; CD 9.6–23; Martyn 1997, 546).

12. Thus, it is not possible to draw as sharp a distinction between Martyn's reading of Gal 6:1 in terms of Jewish sectarianism and apocalyptic warfare and the appeal to philosophic traditions of moral pedagogy in Betz, as Martyn (1997, 546–47) asserts.

13. If Paul had intended to go on from this point to offer an explanation for the existence of transgressions, he would presumably have continued in the second-person plural as in 5:17c and not switched to the indefinite *anthrōpos* ("a person").

14. It also has analogies to the philosophical tradition concerning the proper forms of correction—harsh, stinging rebuke, or gentle correction. Gentleness means that the procedure is aimed at assisting those making moral progress. It is not directed toward punishment or condemnation (Betz 1979, 297).

15. Betz (1979, 298) suggests that v. 1c may have circulated as an independent maxim in the Socratic tradition calling for self-knowledge.

16. Since most commentators do not consider moral perfection as depicted in ancient sources to be more than a set of ideal cases, they treat the injunction as safeguarding against self-righteousness (so Longenecker 1990, 274). Dunn's hypothesis—that those who engage in correcting others might become involved in the same failure because of genuine sympathy for the individual (1993, 321)—is pure pop psychology.

17. So Longenecker 1990, 275–76, associated with his view of a libertine crisis in Galatia. He treats Gal 6:2 as equivalent to 1 Cor 9:21: "[It] stands in Paul's thought for those prescriptive principles stemming from the heart of the gospel (usually embodied in the example and teachings of Jesus) which are meant to be applied to specific situations by the direction and enablement of the Holy Spirit" (Longenecker 1990, 275–76).

18. Since, as far as Paul is concerned, the Jewish law does not enshrine the will of God for humanity (cf. Rom 2:18; Murphy-O'Connor 1996, 156).

19. There is no reason to treat this section as "personal" rather than "corporate," as Barclay (1988, 149) does, since all contests for personal honor among males in antiquity are public and communal. Paul is not recommending some form of private contemplation to increase one's humility.

20. Faced with the Corinthian pretensions to wisdom and sophistic rhetoric as modes of self-exaltation, Paul adopts just such a posture concerning his own apostleship. He accepts the "degrading" conditions of manual labor in order not to become indebted to Corinthian patrons, to impose the burden of supporting the one who preaches the gospel (1 Cor 9:1–23). In so doing, Paul exhibits the freedom with which he preaches the gospel. Had Paul wished to recommend that posture to the Galatians, one would have expected him to return to the motif of freedom enunciated in 5:13.

21. Dunn suggests on the basis of 1 Cor 13:2 that such inflated self-promotion could be the consequence of experiences of the Spirit. However, Paul gives no hint that the problems faced in Corinth had emerged among the Galatians.

22. Therefore, the elaborate reconstruction proposed by Martyn (1997, 549) seems overblown. In his interpretation Paul alludes to the false self-importance of Jerusalem leaders (2:1–10), to authoritarian claims advanced by the opposing teachers on the basis of their authority, and to the hopes of those Galatians allied with the teachers to benefit from imposition of hierarchical relationships in the church. But Martyn is surely right to insist that v. 3 has a more significant place in Paul's argument than "a truly trite maxim" would suggest.

23. Commentators who focus on these maxims as instances of individual self-correction generally miss the social context. Betz (1979, 302–303)

proposes a variant of the familiar Delphic maxim, "know yourself." Dunn (1993, 325) observes that an honest self-appraisal of the impact of sin on one's work would prevent self-glorification. Longenecker (1990, 277) proposes appropriate Christian feelings: "The warning here is not to live as spiritual people in a state of pride or conceit, always comparing one's attainments to those of others . . . Christian feelings of exultation and congratulation should spring from one's own actions as seen in the light of God's approval and not derive from comparing oneself to what others are or are not doing." Such a reading might be appropriate in the context of Paul's polemic against the "super-apostles" at Corinth (e.g., 2 Cor 11:1–21), but is not evident in Galatians.

24. Betz 1979, 305–306, highlighting the use of the maxim that friends have all things in common to describe the relationship between students and teachers in philosophical schools, hypothesizes that there may have been some form of educational institution among the Galatian churches.

25. Martyn's suggestion that the outside teachers sought to replace teachers loyal to Paul with persons of their party (1997, 552) would lead one to expect a more partisan statement of the principle. However, his observation points out that those for whom Paul is recommending support would be assumed to continue the theological tradition reflected in Paul's original instruction and in this epistle.

26. Patterns in the Pauline corpus are not sufficiently rigid to use this feature to argue that the paraenetic elements in Gal 5:13–6:10 are part of the letter's argument, not an independent section. Longenecker 1990, cviii–cix, uses other epistolary indices to include this section in a division of the body of the letter that presents the author's requests (4:12–6:10).

27. Or "to be treated with contempt"; the gesture implied by the verb *muktērizō* involves "turning up the nose" or, in rhetorical terms, speaking with irony or scorn about an opponent (Betz 1979, 306 n. 151).

28. The "persevere in doing good" is sufficiently common in Hellenistic philosophy and apocalyptic texts that its presence need not imply that Paul has some reason to suspect flagging interest on the part of his audience (Betz 1979, 309).

29. One might even translate this use of *kairos* as "a divinely given opportunity" (Longenecker 1990, 283).

30. Similarly, though without discussion of patronage relationships, as the occasion for Judaizing (Martyn 1997, 554).

31. Literally, "in the flesh."

32. Reading simply *oute gar* with p⁴⁶ B Y 075 33 et al. rather than *en gar Christo Iesou*, "for in Christ Jesus . . . not . . ." as in ℵ A B C D F G 0150 6 81 et al.

33. The expression could also have a temporal reference, "from now on," but that makes little sense in the epistolary context (see the discussion in Longenecker 1990, 299).

34. As Longenecker 1990, 299, concluded: "Paul took the affronts to the gospel caused by the Judaizers quite personally, for he had been commissioned apostle to the Gentiles (1:1) and was the one who had evangelized the Galatian churches (cf. 1:8–9; 4:13–15)."

35. Martyn, who rightly insists that Paul is not complaining or appealing for sympathy in this reference to the hardships undergone in preaching the gospel, gives a dramatic rendering of the "scars" as wounds suffered in the great apocalyptic battle: "He does not see his apostolic sufferings as bad luck! On the contrary, as the powers of the present evil age (1:4) sense God's liberating invasion, they put up a bitter fight, wounding God's emissaries" (1997, 568). Martyn includes as a parallel example Antipater's assertion that he bore on almost every part of his body wounds that proved his loyalty to Caesar (Josephus, *War* 1.193).

36. A legal context for the conclusion has also been defended in Betz's treatment of the letter as an apology. He refers to 6:11–18 as a *peroratio*, the last chance to remind the judges/audience of the salient points, to sharpen the issues, and to arouse emotions—perhaps even anger at the opposition (Betz 1979, 313). However, this analysis of the letter as a whole has been challenged on the grounds that the primary agenda in its second half is not defense of the apostle, but deliberative, seeking to win the Galatians over to the actions that Paul wishes them to take (Longenecker 1990, c–cxix). Martyn 1997 (20–23) rejects the "deliberative" category for what he calls "revelatory and performative" rhetoric. Were the legal elements in the subscription more firmly established, one might treat v. 17a as a comment concerning the possibility of introducing *kopoi*, "physical sufferings," as witnesses—presumably against the apostle, although one would expect the "me" to be in a prepositional phrase, not a simple dative of respect, had that been Paul's meaning.

37. Betz (1979, 315) rightly observes that such compulsion cannot be an appropriate description of the historical facts. Paul has treated their rhetorical persuasion as if it were compulsion. We have seen that it would be an extremely risky move for persons in the Jewish community to be seen to actively advocate proselytism among Gentiles.

38. Betz (1979, 316) concludes that it is not possible to determine whether v. 13a has a historical referent or is simply an example of intrasectarian, Jewish polemic. Esler (1998, 183) suggests that Paul wishes to imply that his opponents are neglecting the ethical dimensions of the Law.

39. This identification is even more striking when one observes another unusual feature of Paul's theological language in Galatians. With the exception

of the epithet attached to God in Gal 1:1, "Father who raised him from the dead," Paul does not explicitly mention the resurrection in the letter. Even when resurrection would follow as the presupposition for the life that the apostle experiences in Christ (Gal 2:19–21), he does not introduce it.

40. This catalogue of items coded by the term "world" makes it inappropriate to make the leading image to be the change "from a boasting which focused on God's choice of (ethnic) Israel, to a boasting which focused on the principle of grace in a crucified and cursed messiah" (Dunn 1993, 340). The latter is certainly implied by Paul's boasting in the cross, but the former is not his primary meaning. It may be the consequence of his polemic against Gentiles assimilating to Jewish customs.

41. The apparent social weakness of identification with the Christian group in contrast to their past, socially dominant paganism or the proposed assimilation to Judaism may have provided the impetus for some Galatians to consider circumcision (Adams 2000, 222–24). Adams observes: "By becoming culturally Jewish, the Gentile Galatian believers could take on a more credible social identity among the social categorizations of the day and occupy a more secure place in Galatian society, one less exposed to social censure" (224).

42. As a polemical move, Paul also does an effective job of "trash-talking" the opposition. Not only do they not embody the cross in any of the several forms that Paul mentions, he insists that they do not embody the Torah that circumcision signifies, either. In fact, all they have to show is a cowardly fear of suffering for Christ and the crassest form of self-glorification at the expense of others.

43. Equivalents to "new creation" as a technical term include "new heavens" and "new earth" (Isa 65:17, 66:22; Rev 21:1; 2 Pet 3:13; *1 Enoch* 91:15), "renewed creation" (*4 Ezra* 7:75; *2 Baruch* 32:6; 57:2), "renewal" (1 QS 4.25), "new world" (*2 Baruch* 44:12; Adams 2000, 226).

44. The believers' participation in the Spirit forms a tie to the new age even as the full experience of God's salvation remains an object of hope (1 Cor 7:31b; 15:27–28; Rom 8:19–22; Phil 3:20–21). Adams (2000, 227–28) rightly insists that Paul is not using "new creation" as a metaphor or analogy for conversion. He intends to affirm that the new is present in a proleptic fashion. The community of believers is not the new reality, but does belong to it.

45. Dunn (1993, 345) also opts for a reference to Israel as God's covenant people in this phrase, although he appeals to Paul's later comments about Israel to justify that conclusion.

Bibliography

Commentaries on Galatians
Betz, Hans Dieter. 1979. *Galatians*. Philadelphia: Fortress.
Bruce, F. F. 1988. *Commentary on Galatians*. Grand Rapids: Eerdmans.
Dunn, James D. G. 1993. *The Epistle to the Galatians*. Peabody, Mass.: Hendrickson.
Esler, Philip F. 1998. *Galatians*. London: Routledge.
Fung, Ronald Y. K. 1988. *The Epistle to the Galatians*. Grand Rapids: Eerdmans.
Longenecker, Richard N. 1990. *Galatians*. WBC 41. Dallas: Word.
Martyn, J. Louis. 1997. *Galatians*. AB 33A. New York: Doubleday.
Mussner, F. 1974. *Der Galaterbrief*. HTKNT 9. Freiburg: Herder.
Schlier, H. 1965. *Der Brief an die Galater*. Kritische-exegetisher Kommentar über das NT. 4th ed. Göttingen: Vandenhoeck & Ruprecht.
Williams, Sam K. 1997. *Galatians*. Nashville: Abingdon.

Other Scholarly Works
Aageson, J. 1996. "Control" in Pauline Language and Culture: A Study of Rom 6. *NTS* 42:75–89.
Achtemeier, Paul J. 1987. *The Quest for Unity in the New Testament Churches*. Philadelphia: Fortress.
———. 1996. The Continuing Quest for Coherence in St. Paul: An Experiment in Thought. Pages 132–45 in *Theology and Ethics in Paul and His Interpreters: Essays in Honor of Victor Paul Furnish*. Edited by Eugene H. Lovering and Jerry L. Sumney. Nashville: Abingdon.
Adams, Edward. 2000. *Constructing the World: A Study in Paul's Cosmological Language*. Edinburgh: T&T Clark.
Arnold, Clinton E. 1996. Returning to the Domain of the Powers: Stoicheia as Evil Spirits in Galatians 4:3, 9. *NovT* 38:55–76.
Bachmann, Michael. 1992. *Sünder oder Übertreter: Studien zur Argumentation in Gal 2, 15ff.* WUNT 59. Tübingen: J. C. B. Mohr (Paul Siebeck).
———. 1998. 4QMMT und Galaterbrief, התורה מעשי und ΕΡΓΑ ΝΟΜΟΥ. *ZNW* 89:91–113.

Barclay, J. M. G. 1988. *Obeying the Truth: A Study of Paul's Ethics in Galatians.* Edinburgh: T&T Clark.

————. 1996. *Jews in the Mediterranean Diaspora: From Alexander to Trajan (323 B.C.E.–117 C.E.).* Edinburgh: T&T Clark.

Barrett, C. K. 1998. *The Acts of the Apostles.* Vol. II, *Introduction and Commentary on Acts XV–XXVIII.* ICC. Edinburgh: T&T Clark.

Barton, Stephen C. 1998. Paul and the Limits of Tolerance. Pages 121–34 in *Tolerance and Intolerance in Early Judaism and Christianity.* Edited by Graham N. Stanton and Guy G. Stroumsa. Cambridge: Cambridge University Press.

Bauckham, Richard J. 1979. Barnabas in Galatians. *JSNT* 2:61–70.

Beker, J. C. 1988. Paul's Theology: Consistent or Inconsistent? *NTS* 34:364–77.

Betz, Hans Dieter. 1994a. Transferring a Ritual: Paul's Interpretation of Baptism in Romans 6. Pages 240–71 in *Paulinische Studiem.* Tübingen: J. C. B. Mohr (Paul Siebeck).

————. 1994b. Paul's Ideas about the Origins of Christianity. Pages 272–88 in *Paulinische Studien.*

Boers, Hendrikus. 1994. *The Justification of the Gentiles: Paul's Letters to the Galatians and Romans.* Peabody, Mass.: Hendrickson.

————. 1997. Αγαπη and χαρις in Paul's Thought. *CBQ* 59:693–713.

Bossman, David M. 1996. Paul's Fictive Kinship Movement. *BTB* 26:163–71.

Bowersock, G. W. 1983. *Roman Arabia.* Cambridge, Mass.: Harvard University Press.

Bradley, Keith. 1994. *Slavery and Society at Rome.* Cambridge: Cambridge University Press.

Bändle, Rudolf, and Ekkehard W. Stegemann. 1996. The Formation of the First "Christian Congregations" in Rome in the Context of the Jewish Congregations. Pages 117–27 in *Judaism and Christianity in First-Century Rome.* Edited by K. Donfried and P. Richardson. Grand Rapids: Eerdmans.

Blass, F. and A. Debrunner. 1961 (BDF). *A Greek Grammar of the New Testament and Other Early Christian Literature.* Translated and revised by R. W. Funk. Chicago: University of Chicago.

Brown, Raymond E. 1993. *The Death of the Messiah.* New York: Doubleday.

Bryan, Christopher. 2000. *A Preface to Romans: Notes on the Epistle in Its Literary and Cultural Setting.* Oxford: Oxford University Press.

Byrne, Brendan. 2000. The Problem of Nomos and the Relationship with Judaism in Romans. *CBQ* 62:294–309.

Campbell, R. A. 1996. "Against Such Things There Is No Law"? Galatians 5.23b Again. *ExpTimes* 107:271–72.

Cohen, Shaye J. D. 1999. *The Beginning of Jewishness: Boundaries, Varieties, Uncertainties*. Berkeley: University of California.

Collins, John J. 1995. *The Scepter and the Star: The Messiahs of the Dead Sea Scrolls and Other Ancient Literature*. New York: Doubleday.

———. 1997. *Apocalypticism in the Dead Sea Scrolls*. London & New York: Routledge.

Cooper, Stephen A. 2000. *Narratio* and *Exhortatio* in Galatians According to Marius Victorinus Rhetor. *ZNW* 91:107–35.

Cosgrove, Charles H. 1988. *The Cross and the Spirit: A Study in the Argument and Theology of Galatians*. Macon, Ga.: Mercer.

Crook, J. A. 1967. *Law and Life of Rome: 90 B.C.–A.D. 212*. Ithaca: Cornell University Press.

Danker, Frederick William. 2000. *Greek-English Lexicon of the New Testament and Other Early Christian Literature*. BDAG. 3d ed. Chicago: University of Chicago Press.

Davies, W. D. 1999. Paul from a Jewish Point of View. Pages 678–730 in *The Cambridge History of Judaism*. Vol. 3, *The Early Roman Period*. Edited by W. Horbury, W. D. Davies, and J. Sturdy. Cambridge: Cambridge University Press.

Davies, W. D., and Dale C. Allison. 1997. *The Gospel According to Matthew*. Vol. 3, *Commentary on Matthew xix–xxviii*. ICC. Edinburgh: T&T Clark.

de Lubac, Henri. 1959. *Exégèse Médiévale. Les Quatre Sens de l'Écriture: Première Partie*. Paris: Aubier.

De Vries, C. E. 1975. Paul's "Cutting" Remarks about a Race: Galatians 5:1–12. Pages 115–20 in *Current Issues in Biblical and Patristic Interpretation*. Edited by G. F. Hawthorne. Grand Rapids: Eerdmans.

Dixon, Suzanne. 1992. *The Roman Family*. Baltimore: Johns Hopkins.

Dodd, Brian J. 1996. Christ's Slave, People Pleasers and Galatians 1.10. *NTS* 42:90–104.

Donaldson, Terence L. 1989. Zealot and Convert: The Origin of Paul's Christ-Torah Antithesis. *CBQ* 51:655–82.

———. 1997. *Paul and the Gentiles. Remapping the Apostle's Convictional World*. Minneapolis: Fortress.

Donfried, Karl P., and Peter Richardson. 1996. *Judaism and Christianity in First-Century Rome*. Grand Rapids: Eerdmans.

Dunn, James D. G. 1988. *Romans 1–8*. WBC 38A. Dallas: Word.

———. 1996. "The Law of Faith," "the Law of the Spirit" and "the Law of Christ." Pages 62–82 in *Theology and Ethics in Paul and His Interpreters: Essays in Honor of Victor Paul Furnish*. Edited by Eugene H. Lovering and Jerry L. Sumney. Nashville: Abingdon.

———. 1998. *The Theology of Paul the Apostle*. Grand Rapids: Eerdmans.

———. 1999. Who Did Paul Think He Was? A Study of Jewish Christian Identity. *NTS* 45:174–93.

Elliott, Mark Adam. 2000. *The Survivors of Israel: A Reconstruction of the Theology of Pre-Christian Judaism*. Grand Rapids: Eerdmans.

Elliott, Susan M. 1999. Choose Your Mother, Choose Your Master: Galatians 4:21–5:1 in the Shadow of the Anatolian Mother of the Gods. *JBL* 118:661–93.

Engberg-Pedersen, Troels. 2000. *Paul and the Stoics*. Louisville: Westminster/ John Knox.

Erler, Michael, and Malcolm Schofield. 1999. Epicurean Ethics. Pages 642–74 in *The Cambridge History of Hellenistic Philosophy*. Edited by K. Algra, J. Barnes, J. Manifield, and M. Schofield. Cambridge: Cambridge University Press.

Esler, Philip F. 1995. Making and Breaking an Agreement Mediterranean Style. *BibInt* 3:285–314.

Fee, Gordon D. 1994. *God's Empowering Presence: The Holy Spirit in the Letters of Paul*. Peabody, Mass.: Hendrickson.

Fitzmyer, Joseph A. 1993. *Romans*. AB 33. New York: Doubleday.

———. 1998. *The Acts of the Apostles*. AB 31. New York: Doubleday.

Frantham, Elaine, Helene P. Foley, Natalie B. Kampen, Sarah B. Pomeroy, and H. Alan Shapiro. 1994. *Women in the Classical World: Image and Text*. New York: Oxford.

Frey, Jörg. 1999. Die paulinische Antithese von "Fleisch" und "Geist" und die palästinische-j̲dische Weisheitstradition. *ZNW* 90:45–77.

Gaca, Kathy L. 1999. Paul's Uncommon Declaration in Romans 1:18–32 and Its Problematic Legacy for Pagan and Christian Relations. *HTR* 92:165–98.

Gager, John G. 1992. *Curse Tablets and Binding Spells from the Ancient World*. New York: Oxford.

Garlington, Don. 1997. Role Reversal and Paul's Use of Scripture in Galatians 3.10–13. *JSNT* 65:85–121.

Gaventa, Beverly R. 1986. Galatians 1 and 2: Autobiography as Paradigm. *NovT* 28:309–26.

———. 1990. The Maternity of Paul: An Exegetical Study of Galatians 4:19. Pages 189–201 in *The Conversation Continues: Studies in Paul and John*. Edited by R. T. Fortna and B. R. Gaventa. Nashville: Abingdon.

Glancy, Jennifer A. 1998. Obstacles to Slaves' Participation in the Corinthian Church. *JBL* 117:481–501.

Goodman, Martin. 1994. *Mission and Conversion: Proselytizing in the Religious History of the Roman Empire*. Oxford: Clarendon.

————. 1997. *The Roman World 44 B.C.–A.D. 180*. London: Routledge.

————. 1999. Josephus' Treatise *Against Apion*. Pages 45–58 in M. Edwards, M. Goodman, and S. Price. *Apologetics in the Roman Empire: Pagans, Jews and Christians*. Oxford: Oxford University Press.

Griffin, Miriam. 1996. Cynicism and the Romans: Attraction and Repulsion. Pages 190–204 in *The Cynics: The Cynic Movement in Antiquity and Its Legacy*. Edited by R. B. Branham and M.-O. Goulet-Cazé. Berkeley: University of California.

————. 2000. The Flavians. Pages 1–83 in *The Cambridge Ancient History*. Vol. XI, *The High Empire A.D. 70–192*. Edited by A. K. Bowman, P. Garnsey, and D. Rathbone. Cambridge: Cambridge University Press.

Hansen, G. Walter. 1994. Galatia. Pages 377–96 in *The Book of Acts in Its First Century Setting*. Vol. 2, *Graeco-Roman Setting*. Edited by D. W. J. Gill and C. Gempf. Grand Rapids: Eerdmans.

Hays, Richard B. 1987. Christology and Ethics in Galatians: The Law of Christ. *CBQ* 49:268–90.

————. 1989. *Echoes of Scripture in the Letters of Paul*. New Haven: Yale University Press.

————. 1991. PISTIS and Pauline Christology. Pages 714–29 in *Society of Biblical Literature 1991 Seminar Papers*. Edited by E. Lovering. Atlanta: Scholars Press.

————. 1996. The Role of Scripture in Paul's Ethics. Pages 30–47 in *Theology and Ethics in Paul and His Interpreters: Essays in Honor of Victor Paul Furnish*. Edited by Eugene H. Lovering and Jerry L. Sumney. Nashville: Abingdon.

Hengel, Martin, and Anna Maria Schwemer. 1997. *Paul between Damascus and Antioch: The Unknown Years*. Louisville: Westminster/John Knox.

Hock, Ronald F. 1980. *The Social Context of Paul's Ministry: Tentmaking and Apostleship*. Philadelphia: Fortress.

Holmberg, Bengt. 1978. *Paul and Power: The Structure of Authority in the Primitive Church as Reflected in the Pauline Epistles*. Lund: Gleerup.

————. 1998. Jewish versus Christian Identity in the Early Church? *RB* 105:397–425.

Horbury, W., W. D. Davies, and J. Sturdy, eds. 1999. *The Cambridge History of Judaism*. Vol. 3, *The Early Roman Period*. Cambridge: Cambridge University Press.

Hübner, H. 1984. *Law in Paul's Thought*. Edinburgh: T&T Clark.

Hultgren, A. J. 1976. Paul's Pre-Christian Persecutions of the Church: Their Purpose, Locale and Nature. *JBL* 96:5–17.

Inwood, Brad, and Pierluigi Donini. 1999. Stoic Ethics. Pages 675–738 in *The Cambridge History of Hellenistic Philosophy*. Edited by K. Algra, J. Barnes, J. Mansfeld, and M. Schofield. Cambridge: Cambridge University Press.

Jegher-Bucher, Verena. 1991. *Der Galaterbrief auf dem Hintergrund antiker Epistolographie und Rhetorik: Ein anderes Paulusbild.* AthANT 78. Zürich: Theologischer Verlag.

Jewett, R. 1971. The Agitators and the Galatian Congregation. *NTS* 17:198–212.

Kern, Philip H. 1998. *Rhetoric and Galatians: Assessing an Approach to Paul's Epistle.* SNTSMS 101. Cambridge: Cambridge University Press.

Kim, C.-H. 1972. *Form and Structure of the Familiar Greek Letter of Recommendation.* SBLDS 4. Missoula: Scholars Press.

Klauck, Hans-Josef. 2000. *The Religious Context of Early Christianity.* Edinburgh: T&T Clark.

Kloppenborg, John. 1993. Edwin Hatch, Churches and *Collegia.* Pages 212–38 in *Origins and Method: Towards a New Understanding of Judaism and Christianity.* Edited by B. H. McLean. Sheffield: Sheffield Academic Press.

Kondoleon, Christine. 2000. *Antioch: The Lost Ancient City.* Princeton: Princeton University Press in collaboration with the Worcester Art Museum.

Kraus, Wolfgang.1999. *Zwischen Jerusalem und Antiochia: Die "Hellenisten," Paulus und die Aufnahme der Heiden in das endzeitliche Gottesvolk.* SBS 179. Stuttgart: Katholisches Bibelwerk.

Lambrecht, J. 1997. Paul's Coherent Admonition in Galatians 6, 1–6: Mutual Help and Individual Attentiveness. *Biblica* 78:33–56.

Levine, L. I. 1999.The Hellenistic-Roman Diaspora C.E. 70–C.E. 235: The Archaeological Evidence. Pages 991–1024 in *The Cambridge History of Judaism.* Vol. 3, *The Early Roman Period.* Edited by W. Horbury, W. D. Davies, and J. Sturdy. Cambridge: Cambridge University Press.

Levinskaya, Irina. 1996. *The Book of Acts in Its Diaspora Setting.* Grand Rapids: Eerdmans.

Lieu, Judith. 1995. The Race of the God-Fearers. *JTS* ns 46:483–501.

Lim, Timothy H. 2000. Kittim. Pages 469–71 in *Encyclopedia of the Dead Sea Scrolls.* Edited by L. H. Schiffman and J. C. Vanderkam. Oxford: Oxford University Press.

Longenecker, Bruce W. 1999. "Until Christ Is Formed in You": Suprahuman Forces and Moral Character in Galatians. *CBQ* 61:92–108.

Lull, D. J. 1986. "The Law Was Our Pedagogue": A Study in Galatians iii.19–25. *JBL* 105:481–98.

Malherbe, Abraham. 2000. *The Letters to the Thessalonians.* AB 32B. New York: Doubleday.

Martin, Dale P. 1990. *Slavery as Salvation.* New Haven: Yale University Press.

———. 1995. *The Corinthian Body.* New Haven: Yale University Press.

Martin, Troy. 1995. Apostasy to Paganism: The Rhetorical Stasis of the Galatian Controversy. *JBL* 114:437–61.

Martyn, J. Louis. 1985a. Apocalyptic Antinomies in Paul's Letter to the Galatians. *NTS* 31:410–24.

———. 1985b. Law-Observant Mission to Gentiles: The Background of Galatians. *SJT* 38:307–24.

———. 1995. Christ, the Elements of the Cosmos, and the Law in Galatians. Pages 16–39 in *The Social World of the First Christians*. Edited by L. M. White and L. Yarbrough. Minneapolis: Fortress.

———. 1996. The Crucial Event in the History of the Law. Pages 48–61 in *Theology and Ethics in Paul and His Interpreters: Essays in Honor of Victor Paul Furnish*. Edited by Eugene H. Lovering and Jerry L. Sumney. Nashville: Abingdon.

Mason, Steven. 1990. Paul, Classical Anti-Jewish Polemic, and the Letter to the Romans. Pages 181–223 in *Self-Definition and Self-Discovery in Early Christianity: A Study in Changing Horizons*. Edited by D. J. Hawkin and T. Robinson. Lewiston, Maine: Edwin Mellen.

Matera, Frank J. 2000. Galatians in Perspective. *Int* 54:233–43.

Meeks, Wayne A. 1973/74. The Image of the Androgyne: Some Uses of a Symbol in Earliest Christianity. *HR* 13:165–208.

———. 1981. *First Urban Christians*. New Haven: Yale University Press.

Mitchell, Margaret M. 1992. New Testament Envoys in the Context of Greco-Roman Diplomatic and Epistolary Conventions: The Example of Timothy and Titus. *JBL* 111:641–62.

Mitchell, S. 1993. *Anatolia: Land, Men, and Gods in Asia Minor*. 2 vols. Oxford: Oxford University Press.

Mullins, T. Y. 1972. Formulas in New Testament Epistles. *JBL* 91:380–90.

Murphy-O'Connor, Jerome. 1996. *Paul: A Critical Life*. Oxford: Clarendon Press.

———. 1999. The Irrevocable Will (Gal 3:15). *RB* 106:224–35.

———. 2000. To Run in Vain (Gal 2:2). *RB* 107:383–89.

O'Neill, J. C. 1998. "Did You Receive the Spirit by the Works of the Law?" (Gal 3:2): The Works of the Law in Judaism and the Pauline Corpus. *AusBibRev* 46:70–84.

Neyrey, J. H. 1988. Bewitched in Galatia: Paul and Cultural Anthropology. *CBQ* 50:72–100.

Nickelsburg, George W. E. 1998. Abraham, the Convert: A Jewish Tradition and Its Use by the Apostle Paul. Pages 151–75 in *Biblical Figures Outside the Bible*. Edited by M. E. Stone and T. A. Bergren. Harrisburg, Pa.: Trinity Press International.

Painter, John. 1997. *Just James: The Brother of Jesus in History and Tradition*. Columbia: University of South Carolina.

Perkins, Pheme. 1994. *Peter: Apostle for the Whole Church*. Columbia: University of South Carolina.

Rabens, Volker. 1999. The Development of Pauline Pneumatology: A Response to F. W. Horn. *BZ* 43:161–79.

Räisänen, H. 1983. *Paul and the Law.* WUNT 29. Tübingen: J. C. B. Mohr (Paul Siebeck).

Reinbold, Wolfgang. 2000. Gal 3, 6–14 und das Problem der Erfüllbarkeit des Gesetzes bei Paulus. *ZNW* 91:91–106.

Richardson, Peter. 1996. Augustan-Era Synagogues in Rome. Pages 17–29 in *Judaism and Christianity in First-Century Rome.* Edited by K. Donfried and P. Richardson. Grand Rapids: Eerdmans.

Sampley, J. Paul. 1995. The Weak and the Strong: Paul's Careful and Crafty Rhetorical Strategy in Romans 14:1–15:13. Pages 40–52 in *The Social World of the First Christians.* Edited by L. M. White and O. L. Yarbrough. Minneapolis: Fortress.

Schäfer, Peter. 1997. *Judeophobia: Attitudes Toward the Jews in the Ancient World.* Cambridge, Mass.: Harvard University Press.

Schürer, Emil. 1986. *The History of the Jewish People in the Age of Jesus Christ (174 B.C.–A.D. 135).* Revised and edited by G. Vermes, F. Millar, and M. Goodman. Edinburgh: T&T Clark.

Smallwood, E. Mary. 1999. The Diaspora in the Roman Period before C.E. 70. Pages 168–91 in *The Cambridge History of Judaism.* Vol. 3, *The Early Roman Period.* Edited by W. Horbury, W. D. Davies, and J. Sturdy. Cambridge: Cambridge University Press.

Smiles, Vincent M. 1998. *The Gospel and the Law in Galatia: Paul's Response to Jewish-Christian Separatism and the Threat of Galatian Apostasy.* Collegeville, Minn.: Liturgical Press (Michael Glazier).

Smith, C. C. 1996. "Ekkleisai in Galatians 4.17": The Motif of the Excluded Lover as a Metaphor of Manipulation. *CBQ* 58:480–99.

Smith, Morton. 1999. The Gentiles in Judaism 125 B.C.E.–C.E. 66. Pages 192–249 in *The Cambridge History of Judaism.* Vol. 3, *The Early Roman Period.* Edited by W. Horbury, W. D. Davies, and J. Sturdy. Cambridge: Cambridge University Press.

Spilsbury, Paul. 1998. *The Image of the Jew in Flavius Josephus' Paraphrase of the Bible.* Texte und Studien zum Antiken Judentum 69. Tübingen: J. C. B. Mohr (Paul Siebeck).

Stanley, Christopher D. 1996. "Neither Jew nor Greek": Ethnic Conflict in Graeco-Roman Society. *JSNT* 64:101–24.

Stanton, Graham N., and Guy G. Stroumsa. 1998. *Tolerance and Intolerance in Judaism and Christianity.* Cambridge: Cambridge University Press.

Stark, Rodney. 1996. *The Rise of Christianity.* Princeton: Princeton University Press.

Stowers, S. K. 1981. *The Diatribe and Paul's Letter to the Romans.* SBLDS 57. Chico, Calif.: Scholars Press.

Strecker, Christian. 1999. *Die Liminale Theologie des Paulus: Zugänge zur paulinischen Theologie aus kulturanthropologisher Perspektive.* FRLANT 185. Göttingen: Vandenhoeck & Ruprecht.

Thiselton, Anthony C. 2000. *The First Epistle to the Corinthians.* Grand Rapids: Eerdmans.

Thrall, Margaret E. 2000. *The Second Epistle to the Corinthians.* Vol. II, *Commentary on II Corinthians VIII–XVIII.* Edinburgh: T&T Clark.

Thurén, Lauri. 2000. *Derhetorizing Paul: A Dynamic Perspective on Pauline Theology and the Law.* WUNT 124. Tübingen: Mohr-Siebeck.

Trebilco, Paul. 1991. *Jewish Communities in Asia Minor.* SNTSMS 69. Cambridge: Cambridge University Press.

Trobisch, David. 1994. *Paul's Letter Collection: Tracing the Origins.* Minneapolis: Fortress.

Udoh, Fabian E. 2000. Paul's Views on the Law: Questions about Origins (Gal 1:6–2:21; Phil 3:2–11). *NovT* 42:214–37.

Walters, James C. 1996. Romans, Jews, and Christians: The Impact of the Romans on Jewish/Christian Relations in First-Century Rome. Pages 175–95 in *Judaism and Christianity in First-Century Rome.* Edited by K. Donfried and P. Richardson. Grand Rapids: Eerdmans.

White, John L. 1986. *Light from Ancient Letters.* Philadelphia: Fortress.

———. 1999. *The Apostle of God: Paul and the Promise of Abraham.* Peabody, Mass.: Hendrickson.

White, L. Michael. 1996. Synagogues and Society in Imperial Ostia: Archaeological and Epigraphic Evidence. Pages 30–68 in *Judaism and Christianity in First-Century Rome.* Edited by K. Donfried and P. Richardson. Grand Rapids: Eerdmans.

Williams, Margaret. 1999. The Contribution of Jewish Inscriptions to the Study of Judaism. Pages 75–93 in *The Cambridge History of Judaism.* Vol. 3, *The Early Roman Period.* Edited by W. Horbury, W. D. Davies, and J. Sturdy. Cambridge: Cambridge University Press.

Williams, Sam K. 1987. Justification and the Spirit in Galatians. *JSNT* 29:91–100.

———. 1988. Promise in Galatians: A Reading of Paul's Reading of Scripture. *JBL* 107:709–20.

Winger, Michael. 1992. *By What Law? The Meaning of Nomos in the Letters of Paul.* SBLDS 128. Atlanta: Scholars Press.

———. 2000. The Law of Christ. *NTS* 46:537–46.

Young, Norman. 1998. Who's Cursed—And Why? (Galatians 3:10–14). *JBL* 117:79–92.

Ancient Sources

Old Testament Pseudepigrapha (OTP). 1983–85. Edited by J. H. Charlesworth. 2 vols. New York: Doubleday.

Apuleius. 1989. *The Golden Ass* or *Metamorphoses (Metam.).* Translated by J. A. Hanson. 2 vols. LCL. Cambridge: Harvard University Press.

Aristeas. *Letter of Aristeas.* Translated by R. J. H. Schutt. *OTP* 2:7–34

Aristotle. 1991. *Art of Rhetoric (Rhet.).* Translated by J. H. Freese. LCL. Cambridge: Harvard University Press.

————. 1999. *Nichomachean Ethics (Eth nic.).* Translated by T. H. Irwin. 2d ed. Indianapolis: Hackett.

Athenaeus. 1927–1941. *Deipnosophistae (Deipn.)* or *The Learned Banquet.* Translated by C. B. Gulick. LCL. Cambridge: Harvard University Press.

2 Baruch or *Syriac Apocalypse.* Translated by A. F. J. Klijn. *OTP* 1:615–52.

Cassius Dio. 1914–1927. *Roman History (Hist.).* Translated by E. Cary. LCL. Cambridge: Harvard University Press.

Catullus. 1913. *Poems.* Translated by F. W. Cornish. LCL. Cambridge: Harvard University Press.

Cicero. 1971. *On the Good Life.* Translated by M. Grant. Baltimore: Penguin. Reprint 1992. *On Friendship* or *De Amicitia (Amic.).* Edited by H. E. Gould and J. L. Whiteley. Wauconda, Ill: Bolchazy-Carducci.

Dio Chrysostom. 1932. *Discourses (Or.).* Translated by J. W. Cohoon. LCL. Cambridge: Harvard University Press.

Diodorus Siculus. 1933–1967. *Bibliotheke (Hist.)* or *Library.* Translated by C. H. Oldfather et al. LCL. Cambridge: Harvard University Press.

Diogenes Laertius. 1925. *Lives of Eminent Philosophers (Lives).* Translated by R. D. Hicks. LCL. Cambridge: Harvard University Press.

1 Enoch or *Ethiopic Apocalypse.* Translated by E. Isaac. *OTP* 1:5–90.

Epictetus. 1925. *The Discourses as Reported by Arrian* or *Diatribae/Dissertationes (Diatr.).* Translated by W. A. Goldfather. LCL. Cambridge: Harvard University Press.

Genesis Rabbah. 1965. *Midrash Bereshit Rabba: Critical Edition with Notes and Commentary (Gen. Rab.).* Edited by J. Theodor and C. Albeck. Jerusalem: Wahrman.

Herodotus. 1998. *The Histories (Hist.).* Translated by Robin Waterfield. Oxford: Oxford University Press.

Horace. 1973. *The Satires of Horace and Persius (Sat.).* Translated by N. Rudd. London: Penguin.

Irenaeus. 1969–1982. *Adversus Haereses (Haer.)* or *Against Heresies. Contre les Hérésies. Livres I–V.* SC. Edited by A. Rousseau et al. Paris: Cerf.

Jerome. 1884. *Commentariorum in Epistulam ad Galatas (Comm. Gal.)* or *Commentary on the Epistle to the Galatians. PL* 26. J. P. Migne, ed. *Patrologiae cursus completus Series Latina.* Paris.

Josephus. 1926. *Against Apion. The Life, Against Apion (C. Ap.).* Translated by H. St. J. Thackeray. LCL. Cambridge: Harvard University Press.

———. 1926. *Life. The Life, Against Apion (Life).* Translated by H. St. J. Thackeray. LCL. Cambridge: Harvard University Press.

———. 1927. *The Jewish War (War).* Translated by H. St. J. Thackeray. LCL. Cambridge: Harvard University Press.

———. 1933–1969. *Jewish Antiquities (Ant.).* Translated by R. Marcus, L. H. Feldman et al. LCL. Cambridge: Harvard University Press.

Jubilees. Translated by O. S. Wintermute. *OTP* 2:35–142.

Juvenal. 1991. *The Satires (Sat.).* Translated by N. Rudd. LCL. Cambridge: Harvard University Press.

Livy. 1922–1951. *History (Hist.).* Translated by B. D. Foster and A. G. Schlesinger. LCL. Cambridge: Harvard University Press.

Lucian. 1925. *De syria dea* or *The Goddess of Syria (Syr. d.).* Translated by A. M. Harmon. *Lucian IV.* LCL. Cambridge: Harvard University Press.

———. 1925. *Toxaris* or *Friendship (Tox.).* Translated by A. M. Harmon. Lucian V. LCL. Cambridge: Harvard University Press.

Lysias. 1930. *Orationes (Lysias).* Translated by W. R. M. Lamb. LCL. Cambridge: Harvard University Press.

Origen. 1965. *Contra Celsum (Cels.).* Translated by Henry Chadwick. Cambridge: Cambridge University Press.

Pesiqta de Rab Kahana. 1962. *Pesiqta de Rab Kahana (Pesiq. Rab. Kah.).* Edited by B. Mandelbaum. 2 vols. New York.

Petronius. 1965. *The Satyricon (Satyr.).* Translated by J. P. Sullivan. LCL. Cambridge: Harvard University Press.

Philo. 1929. *De cherubim* or *On the cherubim (Cher.).* Translated by F. H. Colson. *Philo II.* LCL. Cambridge: Harvard University Press.

———. *De congressu eruditionis gratia* or *On the Preliminary Studies (Congr.).* Translated by F. H. Colson and G. H. Whitaker. *Philo IV.* LCL. Cambridge: Harvard University Press.

———. *De migratione Abrahami* or *On the Migration of Abraham (Migr.)* Translated by F. H. Colson and G. H. Whitaker, *Philo IV.* Cambridge: Harvard University Press.

———. 1929. *De opificio mundi* or *On the Creation of the World (Opif.).* Translated by F. H. Colson and G. H. Whitaker. *Philo I.* Cambridge: Harvard University Press.

———. 1929. *Legum allegoriae* or *Allegorical Interpretation (Leg.)*. Translated by F. H. Colson and G. H. Whittaker. *Philo I.* LCL. Cambridge: Harvard University Press.

———. 1932. *De vita Mosis* or *On the Life of Moses (Mos.)*. Translated by F. H. Colson. *Philo VI.* Cambridge: Harvard University Press.

———. 1932. *Quis rerum divinarum heres sit* or *Who Is the Heir? (Her.)*. Translated by F. H. Colson and G. H. Whitaker. *Philo IV.* Cambridge: Harvard University Press.

———. 1934. *De somniis* or *On Dreams (Somn.)*. Translated by F. H. Colson and G. H. Whitaker. *Philo V.* LCL. Cambridge: Harvard University Press.

———. 1935. *De Abrahamo* or *On the Life of Abraham (Abr.)*. Translated by F. H. Colson. *Philo VI.* LCL. Cambridge: Harvard University Press.

———. 1937. *De specialibus legibus* or *On the Special Laws (Spec.)*. Translated by F. H. Colson. *Philo VII.* LCL. Cambridge: Harvard University Press.

———. 1939. *De virtutibus* or *On the Virtues (Virt.)*. Translated by F. H. Colson. *Philo VIII.* Cambridge: Harvard University Press.

———. 1941. *De vita contemplativa* or *On the Contemplative Life (Contempl.)*. Translated by F. H. Colson. *Philo IX.* Cambridge: Harvard University Press.

———. 1941. *In Flaccum* or *Against Flaccus (Flacc.)*. Translated by F. H. Colson. *Philo IX.* LCL. Cambridge: Harvard University Press.

———. 1953. *Quaestiones et solutiones in Exodum (QE 1, 2)*. *Philo. Supplement II.* LCL. Cambridge: Harvard University Press.

———. 1962. *Legatio ad Gaium* or *Embassy to Gaius (Legat.)*. Translated by F. H. Colson. *Philo X.* LCL. Cambridge: Harvard University Press.

Plato. 1997. *Complete Works (CW)*. Edited by John M. Cooper. Indianapolis: Hackett.

———. *Apology (Apol.)*. Pages 17–36 in *CW*. Translated by G. M. A. Grube.

———. *Republic (Resp.)*. Pages 971–1223 in *CW*. Translated by G. M A. Grube. Revisions by C. D. C. Reeve.

Pliny, the elder. 1991. *Natural History: A Selection (Nat.)*. Translated by John F. Healy. Baltimore: Penguin.

Plutarch. 1914–1926. *Lives*. Translated by B. Perrin. LCL. Cambridge: Harvard University Press.

———. *Lucullus (Luc.)*.

———. *Pompey (Pomp.)*.

———. *Theseus (Thes.)*.

———. 1935–1976. *Moralia (Mor.)*. Translated by F. C. Babbitt et al. LCL. Cambridge: Harvard University Press.

———. *De curiositate* or *On Curiosity (Curios.)*.

———. *De fraterno amore* or *On Brotherly Love (Frat. amor.)*.
———. *Quaestionem convivialum* or *Table Talk (Quaest. conv.)*.
———. *Quaestiones romanae* or *Roman Questions (Quaest. rom.)*.
———. *De tuenda sanitate praecepta* or *Advice on Health (Tu. san.)*
———. 1993. Plutarch, *Selected Essays and Dialogues*. Translated by D. Russell. Oxford: Oxford University Press.
Psalms of Solomon. Translated by R .B. Wright. *OTP* 2:639–70.
Ptolemy, Claudius. 1991. *Geography*. Trans. E. L. Stevenson. New York: Dover. Reprint of 1932 edition.

Qumran: Dead Sea Scrolls and Other Essene Writings
García Martínez, F. and E. J. C. Tigchelaar, eds. *The Dead Sea Scrolls Study Edition (DSSSE)*. 2 vols. Leiden: Brill/Grand Rapids: Eerdmans, 1997–1998.

CD	Damascus Document. *DSSSE*:550–627.
1 QH	1Q Hodayot. *DSSSE*:146–205.
1 QS	1Q Rule of the Community. *DSSSE*:69–99.
4 QFlor	4Q Florilegium. *DSSSE*:352–55.
4 QMMT	Q Halakhic Letter. *DSSSE*:790–805.
4QpNah	Nahum Pesher. *DSSSE*:334–41.
4Q164	4Q Isaiah Pesher[d]. *DSSSE*:326–27.
4Q 416–18	4Q Instruction[b-d]. *DSSSE*:846–77.
11 QT	11Q Temple Scroll. *DSSSE*: 228–1305.

Sibylline Oracles (Sib. Or.). Translated by J. J. Collins. *OTP* 1: 317–472.
Strabo. 1917–1932. *Geography (Geogr.)*. Translated by H. L. Jones. LCL. Cambridge: Harvard University Press.
Suetonius. 1979. *Claudius (Claud.)*. *The Twelve Caesars*. Translated by R. Graves. Revised by M. Grant. Baltimore: Penguin.
———. *Tiberius (Tib.)*. *The Twelve Caesars*.
Tacitus. 1971. *Annals (Ann.)*. 2d ed. Translated by R. Grant. Baltimore: Penguin.
———. 1997. *The Histories (Hist.)*. Translated by W. H. Fyfe. Revised by D. S. Levene. Oxford: Oxford University Press.

Targums
Sperber, A. 1959–1973. *The Bible in Aramaic*. Leiden: Brill.

Talmud, Babylonian
Targum Isaiah (Tg.-Isa.). 1987. Translated by B. Chilton. *The Isaiah Targum: Introduction, Translation, Apparatus and Notes*. Wilmington: Michael Glazier.

Targum Pseudo-Jonathan (Tg. Ps.-J). 1984. *Targum Pseudo-Jonathan of the Pentateuch: Text and Concordance*. Edited by E. G Clarke et al. Hoboken, N.J.

Tractate, Sanhedrin (*b. Sanh.*) 1941. Translated by Israel Epstein. *The Babylonian Talmud*. London: Soncino.

Testaments of the XII Patriarchs.
Testament of Judah. Translated by H. C. Kee. *OTP* 1:795–802.
Testament of Levi. Translated by H. C. Kee. *OTP* 1:788–95.

Tertullian. 1972. *Adversus Marcionem* or *Against Marcion (Marc.)*. Edited by E. Evans. Oxford: Oxford University Press.

Theocritus. 1982. *Idylls and Epigrams (Id.)*. Translated by D. Hine. New York: Atheneum.

Index of Scriptural Texts

Index of Subjects and
Modern Authors